P9-CSW-277

PENGUIN BOOKS

Three Plays

FIVE FINGER EXERCISE
SHRIVINGS
EQUUS

One of the foremost dramatists of our time, Peter Shaffer was born in Liverpool and educated at St Paul's School and Trinity College, Cambridge. He had several varied jobs before earning fame as a playwright – working as a 'Bevin Boy' in the coal mines during the Second World War, in the acquisitions department of the New York Public Library and for the London music-publishing firm of Boosey & Hawkes.

His first big success came in 1958 with *Five Finger Exercise*. The play ran for nearly two years at the Comedy Theatre in London, won the *Evening Standard* Drama Award and was subsequently presented, with great acclaim, in New York City. Other Shaffer successes include *The Private Ear: The Public Eye* (which, like *Lettice and Lovage*, starred Maggie Smith and played at the Globe Theatre); *The Royal Hunt of the Sun*, an epic drama concerning the Spanish conquest of the Inca Empire; the hilarious farce *Black Comedy; The Battle of Shrivings*; *Equus*, a sensational triumph in London and in New York where it received the 1975 Tony Award for Best Play of the year; and *Amadeus*, which also won the same prize, as well as the 1979 *Evening Standard* Drama Award, the *Plays and Players* Award, and the London Theatre Critics' Award. Both these last-mentioned plays boast the rare distinction of having run for over a thousand performances on Broadway, and in 1984 the film of *Amadeus* won the Academy Award for both script and picture. His most recent plays are *Yonadab*, *Lettice and Lovage*, which received the *Evening Standard* Drama Award for the best comedy of 1988, and *The Gift of the Gorgon*. Penguin publish a number of his plays. Peter Shaffer was awarded the CBE in the 1987 Birthday Honours List.

PETER SHAFFER

*

Three Plays

Five Finger Exercise
Shrivings
Equus

Penguin Books

PENGUIN BOOKS

Published by the Penguin Group
Penguin Books Ltd, 27 Wrights Lane, London W8 5TZ, England
Penguin Books USA Inc., 375 Hudson Street, New York, New York 10014, USA
Penguin Books Australia Ltd, Ringwood, Victoria, Australia
Penguin Books Canada Ltd, 10 Alcorn Avenue, Toronto, Ontario, Canada M4V 3B2
Penguin Books (NZ) Ltd, 182–190 Wairau Road, Auckland 10, New Zealand

Penguin Books Ltd, Registered Offices: Harmondsworth, Middlesex, England

Five Finger Exercise first published by Hamish Hamilton 1958
Published in Penguin Books 1962
Copyright © Peter Shaffer, 1958

Shrivings first published by André Deutsch 1974
Copyright © Peter Shaffer, 1974

Equus first published by André Deutsch 1973
Published in Penguin Books 1977
Copyright © Peter Shaffer, 1973

This collection first published in Penguin Books 1976
11 13 15 17 19 20 18 16 14 12

Copyright © Peter Shaffer, 1958, 1973, 1974, 1976
All rights reserved

Printed in England by Clays Ltd, St Ives plc
Set in Monotype Bembo

Contents

Five Finger Exercise

FOR

HARRY AND JEAN

FIVE FINGER EXERCISE

First produced at the Comedy Theatre, London, on 16 July 1958, with the following cast:

STANLEY HARRINGTON, *a furniture manufacturer; in his middle forties*   Roland Culver

LOUISE, *his wife; in her middle forties*   Adrianne Allen

CLIVE, *his son; nineteen*   Brian Bedford

PAMELA, *his daughter; fourteen*   Juliet Mills

WALTER LANGER, *a German boy; twenty-two; employed by Mrs Harrington as tutor to her daughter*   Michael Bryant

Produced by John Gielgud

The action of this play takes place in the Harringtons' week-end cottage in Suffolk. The time is the present.

ACT ONE

SCENE 1: *A Saturday morning in early September. Breakfast*

SCENE 2: *A Saturday night two months later. After dinner*

ACT TWO

SCENE 1: *The following (Sunday) morning. Breakfast*

SCENE 2: *Sunday night. After dinner*

THE SETTING

THE setting is the week-end cottage of the Harrington family in
Suffolk. A multiple set enables us to see a fair amount of this house:
the living-room, the hall, the landing, and the schoolroom where
Pamela has her lessons.

The living-room occupies all of the stage on the ground floor. It is
well furnished, and almost aggressively expresses Mrs Harrington's
personality. We are let know by it that she is a Person of Taste; but
also that she does not often let well alone. There is more here of the
town, and of the expensive town, than is really acceptable in the
country: the furnishings are sufficiently modish and chic to make her
husband feel, and look, perpetually out of place. To the left – *from
the viewpoint of the audience* – there is a sofa or banquette, and a
coffee-table. To the left of the sofa and just downstage of the front
door is a table with a lamp and their telephone. A comfortable armchair, with a round table to the right of it, bridges the gap between
the social centre of the room and its eating centre. This last is to the
right, and slightly more upstage is a dining-table with three matching
chairs and an upholstered bench downstage of the table. The wall
upstage, running parallel to the table, is made of brick and contains
a large fireplace. Built into the wall is a brick bench, covered with a
red cushion. Inside the fireplace, which actually begins at the height
of the bench, we see polished andirons and a brass bowl of green
leaves. The right wall contains the french window, through which
comes all the light the room receives – autumn light from an old
garden. Below the window is a built-in window-seat – high enough
for Mrs Harrington to use it as a sideboard. There is a lamp there, also
a decorative bowl of grapes and leaves. The door to the garden is
downstage of the window-seat. Left of the window, and on the same
wall as the fireplace, is the kitchen door. Up centre against the back

wall stands a commode bearing a crystal candelabra, a tray with whisky decanter, pitcher of water, and glasses, and a lamp. Under the stairway, left of the commode, is a china umbrella-stand filled with green leaves.

The hall can be seen behind the sofa. It is quite small and contains the usual paraphernalia of cottage halls: a mirror on the wall, a hall tree with hats and coats on the pegs. The front door opens into it, left, and the staircase of the cottage leads out of it, right, on to –

The landing. This occupies a fairly small but important central area upstage and above the living-room. Walter's bedroom door opens on to it, right: the door must be recessed and not too prominent. On the left of this, a corridor leads off to two bedrooms (Clive's and his parents') and the bathroom, all of which are invisible. We do, however, see a window on the upstage wall. On the extreme left, a further short flight of steps leads up to a doorway into –

The schoolroom, which is directly above the sofa area of the living-room. This is very much Pamela's room, it is littered with her possessions, her books, and old toys. Down centre is an oval table where her studies are done, and two chairs. The upstage wall contains the door to her bedroom, a bookcase, and a gas-fire. The left wall has the window, gaily framed in curtains, a wall lamp, and an old school desk. To the right of the desk is an old wooden stool.

The whole stage shows a compact dwelling, disposed with feminine care.

Light switches are located at the following points:

The double switch on the pillar, at the centre edge of the sofa, contains switches for the living-room.

A switch just left of the kitchen door turns on and off the lamp on the sideboard.

A switch left of Walter's door on the landing controls the lights for the landing.

The switch for Pamela's schoolroom is right of the schoolroom door.

ACT ONE

SCENE I

A bright Saturday morning in early September.

STANLEY *and* LOUISE *are seen at rise;* STANLEY *in the armchair smoking his pipe and reading the newspaper;* LOUISE *is seated at the table finishing her coffee.*

STANLEY *is a forceful man in middle age, well built and self-possessed, though there is something deeply insecure about his assertiveness.* LOUISE *is a smart woman in her forties, dressed stylishly, even ostentatiously, for a country week-end. Her whole manner bespeaks a constant preoccupation with style, though without apparent insincerity or affectation. She is very good looking, with attractive features, which are reflected – though with greater instability – in her son.*

[STANLEY *looks at his watch.*]

STANLEY: Is Clive coming down at all today?

LOUISE: I've left him to sleep. He was very late last night.

STANLEY: What time did he get in?

LOUISE: I haven't the faintest idea. I didn't wait up for him.

STANLEY: That's a wonder.

[*She looks at him with irritation and returns to her coffee. Upstairs,* CLIVE *appears on the landing. He is a boy of nineteen, quick, nervous, taut, and likeable. There is something about him oddly and disturbingly young for his age, the nakedness of someone in whom intellectual development has outstripped the emotional. He calls up towards the schoolroom.*]

CLIVE: Pam! [*There is no answer. He goes on downstairs. He enters hesitantly, conscious of being very late.*] Good morning.

STANLEY: Good afternoon. What do you think this place is – a hotel?

CLIVE: I'm sorry.

LOUISE [*being extra friendly and welcoming for* STANLEY'*s benefit*]: Good morning, Jou-Jou! How did you sleep, darling?

CLIVE [*crossing and sitting above the table*]: Very well, thank you.

LOUISE: Don't I get a kiss this morning? [*He kisses her.*] That's better . . . [*Looking at the plate of eggs she has placed before him.*] I'm afraid those eggs are quite horrid now. Let me make you some more.

CLIVE: No, these are all right. Really.

LOUISE: It's no trouble, darling.

CLIVE: They are fine, thank you, Mother . . . Where's Pam?

LOUISE [*knowing this is going to come as a surprise*]: She's out walking with her tutor.

CLIVE: What on earth do you mean?

LOUISE [*mischievously as she pours* CLIVE'*s coffee*]: Her tutor, dear. You know – the German boy I engaged in London to come in every morning and give Pamela her lessons. Well, he's going to live with us. As part of the family.

CLIVE: You mean . . . he's here? Now?

LOUISE [*delighted with her effect*]: Yes. Isn't it amusing? He came down with us last night on the 6.30 train! It's my big surprise. Don't you like it? Pamela's mad about the idea and I thought you would be too.

CLIVE: Why should I be? I hardly know him.

LOUISE: Well, you will now. He's terribly nice. And anyway, it's time you had some well-bred friends for a change. He's marvellously educated and has the most divine manners. I always say it takes a Continental to show us just how ignorant we really are.

[*She exits into the kitchen.*]

CLIVE [*dumbfounded*]: Well!!! And when was all this decided?

STANLEY: Yesterday morning in London – after you left the house. You like the idea, I suppose?

CLIVE: No ... as a matter of fact, I think it's ridiculous ... I mean unnecessary ...

STANLEY: Your mother thinks different. Apparently the Best People have private tutors, and since we're going to be the Best People whether we like it or not, we're going to have a tutor too. We don't send our daughter to anything so common as a school. Oh, I can afford it. What's money after all? We have a town place, so we've simply got to have a country place.

[LOUISE *enters from the kitchen with toast for* CLIVE.]

LOUISE: You always said you wanted a country place!

STANLEY: I meant a little week-end cottage. Not a damn great fancy place like this. [*Rises. To* CLIVE *again.*] However, now we've got a country place, we've simply got to have a tutor.

LOUISE [*seated – left of dining-table*]: Now look, Stanley. This is Walter's first day down here and I want everyone to be very sweet to him. So just keep your ideas to yourself. We don't want to hear them.

STANLEY: We? Clive agrees with me.

LOUISE: Do you, Clive?

CLIVE: Well, yes, I mean, well, no. Isn't it a bit early for this kind of conversation?

STANLEY: You just said you thought a tutor was ridiculous.

CLIVE [*unhappily*]: Well, not really ridiculous ...

LOUISE: Just get on with your breakfast, darling.

STANLEY [*irritated, rounding on his son*]: Why were you so late last night?

CLIVE [*made nervous*]: I – I got involved. In London. I had some work to do.

STANLEY [*sits right of dining-table*]: Work?

CLIVE: I promised to review something. It's going to be printed.

STANLEY: Oh? In *The Times*, I suppose.

CLIVE: No, it's more of a magazine actually. It's not really famous.

STANLEY: Well, why did they ask you to do it?

CLIVE: It was more me did the asking. Anyway, it was two free tickets.

STANLEY: What for?

CLIVE: A play.

STANLEY [*aloofly*]: Was it any good?

CLIVE: Yes . . . It was splendid, as a matter of fact.

LOUISE: What was it, dear?

CLIVE: *Electra*.

STANLEY: What's that?

LOUISE [*with exaggerated surprise*]: You can't mean it! You just can't mean it.

STANLEY: Mean what?

LOUISE: Really, Stanley, there are times when I have to remind myself about you – actually remind myself.

STANLEY [*quietly*]: Suppose you tell me, then. Go on . . . Educate me.

LOUISE [*loftily*]: Clive dear, you explain it to your father, will you?
[*CLIVE sits eating.*]

STANLEY [*to him*]: Well, go on.

CLIVE [*low*]: It's Greek.

STANLEY: Oh, one of those.

LOUISE [*brightly, putting her husband in his place*]: Who was in it, dear? Laurence Olivier? I always think he's best for those Greek things, don't you? . . . I'll never forget that wonderful night when they put out his eyes – I could hear that scream for weeks and weeks afterwards, everywhere I went. There was something so *farouche* about it. You know the word, dear: *farouche*? Like animals in the jungle.

STANLEY [*to* CLIVE]: And that's supposed to be cultured?

CLIVE: What?

STANLEY: People having their eyes put out.

CLIVE: I don't know what 'cultured' means. I always thought it had something to do with pearls.

LOUISE: Nonsense, you know perfectly well what your father means. It's not people's eyes, Stanley: it's the *poetry*. Of course I don't expect *you* to understand.

STANLEY [*to* CLIVE]: And this is what you want to study at Cambridge, when you get up there next month?

CLIVE: Yes it is, more or less.

STANLEY: May I ask why?

CLIVE: Well, poetry's its own reward, actually – like virtue. All Art is, I should think.

STANLEY: And this is the most useful thing you can find to do with your time?

CLIVE: It's not a question of useful.

STANLEY: Isn't it?

CLIVE: Not really.

STANLEY [*staring at him gravely*]: You don't seem to realize the world you're living in, my boy. [LOUISE *gives* CLIVE *the lighted cigarette from her cigarette holder.*] When you finish at this university which your mother insists you're to go to, you'll have to earn your living. I won't always be here to pay for everything, you know. All this culture stuff's very fine for those who can afford it; for the nobs and snobs we're always hearing about from that end of the table . . . [*Indicating* LOUISE. *He rises and takes a few steps upstage.*] But look here . . . if you can't stand on your own two feet you don't amount to anything. And not one of that pansy set of spongers you're going around with will ever help you do that.

CLIVE: You know nothing about my friends.

STANLEY: Oh yes I do. I've seen them. Arty-tarty boys. Going around London, giggling and drinking and talking dirty; wearing Bohemian clothes . . . Who did you go with last night, for instance?

CLIVE: Chuck.

STANLEY: Chuck? Oh yes, the fellow that never washes. Sings in cafés and wants to stay in school till he's thirty, living on government grants. Such a dignified way to go on. [STANLEY *crosses to the centre table and re-lights his pipe.*]

LOUISE [*sharply. Crosses to her purse which is on the centre table*]: I should have thought it was a sign of maturity to want to become more educated. Unfortunately, my dear, we were not all born orphans; we didn't all go to grammar schools or build up a furniture factory on our own by sheer will-power. [*Takes handkerchief from purse.*] We can never hope to live down these shortcomings, of course, but don't you think you might learn to tolerate them?

17

We just didn't have the advantage of your healthy upbringing in the tough world outside. [*She is holding the chafing dish in one hand, the coffee-pot in the other, and standing to the left of the kitchen door.*] Jou-Jou! *La porte.*

[LOUISE *exits after* CLIVE *opens the door for her.* CLIVE *then crosses left of the dining-table to the bench. Picks up the newspaper and sits on the bench.*]

STANLEY [*gets the golf club from left of the commode*]: Well, I'll see you later. That is, unless you want to walk around with me and Joe Benton. [*Pause.*] No, of course not. [*Pause.*] You'd better get out in the air, I didn't take this place so you could lounge about indoors all week-end. [*He contemplates his son.*] You know, Clive – I don't understand you . . .

[LOUISE *re-enters from the kitchen. Closes the door.*]

I don't understand you at all. Not at all. [*He goes out through the front door.*]

CLIVE: Breakfast as usual.

LOUISE [*crossing right to above chair right of dining-table*]: It was just one of his moods, dear.

CLIVE: Oh yes.

LOUISE: Oh, Jou-Jou, I want you to be very happy down here, darling. Really happy, not pretending. After all, it's why I made Daddy buy this place – to get away from London and all the squabbling. To come into the country and relax in our own little retreat . . . So you see, you've just got to be happy. You can't let me down. Can you? [LOUISE *sits in armchair.*]

CLIVE [*rises, salutes, crosses to his mother, and kneels to her left*]: *Votre Majesté.* My empress!

LOUISE [*permitting her hand to be kissed*]: *Levez-vous!*

CLIVE: The Empress Louise, ill-fated, tragic, dark-eyed Queen from beyond the seas! What is your wish, Madame? I am yours to command.

LOUISE: I've told you already, my little Cossack. *Sois content.* Be happy.

CLIVE: *Bien.* On my honour as a guardsman, and on my beautiful hat of genuine black sheepskin, I promise to you six big laughs a day, and twelve little giggles.

LOUISE: Darling. My darling Jou-Jou!

CLIVE: *Maman!*

[*They embrace very fondly.*]

LOUISE: Now that's a promise, you know. To be happy. Then I can be happy too. Because I can tell when you're not, you know; and that makes me miserable also. So remember; no complexes.

CLIVE: No complexes, *Majesté.*

[*She kisses his forehead.*]

LOUISE [*rises*]: Come on. I'll wash and you dry. It won't take five minutes.

CLIVE: It'll take at least twenty. I can't think why you don't get a maid in.

LOUISE [*crossing to dining-table, where she removes her watch, rings, bracelets, etc. and leaves them on the table*]: You know we've tried all that. Their bicycles break down or there's illness at home; they're always late or they don't come at all. And anyway, dear, house-work's all in the fun. Everyone does it these days.

[CLIVE *allows himself to be coaxed and follows his mother into the kitchen. The kitchen door is left open.*]

PAMELA [*running through the front door and calling back to Walter*]: Hurry up, Walter ... [*Running up the stairs.*] You're the slowest runner I've ever met. You must be in dreadful condition.

[PAMELA *is a girl of fourteen, as quick as her brother and wholly without his melancholy.*]

WALTER [*hanging his coat and cap on the hat rack in the hall*]: I'm older than you are.

[WALTER *is a slim German of twenty-two, handsome, secret, diffident, but happily at ease with his young student.*]

PAMELA [*rushing up to the schoolroom*]: If I get up there first, no French today.

WALTER: Oh, no you don't ... you're not going to get out of it as easy as that. [PAMELA *closes the schoolroom door and stands against it.* WALTER *tries to open it.*] Hey!

PAMELA [*from the schoolroom*]: What?

WALTER: French.

PAMELA: You are invading my privacy, sir.

WALTER: Open the door.

PAMELA: What for?

WALTER: French ... Come on now.

[*Reluctantly* PAMELA *opens the schoolroom door and exits into her bedroom.*]

PAMELA [*from off*]: But it's too cold to think in French, Walter.

WALTER: Is it? Well, I'll light the gas-fire then. Where are the matches?

PAMELA: They're on the window-sill.

[WALTER *gets the matches from the window-sill and lights the fire.* PAMELA *enters from the bedroom with her essay book.*]

WALTER: *Parler:* to talk. Future tense. Now think hard.

PAMELA [*concentrating*]: *Je parlerai?*

WALTER: Good.

PAMELA: *Je parlerai, tu parleras, il parlera, nous parlerons?* [*Nods.*] *Vous parlerez, ils parleront.*

WALTER: Good. That's the first time you have had it right.

PAMELA: Oh phooey to French! I hate it really.

WALTER: Why?

PAMELA: Because the French are a decadent nation. Personally I think we all ought to study Russian and American.

WALTER: But American is the same as English.

PAMELA: Oh, no it isn't ... When they say 'dame' they mean young girl, and when we say 'dame' we mean old girl. But when we call someone 'old girl' we really mean what they call a dame. So you see ...

WALTER: No.

PAMELA: Well of course. I know all about America from Mary. You've still to meet her. She's my only friend here.

WALTER: Where does she live?

PAMELA: Over the stables in Craven Lane. You'll just fall when you see her.

WALTER: How? In love?

PAMELA: Of course. Mummy says she's common, but that's just because she wears shocking pink socks and says 'Drop dead' all the time. I know her mother drinks and has lovers and things. But her husband's dead and so you really can't blame her, can you? Just like Clive says. There-but-for-the-Grace-of-God Department.

WALTER: And she knows all about America because she says 'Drop dead'?

PAMELA [*loftily*]: Of course not. How can you be so brutish? For one thing she's got an American boy friend in the Air Force.

WALTER: How old is she?

PAMELA [*airily*]: Sixteen, But that's all right; they like them young. I don't think they actually . . . well, you know . . . Sometimes, she gets decked up in her black jeans and goes off to some sexy club in Ipswich under a Polish restaurant. But her mother doesn't like her going round the streets looking like that, so she has to sneak off when no one's looking.

WALTER: Like witches.

PAMELA: Witches?

WALTER: Going to their Sabbath.

PAMELA: What's that?

WALTER: When they used to worship the Devil. They used to sneak off just like that. It was the same thing like your English Teddy Boys. You make yourself very excited, then people give you a bad name and start being afraid of you. That's when you really do start worshipping the Devil.

PAMELA: Oh, phooey.

WALTER [*more gravely*]: Not phooey.

PAMELA: You talk as if you'd seen him.

WALTER: The Devil? I have.

PAMELA: Where?

WALTER: Where he lives.

PAMELA: Where's that?

WALTER: Where I was born.

PAMELA: And what was he doing?

WALTER: Sitting down.

PAMELA: Where?

WALTER: Behind people's eyes ... [*Seeing her confusion.*] Well, isn't that a good place to sit?

PAMELA: D'you miss it?

WALTER: What?

PAMELA: Your home.

WALTER: It's not my home.

PAMELA: Still, there must be things you miss. Birthdays or Christmases or something.

WALTER: Christmas, yes ... Where I was born it was better. It's called Muhlbach. The stars are more clear there.

PAMELA: Just the stars?

WALTER [*with a small spurt of excitement*]: No, ice too. Ice grows all down the river, and at night you go skating all alone, all alone for miles in the black, and it's terribly cold and fast – and suddenly you see torches coming towards you, and voices come, and there's a crowd of happy people with nuts and fruit and hot rum, kissing you a good New Year.

PAMELA: Oh, wonderful!

WALTER [*with reservation*]: Yes, it is for that ...

PAMELA: Let's go! [*Rises.*] Just for Christmas, you and me. You can teach me enough German in twelve weeks so I can understand everyone – Oh, I'm sorry. I forgot. You don't teach German.

WALTER: No.

PAMELA: Walter, I never asked before – but why not? I mean you'd make more money doing that than anything else.

[WALTER *shakes his head slowly 'No'.* PAMELA *crosses above table to stool left of desk.*]

You're really a very strange young man.

WALTER: Am I?

PAMELA [*kindly*]: I suppose part of it's living in a foreign country all the time.

22

WALTER: It's not foreign. I've been here five years, and soon I get my citizenship.

PAMELA: Then you'll be English?

[WALTER *nods 'Yes'*.]

Then you'll like Christmas here too, because this'll be home and you'll spend it with us here in the country. Don't you have any family at all?

[WALTER *shakes his head*.]

No one?

WALTER: No.

PAMELA: But that's the wrong answer now. When I say 'Have you got no family?' you must say: 'Yes, of course I have a family, and a very fine one too.' Now repeat after me. 'My family lives at 22 Elton Square, London and The Retreat, Lower Orford, Suffolk.' Come on.

WALTER: My family lives at 22 Elton Square, London and The Retreat, Lower Orford, Suffolk.

PAMELA [*crossing above* WALTER]: Good. Ten out of ten. Now you look much happier . . . you should wear a high collar and one of those floppy ties. Then you'd look like Metternich or someone. And wear your hair very sleek and romantic. [*She smooths his hair*.] Like this . . .

WALTER: Stop that!

PAMELA [*going to the schoolroom door*]: No, it's terribly becoming . . . [*Opens the door*.] Count Walter Langer, Knight of the Holy Golden Soup-ladle!

WALTER [*picking up the wild flowers from the table and crossing to the door*]: Pamela, no! [*He runs down the stairs on to the landing. She chases him. The schoolroom door is left open*.] Stop it! You're not to –

PAMELA: Pompous, pompous, pompous!

LOUISE [*at the kitchen door, wearing apron and carrying a dish towel*]: Walter!

WALTER: There's your mother calling me.

LOUISE: Walter! [*Returns to the kitchen*.]

WALTER: I go now. You go and get on with your history. What's that in French – 'I go?'

PAMELA [*at the schoolroom door*]: *Je allez?*

WALTER: No, I've told you one million times. *Je vais.*

PAMELA: *Je vais.* [*She climbs the stairs to the schoolroom. Stops at the door.*] Hey!

WALTER: Yes?

PAMELA: See you anon, Mastodon.

WALTER: Quarter to four, Dinosaur!

[*He goes downstairs to the living-room.* PAMELA *enters the schoolroom, closes the door, and applies herself to the history book. She sits at the table.* CLIVE *comes in from the kitchen and goes to the dining-table.*]

CLIVE [*to* WALTER, *as he enters*]: Hello.

WALTER: Hello.

CLIVE: Welcome to the family.

WALTER: Thank you.

CLIVE: What do you think of our house?

WALTER: Oh, it's wonderful. Very elegant.

CLIVE [*dryly*]: It's certainly that.

WALTER: I think your mother was calling me.

CLIVE: She's in the music room. Through there.

WALTER: You have a music room here?

CLIVE: Oh, yes. It used to be an outside privy. But mother wasn't daunted by that. She bought a baby grand for fifteen pounds and knocked down a wall to get it in. It's lucky it's at the back because His Godship doesn't care for music.

WALTER: Oh . . . I brought my record-player down with me. I was playing it in my room last night. I'm sorry.

CLIVE: He'll soon let you know if he minds.

[WALTER *puts the wild flowers on the centre table.*]
How do you like being tutor to our little hepcat?

WALTER: Oh, she's delightful. When your mother first met me, and engaged me to teach her, I was so pleased. My last job was not so easy . . . and now that I have been invited to live with you, I am

24

very happy. [*He is very shy at saying this.* CLIVE *reacts kindly to this. He starts to fold the table-cloth.*] Let me help you.

CLIVE [*folding cloth with* WALTER]: Have you never lived with a family before?

WALTER: No, I had a flat in North London.

CLIVE: Did you?

WALTER: Well, it was more of a basement, really.

CLIVE: I can imagine.

WALTER: This is my first family.

CLIVE: Yes? [*Crossing to the commode to put the table-cloth in the top drawer.*] Well, let me give you a word of warning. This *isn't* a family. It's a tribe of wild cannibals. Between us we eat everyone we can. You think I'm joking?

WALTER [*putting the bowl of flowers back on the table*]: I think you are very lucky to have a family.

CLIVE: And I think you're very lucky to be without one ... I'm sorry. [*Crosses to the coffee-table.*] Actually we're very choosey in our victims. We only eat other members of the family.

WALTER [*crossing to above the armchair*]: Then I must watch out. Your sister thinks I'm almost a member already.

CLIVE: Pam? [*Offers* WALTER *a cigarette.* WALTER *declines.*] You know, I don't like the way she's growing up at all. She wants to include people all the time. She doesn't seem to want to exclude or demolish anybody.

WALTER: Perhaps that's because she takes after her mother.

CLIVE [*sits on sofa*]: Well, of course, a girl who took after my father would be almost unthinkable ...

[WALTER *starts to cross left.*]

You're not at all like a German.

WALTER: Am I not?

[*Enter* LOUISE, *holding music album.*]

LOUISE: Walter, my dear, I do hope I didn't disturb your lesson. But I'm longing for us to start ours. [*She gives album to* WALTER.] Actually I thought this morning *you* could do the playing and I'd just watch. I mean, you could try my little piano – see what it's capable of . . . [*She sits in chair right of dining-table.*]

WALTER: I'd be delighted, Mrs Harrington.

LOUISE: You have such beautiful hands. [*She takes one of his hands.*] I remember once shaking hands with Paderewski. Of course it was many years ago, and I was only a girl, but I've never forgotten it. He had hands almost exactly like yours, my dear boy. Much older of course – but the same bone formation, the same delicacy . . . This was my mother's album.

WALTER: It's charming.

LOUISE: What are you going to play for me? Something Viennese, of course.

WALTER [*sits on bench below dining-table*]: What would you like? Beethoven? – Brahms?

LOUISE: Wonderful! And you can explain to me all about it. I mean where it was written and who for. I always think it so much increases one's enjoyment if you know about things like that. Take the 'Moonlight', for example. Now what was the true story about that?

CLIVE: Well it wasn't really moonlight at all, Mother. Moonlight was the name of the brothel where Beethoven actually was when he started writing it.

LOUISE [*rises, shocked*]: Jou-Jou!

CLIVE: He got one of the girls to crouch on all fours so he could use her back for a table. It's in one of the biographies, I forget which.

LOUISE [*to* WALTER]: He's being very naughty, isn't he? Really, Jou-Jou!

WALTER [*going to centre table and picking up posy of wild flowers*]: I found these in the lane. They're quite rare for this time of year – I thought you might be interested –

LOUISE [*taking posy*]: How charming! I am very touched. Thank you, my dear. [*Pause.*] You know, I must give you a nickname. Walter is much too formal. Wait. Of course! Clive's Jou-Jou so you can be Hibou. Perfect. Hibou, the owl. [*To* CLIVE.] He looks rather like a little owl, doesn't he?

CLIVE: Why not Pou? That's better still.

LOUISE: Oh, he's impossible this morning. Your father's right, a walk in the fresh air would do you a lot of good.

[PAMELA *snaps her book shut and comes bounding out of the school-room and down the stairs.*]

PAMELA [*running downstairs*]: Mother! Mother . . . !

LOUISE: Good heavens, what a noise that girl makes. [*To* WALTER.] I'm afraid you're going to have to teach her some etiquette as well.

[PAMELA *comes bursting into the living-room.*]

PAMELA: Mother!

LOUISE: Quietly, dear. Quietly.

[WALTER *crosses to kitchen door.*]

PAMELA [*breathless*]: Sorry. Mother, will you test me on my history?

LOUISE: Ask Clive, will you dear? I'm busy now. [*Picks up glass of wild flowers.*] We're going to *our* lesson. Walter's going to play for me.

PAMELA: Are you, Walter? How lovely!

LOUISE [*to* WALTER]: Come along, my dear.

[LOUISE *goes out with* WALTER *into the kitchen.* CLIVE *lies down on the sofa and covers his face with his handkerchief.* PAMELA *studies her brother, then knocks on the commode.*]

PAMELA: General Harrington.

CLIVE [*as if deaf. Sits up*]: Eh? . . . Eh? . . . What's that? . . . Who's there? . . .

PAMELA: It's only me, General. May I come in?

CLIVE: What! [*He uses the rolled-up magazine as a telescope and studies her. He speaks broadly and heavily.*] Well, bless my soul! . . . If it isn't little Daphne. Spike my cannon! Come in, me dear. Come in.

PAMELA [*sits to the left of* CLIVE]: Thank you.

CLIVE: That's the way. Don't be afraid. I must say it's damned decent of you to call on a boring old soldier like me.

PAMELA [*coyly*]: Oh, it's nothing.

CLIVE [*putting his hand on her knee*]: Well, how are you, my dear? Eh?

27

PAMELA [*removing it*]: Fine, thank you. And how's the – [*Whispers.*] you-know-what?

CLIVE [*normal voice*]: Do I?

PAMELA [*normal voice*]: Gout.

CLIVE [*General's voice*]: Oh, it comes and goes, y'know. Comes and goes.

PAMELA [*Daphne's voice again, gushing*]: I think it's wonderful of you to take it so well. I'm sure I'd be complaining all the time. I'm a real silly-billy about pain.

CLIVE: Nonsense, me dear. Lord, though, how yer remind me of yer dear mother. Hair just like hers.

PAMELA: Ow?

CLIVE: Yellow as a cornflower, I always used to say.

PAMELA [*normal voice*]: There's something wrong about that.

CLIVE [*normal voice*]: Is there? What?

PAMELA: Cornflowers are blue.

CLIVE: Well, your mother certainly didn't have blue hair.

PAMELA [*archly*]: That's all you know ... Anyway, you've got to test my history. Come on.

CLIVE [*beckoning*]: Your bow.

[*Automatically she leans to him for it to be tied. The sound of piano music from the music room. Brahms – 'Capriccio in B minor'.*]

PAMELA [*listening*]: He's the best, isn't he?

CLIVE: Is he?

PAMELA: Oh, you can tell. I knew just as soon as he came in the door.

[*They listen for a moment.*]

CLIVE: How d'you get on together?

PAMELA [*rises. Crosses to armchair. Sits*]: Oh, we simply adore each other.

CLIVE: Is he going to teach you anything?

PAMELA: Everything, my dear. Just wait and see, I'll be the most erudine girl for my age in London.

CLIVE: Dite.

PAMELA: What?

CLIVE: Eru*dite*. Come on, let's make a start. [CLIVE *studies the list* *earnestly for a moment.*] Which was the most uncertain dynasty in Europe.

PAMELA: I haven't the faintest.

CLIVE [*as if reading*]: The Perhapsburgs.

PAMELA: Who?

CLIVE: The Perhapsburgs.

PAMELA: Now, Clive, really –

CLIVE [*enthusiastically*]: I don't know much about them yet, but I'm working on it. So far there's just Thomas the Tentative – a successor of Doubting Thomas, of course – and Vladimir – the Vague.

PAMELA: That's marvellous! How about a woman?

CLIVE: By all means.

PAMELA: Dorothea.

CLIVE: Nice.

PAMELA: Dorothea the – the Downright.

CLIVE: But that's just the opposite. There's nothing Perhaps about her.

PAMELA: Well, she could be the black sheep of the family.
     [*Music stops.*]

CLIVE: We'll see . . . Now. [*He consults the list.*] Pay attention. Who was known as the Crying Cavalier?

PAMELA [*protesting*]: Now, Clive, really . . .

CLIVE: Answer me. Who?

PAMELA: I don't know.

CLIVE: Who was the Unknown Civilian?

PAMELA: I don't know.

CLIVE: Who was the Curable Romantic?

PAMELA: I don't know. I don't know . . . ! [*She throws herself at* CLIVE.]

CLIVE: Really, you are the most impossibly ignorant child . . . [*Struggling with her happily.*] Hepcat! Hepcat! Hepcat . . .

PAMELA: Clive!

CLIVE: What?

PAMELA [*springing away from* CLIVE]: Tell me a story!

CLIVE: Sweet or sour?

PAMELA: Sour.

CLIVE [*sitting right of dining-table*]: All right. Once upon a time there was a little girl who lived all by herself in a prison.

PAMELA: Why? What had she done?

CLIVE: Nothing: that's just the point. They took away all her clothes and made her wear blankets instead.

[WALTER *enters from the kitchen.*]

WALTER: Excuse me. Mrs Harrington was asking for her handbag.

PAMELA: Here it is. [*Takes handbag from centre table and hands it to* WALTER.] Stay with us. Clive's telling me a story.

WALTER: A story? About history?

PAMELA: About a prison.

CLIVE [*showing off to* WALTER]: Yes, it's going to be brilliant! [*Rises and goes to* WALTER.] All Gothic darkness and calamities. It's called the 'Black Hole of East Suffolk'. [*Mock grave.*] Sit down and I'll unfold.

WALTER: No, excuse me. Mrs Harrington is waiting.

[*He gives* CLIVE *a short bow and leaves.* CLIVE *stares after him.*]

PAMELA: What's wrong?

CLIVE: Nothing.

PAMELA: What about the little girl in prison?

CLIVE [*turns and looks at her. He speaks with sudden energy, rather bitterly*]: It wasn't a girl. It was a little boy. A little German boy with blond hair, who played the piano rather well. He walked straight into the prison of his own free will and shut the door behind him.

[CLIVE *leaves through the front door. We hear the piano again playing the same piece as the gramophone.*]

SCENE 2

A Saturday night two months later.

The family has finished dinner and is taking coffee, at least STANLEY *and* LOUISE *are.* CLIVE *is at the sideboard up centre, pouring himself a whisky. We hear* PAMELA *practising the piano – first scales, then plays Bach's 'Preludio XI'.*

LOUISE [*to* CLIVE]: Don't you want any coffee?

CLIVE: No, thanks.

LOUISE: I do think you might have caught an earlier train from Cambridge. I cooked a special dinner for you to welcome you home. All your favourite things.

CLIVE [*crosses to sofa. Sits right of* LOUISE]: I'm sorry. Actually, I had a perfectly good sandwich from British Railways.

LOUISE [*to Clive as he sits next to her*]: I think you've got into some rather bad habits in Cambridge. Isn't that your third drink already?

CLIVE: No, I don't think so.

LOUISE: Well, what if it is? It's a special week-end, isn't it?
  [*She smiles at him lovingly.* STANLEY *watches this with irritation.* WALTER *comes out of the kitchen and picks up the record from the commode.*]

STANLEY [*referring to the piano practising*]: How much longer is that row going on, may I ask?

LOUISE: For another half hour, I hope. [*To* WALTER.] How's she getting on, dear?

WALTER: Oh, very well, Mrs Harrington. [*To* STANLEY.] We've only been working for six weeks, you know, sir.

LOUISE: Yes, it's amazing, isn't it? Oh, Walter, would you mind taking Clive's suitcase upstairs as you go?

WALTER: No, of course not, Mrs Harrington. [*He goes up the stairs and takes the suitcase into the hall.*]

LOUISE: Thank you so much. [*To* CLIVE.] I don't know why you can't put your own things away.

STANLEY [*to* CLIVE]: And that's what you call great music? Is that right? Great music?

CLIVE [*with an attempt at humour*]: Let's say it's a little distorted at the moment.

STANLEY: Distorted? It's driving me mad.

CLIVE [*unhappily*]: I suppose we can't expect her to be an expert in two months. Run-before-you-walk Department.

LOUISE [*rises and picks up tray from coffee-table. Starts to the kitchen*]: Your father imagines that everything can be done without hard work. Everything except making money out of the furniture business.

[WALTER *re-enters from the hall and goes into his room, where he turns on the lights.*]

[*To* STANLEY.] Really you are absurd. How do you think Paderewski sounded when he was practising? What is that piece she's learning, dear? Mozart? [*He shrugs, embarrassed.*] Jou-Jou, I'm talking to you.

CLIVE [*low*]: Bach.

LOUISE: You could play too if you wanted to. You've got the hands for it.

[LOUISE *goes out to kitchen.* CLIVE *smiles faintly. There is a pause.*]

STANLEY [*carefully*]: Clive, do you remember coming to the factory for your allowance the day you went up to Cambridge?

CLIVE: Yes, I do.

STANLEY: Did you have a talk to my manager while you were waiting?

CLIVE: Did I . . . I suppose I did.

STANLEY: Is it true you told him you thought the furniture we make was – what was it – 'shoddy and vulgar'? [*Pause.*] Well?

CLIVE: I think I said it – it lacked . . .

STANLEY: What?

CLIVE: Well, that it didn't use materials as well as it might. Wood, for example. [*He smiles hopefully.*]

STANLEY: And the design was shoddy and vulgar?

CLIVE: Well, yes, I suppose I gave that impression. Not all of it, of course – just some things . . .

STANLEY: What things?

CLIVE [*plucking up a little courage*]: Well, those terrible oak cupboards, for example. I think you call it the Jacobean line. And those threepiece suites in mauve plush. Things like that . . .

STANLEY [*impassive as ever*]: Mr Clark said you called them 'grotesque'.

[CLIVE *lowers his eyes.*]

Is that right – grotesque?

CLIVE [*rises, crosses to commode for book, takes it to chair right of diningtable*]: I think they are, rather.

STANLEY: And I suppose you think that's clever. That's being educated, I suppose; to go up to my manager

[LOUISE *enters.*]

in my own factory and tell him you think the stuff I'm turning out is shoddy and vulgar . . . Is it?

LOUISE [*crossing to the sofa*]: Just because *you've* got no taste, it doesn't mean we all have to follow suit.

[STANLEY *gives her a look which silences her, then turns again to his son.* CLIVE *continues to sit rigid at the table.*]

STANLEY: Now you listen to me, my boy. You get this through your head once and for all; I'm in business to make money. I give people what they want. I mean ordinary people. Maybe they haven't got such wonderful taste as you and your mother; perhaps they don't read such good books – what is it? – *Homes and Gardens*? – but they know what they want. If they didn't want it, they wouldn't buy it, and I'd be out of business.

[*Piano stops.*]

Before you start sneering again, young man, just remember something – you've always had enough to eat.

[*The explosive opening of the Brahms Third Symphony is heard from Walter's room.*]

33

[*Looking up, dangerously.*] One stops, the other starts. I'm going out.

[STANLEY *stands up.*]

LOUISE: Where to – Mr Benton?

STANLEY: And if I am, at least I can get some peace there.

LOUISE: Ssh.

STANLEY: Don't you ssh me.

LOUISE: This is the first week-end we've all been here together since Clive went up to Cambridge. I think the least you can do is stay home, the first evening. Why must you be so disagreeable? [*She goes to the landing and calls.*] Walter! Walter! [*She turns on the landing lights.*]

WALTER [*coming from his room*]: Did you call, Mrs Harrington?

LOUISE: Do you think you could play your records another time, dear? Mr Harrington has got a slight headache.

WALTER: Of course, Mrs Harrington. I'm so sorry. So very sorry. [*He reaches into his room and turns off the machine.*]

LOUISE: That's quite all right, dear. I hate to disturb your concentration.

WALTER: Oh, no.

LOUISE: Come down when you want to. I've got some delicious *petits fours* and I'll make you some fresh coffee. [*She turns off the landing lights.*]

WALTER: Thank you, Mrs Harrington. [*He goes into his room.*]

LOUISE [*coming down the stairs and into the living-room.* STANLEY *is again in the armchair*]: I don't know! You say you can't stand London. I go to all the trouble fixing this place for you, and you can't stay in it a single minute. Now try and be a bit more pleasant will you. [*To* CLIVE *as she removes jewellery at the commode.*] Jou-Jou, it's washing-up time. Are you going to help me?

CLIVE: Can't we leave it for once?

LOUISE: It's all right. I can manage perfectly well without you. [*She goes into the kitchen.*]

CLIVE: I'm sorry I said that about the furniture, Father. I suppose it was tactless of me.

STANLEY: Never mind. How are you settling down at Cambridge? What about the other boys, do you get on with them?

CLIVE: It's not exactly like prep school, you know. You rather pick your own friends.

STANLEY: Yes, I suppose you do. Well, what do they do there? I mean apart from lessons.

CLIVE: Anything you like. There are all sorts of clubs and societies.

STANLEY: Do you belong to any?

CLIVE: Yes, I joined a Dramatic Society as a matter of fact.

STANLEY: You mean for acting?

CLIVE: It's quite professional, you know. They have their own theatre and get reviews in *The Times*.

STANLEY: Don't any of your friends play games?

CLIVE: Yes, but – the cricket and football are sort of professional standards. I thought of taking up fencing, it's not as odd as it sounds. It's meant to be very good for coordination –

STANLEY: What's that?

CLIVE: Muscles, I think.

STANLEY: Clive, as you know your mother and I didn't see eye to eye about sending you to University. But that's past history now. The point is what use are you going to make of it? Well?

CLIVE: That's rather as it turns out, I should have thought. I mean you can't judge things in advance, can you?

STANLEY: Ah now, that's just what I mean. If you don't know where you're going you might just as well pack up.

CLIVE: Why?

STANLEY: It's quite simple, I should have thought.

CLIVE: It isn't. It just isn't like that. I mean if I knew where I was going I wouldn't have to go there would I? I'd be there already.

STANLEY: What kind of silly quibble is that?

CLIVE: It's not a quibble. Look, education – being educated – you just can't talk about it in that way. It's something quite different – like setting off on an expedition into the jungle. Gradually all the things you know disappear. The old birds fly out of the sky, new ones fly in you've never seen before, and everything surprises you too. Trees you expected to be a few feet high grow right up overhead, like the nave of Wells Cathedral. Anyway if you had seen all this before, you wouldn't have to go looking. I think education is simply the process of being taken by surprise, do you see?

CLIVE: Be that as it may.

CLIVE: You don't see.

STANLEY [rises – crosses to above dining-table]: Clive, I'm not talking about education. By all means, take advantage of your lessons. Look here boy, let's not pretend. Everyone doesn't get to Cambridge, you know it and I know it. You're in a privileged position and you must make the most of it. What you do now will influence the rest of your life. You know that, don't you?

CLIVE: Yes, I suppose it will.

STANLEY: Take your friends for example. What kind of friends do you have?

CLIVE: Do you want a list?

STANLEY: Now don't start getting on any high-horse. I'm simply saying this ... [Sits above the dining-table. Leans toward CLIVE.] People still judge a man by the company he keeps. You go around with a lot of drifters and arty boys, and you'll be judged as one of them.

CLIVE: I don't ...

STANLEY [cuts him off immediately and closes his book]: I don't say you do, and you're old enough to decide for yourself anyway. Right?
  [CLIVE nods.]
Number two is this. Now's the time for you to be making contacts with the right people, I mean people who will be useful to you later on. I don't mean the smart people or the fancy la-de-da people your mother's always on about. I mean the people that matter. The people who will have influence. Get in with them now and you won't go far wrong. I never had your opportunities, the contacts I made I had to work up myself. So I know what I'm talking about. Do you understand?

CLIVE: Yes, I do.

STANLEY: Good. Now you've got a good brain and I'll see to it you've got enough money. There's no harm in having a few pounds in your pocket, you know.

[LOUISE *enters. Closes kitchen door.*]

Never be so foolish as to look down on money. It's the one thing that counts in the end.

LOUISE [*at the commode putting on her jewellery*]: Money! Is that all you ever think about? Money!

STANLEY: You don't have any difficulty spending it, I notice. [*To* CLIVE.] Now let's see, how long have you been at Cambridge? Is this your half-term holiday?

LOUISE [*crossing to the sofa above the armchair*]: Half-term! You talk about it as if it were a grammar school instead of our leading University. Really, Stanley. I don't know how one can even begin to talk to you.

STANLEY [*rises, crosses right a few steps as if to answer* LOUISE. *Then turns to* CLIVE]: Would you like to walk with me over to Benton's?

CLIVE: I – I've got some reading to do actually.

STANLEY: We can stop in at the Red Lion for a quick one.

CLIVE: No. I don't think so really.

STANLEY: Very well.

CLIVE: It's important, or I would.

[STANLEY *nods and goes out of the front door.*]

LOUISE: Are you going to be intense?

CLIVE: No.

LOUISE [*rises. Crosses to armchair – sits*]: Oh, Jou-Jou! *Mon petit Cossack. Embrasse-moi . . . Non? . . .* It's your Empress.

[WALTER *comes from his room and turns the light off there.*]

CLIVE: Your *Majesté.*

LOUISE: Oh, come on, every family has its rows, you know.

[WALTER *enters the living-room carrying a book.*]

Oh, here you are, Hibou! I'm so sorry about your music.

WALTER: Oh, it's me to be sorry . . . How is Mr Harrington?

LOUISE: It's nothing serious, my dear. He's gone out to clear his head. I'll get the fresh coffee. It must be ready. [*To* CLIVE *as she goes*

37

to the kitchen.] Don't sulk, Jou-Jou. There's no need to take everything as if it were one of your Greek tragedies. [*She exits.*]

WALTER: I'm so sorry about the noise. If I had known I would not have played the machine.

CLIVE [*rises. Goes to the commode*]: Yes, it's a pity. Music always affects him that way. The better the music the stronger the headaches. Do you want a drink?

WALTER: No, thank you.

CLIVE: Was that your new record?

WALTER [*crossing to the sofa and sitting*]: Yes. It's 'high fidelity' sound . . . more bright and clear.

CLIVE [*crossing to the right of the armchair and then sitting*]: It sounds like the motto of a matrimonial agency. 'High Fidelity Guaranteed.'

WALTER: It's nice to see you back, Clive. Tell me, how are you liking Cambridge?

CLIVE: It's all right, I suppose.

WALTER: Is that all? Just all right?

CLIVE: No, it's wonderful, really. Like going to a new country. I suppose one of the thrills of travel is hearing people speak a foreign language. But the marvellous thing about this is hearing them speak my own for the first time.

WALTER: I know.

CLIVE: Pam speaks a few words of it, of course, but it isn't quite enough. Where is she?

WALTER: I don't know.

CLIVE: I suppose she's gone for a walk.

WALTER: It's a beautiful night.

CLIVE: Oh yes. A night for walks. Pam tripping along so gaily . . . Father marching along so . . . rightly. And I should be by his side. Or better still, a pace or two behind. 'Clive, to heel, sir. Heel!' Let me introduce myself: [*Raises his glass in a toast.*] 'Spaniel Harrington.' [*Drinks.*] What's the matter?

WALTER: Nothing.

CLIVE: Fathers should not be spoken to like that . . . is that it?

38

WALTER: I think, if you forgive me . . .

CLIVE: Well?

WALTER: I think you have a duty to your father.

CLIVE: A duty? What a very German thing to say. I'm sorry, I'm not quite sober.

WALTER: I did not mean duty in that sense. I meant that it seems to me . . . Clever children have a duty – to protect their parents who are not so clever.

CLIVE: Protect?

WALTER: I do not put it very well perhaps.

CLIVE: You know when I was on the train tonight, I was so looking forward to seeing them again. I know I've only been away a few weeks, but so much has happened to me . . . and I thought, I don't know why, they would have changed as much as I have. But everything's exactly the same.

[LOUISE *enters with tray holding pot of coffee, plate of* petits fours, *cups and saucers.* WALTER *meets her and takes the tray to the coffee-table.* LOUISE *turns off the lamp on the window-seat. Then she crosses to the sofa.*]

LOUISE: Isn't this nice? Well now, we seem to have the hour to ourselves. What are we going to do? I know! Walter shall recite some beautiful poetry for us in German.

CLIVE: You don't understand German.

LOUISE: It's not the meaning, it's the sound that counts, dear. And I'm sure this boy will speak it adorably. Most people make it sound like a soda siphon, but when you speak it I'm sure I'll feel exactly what the poet wanted to say – [*gives cup to* WALTER] even more than if I actually knew the language and had to cope with all those miller's daughters and woodcutters and little people. It's difficult to explain – but you know what I mean.

CLIVE [*takes his empty glass to the commode*]: I don't – I'm going out.

LOUISE: Where?

CLIVE: To the pub.

LOUISE: You can't be serious.

CLIVE: Too vulgar?

LOUISE: Don't be silly, Clive. No, it's just so ... uncivil, dear. There's plenty of drink in the house if you really need it, though I think you've had quite enough already.

CLIVE [*gravely*]: You're right, I have. [*To* WALTER.] Excuse me, I'm sure you recite beautifully. [*He makes for the french windows.*]

LOUISE [*with a resurgence of desperation*]: But your father asked you if you wanted to go to the pub and you said no.

CLIVE: True. [*He goes out.* WALTER *stands stiffly, very uncomfortable.*]

LOUISE: Poor boy. I'm afraid he gets rather upset down here. He's essentially a town person, really, like me. And I get it from my mother. Being French, of course. Like all Parisians she detested the country. She used to say: 'Fields are for cows. Drawing-rooms are for ladies.' Of course, it sounds better in French. If I had my way I'd never stir from London. I did all this [*indicating the cottage*] for Mr Harrington. He's what we call here an open-air type, you know.

WALTER [*smiling*]: Yes. I know this word.

LOUISE: And for Clive's sake, too. We'd all been a little restless in town, and I thought it would be amusing if we could have a little retreat ... Calm ourselves with country air ... And really, it's been quite successful, I think ... On the whole ...

[WALTER *sits on the sofa. She drinks some coffee.*]

A very clever boy I was recommended to did it up for us. Bunny Baily – d'you know him?

WALTER: No, I'm afraid not.

LOUISE [*lightly and rapidly*]: Well you will, I'm sure. He's very up and coming. Not just chic; I mean really *original*. He wanted to make us entirely early Medieval: stone flagging and rushes strewn on the floor. But my husband didn't quite see eye to eye with us on that. [*Drinks more coffee.*] Mr Harrington's very conservative, you know. Well, most men are, aren't they, essentially? ... Englishmen, any-way. The French are different ... And the Germans too. I'm sure. [*She smiles at him and points to the cigarettes on the coffee-table.*] Would you like to smoke?

WALTER [*reaching for the cigarette-box*]: Thank you.

LOUISE: You look a little upset too, Hibou. What's the matter?

WALTER: Oh, it's nothing.

LOUISE: It must be something. Has Clive been teasing you? He can be very naughty sometimes.

WALTER: Oh, no. You know, Mrs Harrington, I think he is not very happy.

LOUISE [*putting cup on table next to armchair*]: He gets that from me too.

WALTER [*impulsively*]: Is there anything that I can do? Anything at all?

LOUISE [*regardless*]: I'm not a very happy person either, you know. [*Rises. Crosses left to below armchair.*] Well, you can see for yourself. Whatever you do, my dear boy, marry a girl who's your equal. If you can find one. I'm sure it'll be hard. When I married I was a very young girl. Believe it or not [*puts cup on table L. of armchair*] I'd hardly met anyone outside Bournemouth. [*Sits in the armchair.*] My parents didn't consider it proper for me to run about on my own. And when I met Stanley, they did everything in their power to encourage the match. You see they weren't very dependable people. My mother was an aristocratic little lady from France who had never learnt to do a thing for herself all her life. And helplessly extravagant as well. Of course, high-born people so often seem to have extravagance as a sort of inherited characteristic, don't they? My father was more stable, at least he was conscious of money though he never made very much. [*Drinks more coffee.*] And when he actually inherited something, he lost it all in speculation. Do you understand that word, dear? Speculation?

WALTER: Oh yes . . . he was a stockbroker.

LOUISE: Heavens, no – a lawyer. Both my parents came from professional people, so naturally they had reservations about marrying me into the furniture business. [*Gives her cup to* WALTER, *who puts it on the tray.*] Still, I was attracted to Stanley. I won't deny it. He had sort of rugged charm, as they say. Obviously I was interested in all kinds of things like art and music and poetry which he, poor man, had never had time for. But when you're young, those things don't seem to matter. It's only later when the first excitement's gone, you start looking a little closer. [*An audible sigh.*] Walter, these past few years have been intolerable. [*Rises and goes towards* WALTER.] There are times when I listen to you playing when I go almost mad with sheer pleasure. Year after year I've had to kill that side of myself. Smother it. Stamp it out. Heaven knows I've tried to be interested in his bridge and his golf and his terrible business friends. I can't do it – I just can't do it. I'm sorry. I didn't mean to talk like this. I'm embarrassing you.

WALTER: No.

LOUISE: I'm being vulgar, aren't I?

WALTER: You could never be.

LOUISE: Dear Hibou ... you know, don't you? You of all people must know. You understand why I stayed. [*Sits in armchair.*] The children. At least I could see that they weren't stifled too ... Do you condemn me?

WALTER [*puts out cigarette*]: How could I condemn – in your house?

LOUISE [*wryly*]: I think we can leave hospitality to one side.

WALTER [*pursuing his own thought*]: No, no. In the house you have given me also to live in, so I can sit here and talk to you as if always I had the right.

LOUISE [*sympathetically*]: Dear Walter ...

WALTER: Where I worked before, I taught the children for two or three hours. I was paid by their mothers and back always to my small room – [*A faint smile.*] – with my cooking which is not so good. You will never know how much I owe to you.

LOUISE: My dear boy ... Tell me about your family. Your people in Germany.

[WALTER *stiffens perceptibly into withdrawal.*]

WALTER: There is nothing to tell.

LOUISE: There must be something.

WALTER: I was an orphan.

LOUISE: Like Stanley.

WALTER [*rises and goes R. to dining-table*]: My parents died when I was too young to remember them. I was brought up by my uncle and his wife.

LOUISE: Were they good to you?

WALTER [*noncommittal*]: Very good, yes.

LOUISE: And – that's all you want to say?

WALTER: There is nothing else.

LOUISE: Don't think I'm being inquisitive ... It's only that you've come to mean so much to us all in this past two months.

WALTER: I do not deserve it.

LOUISE [*warmly. Rises*]: You deserve far more. Far, far more. I knew as soon as I saw you at that terrible cocktail party in London, standing all by yourself in the corner pretending to study the pictures. Do you remember – before even I spoke to you I knew you were something quite exceptional. I remember thinking: such delicate hands ... and that fair hair – [*touching it*] – it's the hair of a poet. And when he speaks he'll have a soft voice that stammers a little from nervousness, and a lovely Viennese accent ...

WALTER [*stiffly*]: I am not Viennese, you know. I am German.

LOUISE: Well, it's not so very different ...

WALTER [*dogged*]: I am German. This is not so poetic. [*He crosses below* LOUISE *to the left end of sofa.*]

LOUISE [*a little intimidated by the darkness in him*]: But Hibou, there's good and bad in all countries – surely?

WALTER [*gently. Crosses below* LOUISE *and the armchair to the left edge of the sofa*]: You are too good to understand. I know how they seem to you, the Germans; so kind and quaint. Like you yourself said: millers' daughters and woodcutters ... But they can be monsters.

LOUISE [*prepared to mock him as she breaks down stage – left of armchair*]: Really now ...

WALTER: Yes! ... [*He is plainly distressed.* LOUISE *looks at him curiously.*]

LOUISE: Even in England we're not all angels.

WALTER: Angels to me! Because this to me is Paradise.

LOUISE: How charming you are.

WALTER [*with increasing heat*]: No, I am sincere. You see . . . here in England most people want to do what's good. Where I come from this is not true. They want only power . . . They are a people that is enraged by equality. They need always to feel ashamed, to breathe in shame – like oxygen – to go on living. Because deeper than everything else they want to be hated. From this they can believe they are giants, even in chains . . . [*Recovering as he sits on the sofa.*] I'm sorry. It's difficult to talk about.

LOUISE: Anything one feels deeply is hard to speak of, my dear.

WALTER: One thing I do know. I will never go back. Soon I'll be a British subject.

LOUISE [*crossing right a few steps*]: You really want to stay here.

WALTER: If you had seen what I have, you would know why I call it Paradise.

LOUISE: I can see for myself how you've suffered. It's in your face . . . [*Extending her hand to him.*] Walter . . . You mustn't torment yourself like this. [*She takes* WALTER's *hand.*] It's not good for you. You're among friends now. People who want to help you. People who love you . . . Doesn't that make a difference?

WALTER: You are so good to me! So good, good . . . [*Impulsively he bends and kisses her hands.*]

LOUISE [*suddenly she takes his head in her hands and holds it close to her. Tenderly*]: Oh, my dear . . . you make me feel ashamed.

[CLIVE *comes in abruptly through the garden door. He stares at them fascinated.*]

It's been so long since anyone has talked like this to me.

[CLIVE *bangs the door.*]

Jou-Jou . . . [*Trying to recover her composure.*] Did you have a nice talk? Did you see Pam?

[CLIVE *remains where he is, still staring at his mother. She rises and crosses to above armchair.*]

It's absurdly late for her to be walking alone. Are you sure you didn't see her? She's probably gone over to that terrible friend of hers, Mary whatever-her-name-is. I think it's high time she found another friend, don't you? [*As* CLIVE *goes on staring, her last remnant*

44

of poise deserts her.] She may be upstairs after all. I'll just go up and see . . .

[*She leaves the room and goes quickly upstairs to her own room.* WALTER *rises.* CLIVE *stays still by the chair left of the dining-table. Now* CLIVE *goes slowly over to* WALTER. *He is evidently fairly drunk, but alcohol does not impair his speech. Rather it gives it energy, and turns of speed. Now it is more disturbed than he himself is aware.*]

WALTER: Clive, what's the matter? Why are you looking at me like that?

CLIVE: . . . Hair is being worn dishevelled this year. The Medusa style. What would have happened if Medusa had looked in a mirror? Are monsters immune against their own fatal charms? Observe, please, the subtle and dialectical nature of my mind. It's the French in me, you understand. An inheritance from my very French, very aristocratic ancestors. Perhaps you've been hearing about them. In actuality, I regret to say, they weren't as aristocratic as all that. My great-grandpa, [*sinks on to sofa*] despite any impression to the contrary, did not actually grant humble petitions from his bedside – merely industrial patents from a run-down little office near the Louvre. The salary was so small that the family would have died of starvation if Hélène, my grandmother, hadn't met an English lawyer on a cycling tour of the Loire Valley, married him, and exchanged Brunoy for Bournemouth. Let us therefore not gasp too excitedly at the loftiness of Mother's family tree. Unbeknownst to Father it has, as you see, roots of clay.

[CLIVE *pours himself some coffee.* WALTER *stares at him in silence, as he gets into his stride.*]

Still, they *are* French roots. I even have them in me. For example – my mother's name for me – Jou-Jou. Toy. More accurately in this case, ornament.

[WALTER *remains silent.*]

Being French, Mother imagines she's real ormolu in a sitting-room of plaster gilt. She suffers from what I might call a plaster-gilt complex,

[WALTER *sits in armchair.*]

if you see what I mean. To her the whole world is irredeemably plebeian – especially Father. The rift you may detect between them is the difference between the Salon and the Saloon. At least that's what she'd have you believe . . . I won't deny that she's only really at home in the Salon; but then where else can you be so continuously dishonest?

WALTER [*stung into speech*]: Please –

CLIVE: Yes?

WALTER [*rises. Takes a few steps to* CLIVE]: I do not wish to hear this.

CLIVE: The young, charming tutor does not wish . . . So delicate; so old-world. A tutor and his employer by the fireside. Paris calls to Vienna. The waltz plays on the deserted boulevard; the leaf falls into the empty wine glass; Europe crumbles. Oh, the charm of it . . .

[*He lights a cigarette, then grabs pillows on the sofa, piles them up in the corner, and leans back on them.* WALTER *turns left – away from* CLIVE.]

Do let's salvage what we can. If we can't afford a château in Brittany, then we can afford a country place in Suffolk, a simple little farm-house which we can decorate out of all existence. If we can't install scholars in our library because we haven't got a library, since nobody reads in our house, then the least we can do is get in a young charming tutor for the girl, someone with tone, of course; nothing grubby out of Night School . . . You see, we're specialists in delicacy.

WALTER [*turns to* CLIVE]: Clive, why do you talk like this?

CLIVE [*rises – crosses to above armchair*]: Because I'm not so damned delicate after all. Because actually, if you want to know, I'm getting less bloody delicate all the time.

WALTER [*crosses right*]: I do not want to hear any more.

CLIVE: Where are you going?

WALTER [*gravely*]: If you had come from Europe, if you had been taken in, as I was – alone – then perhaps.

CLIVE: Taken in! Taken in is right!

WALTER: Excuse me.

CLIVE [*pushes* WALTER *down on the centre table*]: Oh no – taken up!

Like a fashion. Or an ornament; a piece of Dresden, a dear little Dresden owl . . . and believe me, like any other valuable possession, sooner or later you will be used. I know this family, let me tell you.

[*The front door slams.* PAMELA *comes in and runs upstairs.*]

LOUISE [*calling from the U.R. hall*]: Pam, is that you? [*She appears on the landing.*]

PAMELA [*running up the stairs, breathlessly*]: Yes. It's all me!

[*She turns on the light to the schoolroom and then goes into the bedroom where she also turns on the light.* WALTER *crosses to the left of the dining-table –* CLIVE *goes right.*]

LOUISE [*in the schoolroom*]: Where've you been? It's very late. I wish you'd take your walks earlier.

PAMELA [*coming back into the schoolroom*]: I'm sorry.

LOUISE: Where did you go?

PAMELA: Over to Mary's. She's the funniest person in the world. Last week she went to the ballet for the first time. Well, she watched all these girls going up on their toes and dancing about and do you know what she said at the end? 'Mother, why don't they just get taller girls?' [LOUISE *is unamused.*] Don't you think that's funny?

LOUISE: Yes, dear, very funny. Good night, dear.

PAMELA: Good night, Mother.

LOUISE: Don't read tonight. It's too late.

[LOUISE *returns to her room.* PAMELA *closes the schoolroom door, goes to the bookcase, selects a book, and crosses to turn out the schoolroom lights. She then exits to her bedroom.*]

CLIVE [*keeping still and quiet; to himself, as he crosses centre*]: Hepcat – she's the only one who's free with her private star of Grace . . . [*Louder.*] It's a wonderful dispensation; to escape one's inheritance. Oh, I don't mean you, Walter, you're one of the best people who ever came into our house . . .

[WALTER *slowly crosses to the right end of sofa.*]

You think I don't know how lonely you were before you came here. I can smell your loneliness . . . You see, I've only one real talent; being able to see what's true and just what isn't. And that's an awful thing to have. [*With sudden animation after a pause.*] Come away with me.

WALTER [*startled*]: Come away?

CLIVE [*rises and crosses below the armchair to the left end of the sofa. Kneels on it – facing* WALTER]: Look – in four weeks my term ends. We could go somewhere ... anywhere ... to the West Country ... Wells Cathedral is the most astonishing thing in England. It's like walking down the throat of a whale: a great skeleton whale, with the vertebrae showing. No one will be there at Christmas. The Wye Valley without a single charabanc! That's a bus, you know.

WALTER: I know.

CLIVE: Please say yes ... You'd love it.

WALTER [*sits on the sofa. With a shy smile*]: I'm sorry. Christmas is a family time. For so long I have missed it. This year I wish very much to spend it here.

CLIVE [*insistently. Sits left of* WALTER]: Well, afterwards. I could wait.

WALTER [*awkwardly; his whole stance awkward*]: I'm afraid it's not possible. My lessons, you see. I have been paid already to the end of January.

CLIVE: So what? Everyone takes Christmas off.

WALTER: I do not think I can go away.

CLIVE: Because you've been paid?

WALTER: No ...

CLIVE: Then why?

WALTER: I ... I have an ... [*searches for the right word*] obligation.

CLIVE: To my mother?

WALTER: Yes. An obligation.

CLIVE: Is that what you call it – obligation? [*Rises and crosses to above the armchair.*] Well, doff my plumed hat! Gallant Walter Langer ... The Cavalier Tutor to his Mistress! Or do I mean the Cavalier Teuton? ... Don't look so startled. Proper cavaliers have only figurative mistresses. Department of Old World Charm! [*He crosses to the right end of the fireplace, swept into frantic remorse.*] This is quite beyond anything, isn't it?

[WALTER *rises and crosses to the hall.*]

If you came away with me, it would be for my sake – not yours. I need a friend so badly.

WALTER: You are unhappy. [*Crosses left a few steps.*] I am sorry. I really . . .

CLIVE [*the bitterness returning*]: Is that all you can say? 'I'm sorry.' Such an awkward position I put you in, don't I? The poor little immigrant, careful not to offend. So very sensitive. [*With sudden fury.*] When in hell are you going to stop trading on your helplessness – offering yourself all day to be petted and stroked? [*Sits in chair above dining-table.*] Just like I do. O.K., you're a pet. You've got an irresistible accent. You make me sick.

WALTER: Excuse me. [*He makes for the stairs.* CLIVE *seeks to detain him clumsily.*]

CLIVE: Walter, Walter, I didn't – please –

[WALTER *leaves the room and goes up to his own.*]

[*dully*] Please . . .

[*Slowly he goes to the bottle of whisky.* WALTER *reaches the landing, goes to his door, opens it, and turns on his light.* PAMELA *comes out of her room, leaves the door open, in her night clothes on her way to the bathroom.*]

PAMELA [*to* WALTER]: Hullo! [*Turns on the landing lights.*]

[*She stops speaking when she notices the troubled expression on his face.*] What's the matter? You look as if they were going to cut off your head in the morning!

[WALTER *doesn't answer. Pulling open her dressing-gown and revealing her pyjamas.*]

Are you shocked because I'm in my this?

WALTER: Yes, I am. Very.

PAMELA: Then you'd better leave, sir. I'm on my way to the bathroom and I've no wish to cause you embarrassment.

[*He bows. She curtsies and turns off the landing lights.*]

Good night.

WALTER: Good night.

[*He goes into his own room and closes the door. She exits into the up right hall, after turning off the lights. Downstairs* CLIVE *is pouring out another drink.* STANLEY *comes in through the front door, takes off his hat, hangs it on the hat-rack, and comes into the living-room.* CLIVE *puts down the glass guiltily and leaves it on the sideboard.*]

STANLEY: What are you doing?

CLIVE [*breaks downstage*]: Stealing your drink.

STANLEY [*crossing centre*]: Stealing? You don't have to steal from me, Clive. You're old enough to take a drink if you want one. I don't keep it locked up. [*At commode.*] Where's your mother?

CLIVE [*crosses to sofa and sits*]: I don't know – upstairs . . .

STANLEY: You ought to have come with me to Benton's. We went over to the Golf Club. Jolly nice crowd there. [*Crosses to* CLIVE.] The sort of fellows *you* ought to be mixing with. There was a chap there in publishing. You'd have been interested . . . Clive, I've told you before, in this world you want to get in with the people that matter. But you've got to make an effort, my boy. Make yourself a bit popular. And you're not going to do that sitting here drinking by yourself. Are you?

CLIVE [*still low*]: No, I suppose not.

STANLEY: What d'you want to do it for anyway?

CLIVE [*shrugging*]: I don't know.

STANLEY [*crosses to armchair*]: Well, it's damn silly and it's not normal. [*Sits.*] If you want to drink – drink with others. Everyone likes a drink. You come over to the Golf Club with me, you'll soon find that out. I'll make you a member. You'll get in with them in a jiffy if you'll only try.

CLIVE [*rises and goes to stairs*]: Yes. Well . . . I think I'll go to bed now.

STANLEY: Just a minute. What's the matter? Aren't they good enough for you? Is that it?

CLIVE: No, of course it isn't.

STANLEY: Then what?

CLIVE [*gaining courage and coming back into the room*]: Well, all this stuff – right people, wrong people – people who matter. It's all so meaningless.

STANLEY: It's not a bit meaningless.

CLIVE: Well, all right, they matter! But what can I say to them if they don't matter to me? Look, you just can't talk about people in that way. It's idiotic. As far as I'm concerned one of the few people who really matters to me in Cambridge is an Indian.

STANLEY: Well, there's nothing wrong in that. What's his father? A rajah or something?

CLIVE: His father runs a pastry shop in Bombay. [*He sits on sofa.*]

STANLEY: Well, what about him?

CLIVE: He's completely still. I don't mean he doesn't move – I mean that deep down inside him there's this happy stillness, that makes all our family rows and raised voices here like a kind of – blasphemy almost. That's why he matters – because he loves living so much. Because he understands birds and makes shadow puppets out of cardboard, and loves Ella Fitzgerald and Vivaldi, and Lewis Carroll; and because he plays chess like a devil and makes the best prawn curry in the world. And this is him.

STANLEY: Do you want to be a cook?

CLIVE: No, I don't want to be a cook.

STANLEY [*bewildered and impatient*]: Well, Clive, I'm glad to know you've got some nice friends.

CLIVE [*sharp*]: Don't. Don't do that.

STANLEY: What?

CLIVE [*rises and crosses left a few steps*]: Patronize. It's just too much.

STANLEY: I'm not patronizing you, Clive.

CLIVE: Oh yes, you are. That's precisely what you're doing.

STANLEY: That's very unfair.

CLIVE [*working himself into a deep rage*]: Precisely. Precisely! [*Goes to the commode.*] 'I'm glad you have some nice chums, Clive. I had too at your age' ... These aren't my play-pals; they're important people. Important to me. [*He breaks down stage, left of the armchair with the glass of whisky he poured earlier.*]

STANLEY: Did I say they weren't?

[PAMELA *returns from the bathroom. She listens for a brief moment at the top of the stairs, then goes into the schoolroom, closes the door, and on into her bedroom.*]

CLIVE [*frantic*]: Important! It's important they should be alive. Every person they meet should be altered by them, or at least remember them with terrific – terrific excitement. That's an important person. Can't you understand?

STANLEY [*rises, crosses to the commode. Crushingly*]: No, Clive, I told you: I don't understand you at all. Not at all.

[*A slight pause.* CLIVE *subsides. When he speaks again it is to renew the attack in a colder and more accusing voice.*]

CLIVE: You're proud of it too.

STANLEY [*getting angry*]: What now?

CLIVE: That you don't understand me at all. Almost as if it defined you. 'I'm the Man Who Doesn't Understand.' [*Directly, his voice shaking with resentment.*] Has it ever occurred to you that *I* don't understand *you*? No. Of course not. Because you're the one who does the understanding around here – or rather fails to. [*Furiously.*] What work did you put in to being able to understand anybody?

STANLEY: I think you'd better go to bed.

CLIVE [*he puts his glass on the commode*]: I'll go to bed when I'm good and ready! . . . [*Breaks down stage to* STANLEY.] D'you think it falls into your lap – some sort of a grace that enters you when you become a father?

STANLEY: You're drunk.

CLIVE: Yes, you think you can treat me like a child – but you don't even know the right way to treat a child. Because a child is private and important and itself. Not an extension of you. Any more than I am. [*He falls quiet, dead quiet – as if explaining something very difficult. His speech slows and his face betrays an almost obsessed sincerity as he sits in the chair right of the dining-table.*] I am myself. Myself. Myself. You think of me only as what I might become. What I might make of myself. But I am myself now – with every breath I take, every blink of the eyelash. The taste of a chestnut or a strawberry on my tongue is me. The smell of my skin is me, the trees and tables that I see with my own eyes are me. You should want to become me and see them as I see them, but we can never exchange. Feelings don't unite us, don't you see? They keep us apart. [*Rises and goes to sofa.*] And words are no good because they're unreal. We live away in our skins from minute to minute, feeling everything quite differently, and any one minute's just as true about us as any other. That's why a question like 'What are you going to be?' just doesn't mean anything at all – [*Sits during pause.*] Yes, I'm drunk. You make me drunk.

STANLEY: I do?

CLIVE [*losing heart*]: You and everything . . .

STANLEY [*a little afraid now*]: . . . You've given me something to think about, old boy. It's getting a bit late. Don't you think you'd better go upstairs . . . we'll talk about it in the morning. Well, I'll say good night. [*He steps upstage.*] Clive . . . I said good night.

[*Still* CLIVE *takes no notice.* STANLEY *shrugs and goes up the stairs. On the landing,* STANLEY, *conscious of failure, hesitates to go into the hall.* CLIVE *picks up* WALTER's *spectacles from the coffee-table and puts them on; he begins to cry terribly, almost silently. Presently* STANLEY *returns and stands left of the sofa, looking on with a helpless gesture.*]

Clive, don't forget to turn out the lights. [*He notices the boy's sobbing.*] What's the matter, boy? [*He sits on the sofa next to* CLIVE.] What? Come on, now. Out with it. What's the matter – can't you tell me? That's a stupid attitude to take, isn't it? After all, I'm your father. It's what I'm here for.

[CLIVE *shies away from the thought of contact as* STANLEY *makes to touch his shoulder.*]

I say, there's something really wrong, isn't there?

CLIVE [*whispering*]: No. [CLIVE *goes on shaking his head.*]

STANLEY: Did something happen while I was out?

CLIVE: No . . .

STANLEY: Well, what was it? . . . Did your mother say something?

[*Taking spectacles from* CLIVE'*s hand.*] Is it something to do with Walter?

[CLIVE *rises and crosses below* STANLEY. *Sits on the right arm of the armchair.*]

That's it, Walter . . .

[*Then* CLIVE'*s wretched silence goads* STANLEY *beyond control. He grabs the boy's wrists and stares into his face.*]

STANLEY: Clive! What happened with Walter? . . .

CLIVE [*frightened*]: I don't know. I don't know . . .

STANLEY: Tell me! What happened with Walter?

[CLIVE *crosses away from* STANLEY *and goes towards the stairs.* STANLEY *throws* WALTER'*s glasses into the armchair.*]

CLIVE [*slowly turning to face his father*]: It was Mother!

STANLEY: What?

CLIVE: I came in and they were there. [*He points to the sofa.*] He was kissing her. She was half undressed. And he was kissing her, on the mouth. On the breasts. Kissing . . .

[STANLEY *hits him,* CLIVE *falls on sofa.*]

Department of Just Deserts. . . .

ACT TWO

SCENE 1

The following morning. Sunday. A bright, cold day.

PAMELA, *in her riding clothes, is sitting at the breakfast table finishing her coffee and reading one of the better Sunday papers.* WALTER *is sitting on the right end of the fireplace bench, drinking coffee and having a cigarette.*

PAMELA: Walter, what does 'salacious' mean?

WALTER: What word?

PAMELA: 'Salacious' – it's in this article.

WALTER [*rises and looks about for his glasses. He sees them in the armchair where Stanley dropped them the evening before. Puts them on and takes the paper from* PAMELA]: Where? Ah, now, 'salacious'. [*Pause.*] Yes, it means wise. [*Returns the paper to* PAMELA *and goes back to the fireplace.*]

PAMELA: Does it? I suppose I should have guessed. You ought to teach English.

WALTER: I wouldn't dare.

PAMELA: Oh, phooey. I'm sure you'd be miles better than the man at my last school. Anyway, he was a Dutchman . . . Mother says this is the only Sunday paper she'll have in the house. I think it's mean of her. Everyone else has the popular ones with pictures of rapes . . .

[LOUISE *comes from the kitchen.* WALTER *immediately stands.*]

LOUISE: Did you enjoy your kippers?

WALTER: Yes, they were splendid, thank you.

LOUISE: Do sit down, my dear.

[*He does so.*]

PAMELA: Mother, why can't we have Sunday papers with sexy pictures in?

LOUISE: Because they're vulgar, and give you a distorted view of life.

PAMELA: I don't mind.

LOUISE: Well, I do. Where's Clive?

PAMELA: Not down yet.

LOUISE: Really, you children are the limit. [*Goes to the kitchen door with coffee-pot.*] I don't see why you can't all have your breakfast together. It's late enough, heaven knows. Pamela, you'd better hurry up and finish dressing if you're going riding.

[*She goes back to the kitchen, leaving the door open.*]

PAMELA [*rises and goes to chair left of dining-table. Sits*]: Have you ever gone riding?

WALTER: No.

PAMELA: It's the best, absolutely. What games did you play in Germany?

WALTER: I – I used to walk.

PAMELA: You mean on hiking parties, all dressed up in those leather shorts?

WALTER [*sits in chair right of dining-table*]: No. By myself. I liked it better.

PAMELA [*impulsively*]: Are you happy here? Are you really, really happy?

WALTER: Of course.

PAMELA: Who do you like best?

WALTER: You.

PAMELA: No, seriously.

WALTER: I like you all. You and your mother ...

PAMELA: And Clive.

WALTER: Of course and Clive. I like him very much. I'm only sorry he is so unhappy.

PAMELA: Unhappy?

WALTER: I think so, yes.

PAMELA: That's because he was spoilt when he was young.

WALTER: Spoilt? I don't know that.

PAMELA: You know – to spoil someone. Like damage.

WALTER: Oh, damage; yes! . . .

PAMELA [*down right; drinking her coffee*]: I'm sure he ought to get married.

WALTER: Oh, he's so young!

PAMELA: For some people it's the best thing. You must help him find a girl.

WALTER: Why? Has he not had friendships with girls before?

PAMELA [*in her 'affected' voice*]: Not even acquaintanceships, my dear. [*Normal.*] Except for one; a girl called Peggy-Ann who worked in the tobacconist's when we were at the seaside. She used to wear tight leopard-skin trousers and great sort of brass bells in her ears. Clive said they used to go down on the beach and neck, but I bet he was just bragging. So you see, you've got to help him. I'm sure you know hundreds of girls. [*Takes cup to window seat.*]

WALTER [*amused*]: Oh, yes. What kind would you suggest?

PAMELA [*leans on back of straight chair*]: Someone who'll pay him lots of attention. At home, everyone keeps on at him but no one really takes any notice of him. [*Brightly.*] Clive spends his whole time not being listened to.

WALTER: His mother listens, doesn't she?

PAMELA [*closes kitchen door*]: Not really listens, no . . . Well of course you can't expect her to. No mother ever really listens to her children. It's not done.

WALTER: You seem to know a lot about it.

PAMELA: Yes, I do. [*Sits in chair above dining-table.*] Poor Clive. You know, they really only use him to help them when they're rowing. [*Directly.*] Can you understand why they row?

WALTER: I think everyone has quarrels.

PAMELA: Yes, but this is different. With Mother and Daddy the row is never really *about* – well, what they're quarrelling about. I mean . . . well, behind what they say you can feel – well, that Mother did this in the past, and Daddy did that. I don't mean anything *particular* . . . [*She stops, confused.*] Oh, dear . . . marriage is a very difficult subject, isn't it?

WALTER [*humorously; he is a little uncomfortable*]: You don't take your exam in it until you're a little older.

PAMELA [*pursuing her own thoughts*]: I mean, who begins things? Do you see?

WALTER: Please, Pamela –

PAMELA: I know Mother's frightful to him about Culture, and uses music and things to keep him out – which is terrible. But isn't that just because *he* made *her* keep out of things when they were first married? You know he wouldn't even let her go to concerts and theatres although she was dying to, and once he threw a picture she'd bought into the dustbin; one of those modern things, all squiggles and blobs. [*Gestures.*] . . . But then, mightn't *that* just have been because being brought up by himself he was afraid of making a fool of himself. Oh, poor Daddy . . . Poor Mother, too. [*To him, brightly.*] You know, I shouldn't wonder if parents don't turn out to be my hobby when I grow up.

[STANLEY *appears on the landing and descends the stairs.*]

WALTER [*warmly*]: You know something? You have a wonderful mother. Did you know that?

PAMELA: Yes, I suppose so.

WALTER: Is that all? Only suppose?

PAMELA: People who make you feel stupid are always called wonderful.

[STANLEY *comes into the living-room. He looks tired and strained.* PAMELA *crosses to him.*]

Good morning, Daddy.

[WALTER *rises.*]

STANLEY [*kissing her*]: Morning, dear. [*He stares at* WALTER *with a curious unwilling stare.* WALTER *rises rather awkwardly.*]

WALTER: Good morning, sir.

[LOUISE *comes in from the kitchen with the coffee-pot, which she puts on the window-seat.*]

LOUISE: Stanley ...? You might let me know when you come down. Walter, dear, will you come and get Mr Harrington's cereal for me?

WALTER [*eager to help, he takes a used plate, cup, and saucer from the table and starts for the kitchen*]: Of course, Mrs Harrington.

[*She goes into the kitchen again.*]

I hope your headache is better this morning, sir. [*He exits to the kitchen and closes the door.* STANLEY *nods, apparently unable to speak. He sits right of the dining-table.*]

PAMELA [*goes to the window-seat and pours a cup of coffee for Stanley*]: Aren't you playing golf today, Daddy? It's late.

STANLEY: No, not today.

PAMELA: Why? Aren't you feeling well?

STANLEY: Oh, I'm all right ...

PAMELA: Why not come riding with me then?

STANLEY [*wrapped in himself*]: No ... not today. I ... just want to take things easy today.

PAMELA [*mischievously as she gives him the coffee*]: You must be getting old.

[*He looks at her searchingly.*]

STANLEY: When are you going to learn to fix that bow? Come here. [*She kneels to his right. He fixes the ribbon.*] Has Clive come down yet?

PAMELA: No, the lazy pig. You were talking to him late last night, weren't you? I could hear you from upstairs. [*Crosses to centre table.*] Well, really, it seemed more like Clive was talking to you.

[*He stiffens, but she doesn't notice.* WALTER *reappears with porridge.* PAMELA *sits on C. table.*]

WALTER [*placing it before* STANLEY]: Mrs Harrington asks would you prefer eggs or kippers?

STANLEY [*quietly*]: Nothing.

PAMELA: Daddy, you must have something.

STANLEY: Don't fuss, Pam. [*Curtly, to* WALTER.] Nothing.

WALTER [*with a half bow*]: Yes, sir. [*He goes back to the kitchen, deflated.*]

PAMELA: He'd make a wonderful waiter, wouldn't he?

[STANLEY *gets newspaper from bench. Sits there and opens paper.*]

How did you like Clive talking to you man to man? [*Brightly.*] He must have been drunk.

STANLEY: Why do you say that?

PAMELA: Because if he wasn't, he never would have. Not properly, anyway. He'd be too nervous.

[*He looks at her sharply.*]

That's because you like him to answer questions all the time, and he hates to.

STANLEY: Why?

PAMELA: I don't know. I suppose he's just not the answering type. D'you know he even has a dream about you?

STANLEY: Clive does?

PAMELA: Yes. He gets it quite often, so he must think an awful lot about you. You ought to be flattered, though it's not exactly what I'd call a flattering dream . . . [*Recounting it carefully, with increasing drama. She sits right of table.*] Apparently, he's always in bed lying down under thick blankets; and there is a window and he can see into a big garden all covered in snow. It's freezing so hard outside he can hear twigs snapping on the trees. Then suddenly you appear, coming slowly over the snow towards him – crunch . . . crunch . . . crunch. You disappear inside the house and he can hear you coming upstairs – crunch . . . crunch . . . and along the passage to his room. Then the door slowly opens and you come in, and cross the room to see if he's asleep. So while you stand there he pretends to be asleep, as asleep as can be, except that sometimes he starts shivering, which spoils the effect. Then you start taking off the blankets one by one. Clive says there must be about ten blankets on the bed, and with each one you take off he gets colder and colder. Usually he wakes up with all his bedclothes on the floor. Isn't that the silliest dream you ever heard . . .? I told him the next time he heard you coming upstairs he was to wait till you came up to the bed, then sit bolt upright and shout 'Go to hell!'

[STANLEY *has listened to this impassively but with the greatest*

60

attention. He still sits involved in his own silent conflict as LOUISE *returns from the kitchen.* WALTER *follows carrying the picnic basket.*]

LOUISE [*to* PAMELA]: Pamela! Are you still here?

[PAMELA *rises.*]

You're going to be very late for your ride. And I've told you before, unpunctuality is just bad breeding.

PAMELA [*to* WALTER, *who crosses right below the table*]: I've decided you'd make the most wonderful waiter.

LOUISE [*shocked*]: Pamela! What a thing to say.

PAMELA: Well, he would. Can't you just see him bowing to old ladies with Pekineses.

LOUISE: Stop it, Pamela. That's very rude. A waiter! Can't you think of anything else for Walter to be? I only hope one day you'll have a tiny part of his education, and a few of his manners. [*To* PAMELA.] Now hurry up and get dressed.

[WALTER *goes upstairs and into schoolroom to change a book.*]

Your picnic's all ready.

PAMELA [*goes to dining-table. Picks up basket*]: Daddy, can I borrow your lumber jacket? Please say yes.

STANLEY [*quiet*]: Of course – it'll be a bit big for you, won't it?

PAMELA: Oh, yes, but I'll wear it as a cape. Of course I won't look half so good in it as you.

STANLEY: Enjoy the ride.

PAMELA [*intimately*]: You bet.

LOUISE: And tell Clive from me, if he's not down right away he won't get any breakfast.

[PAMELA *goes upstairs and into the hall.* LOUISE *crosses left.*]

Stanley, what are you sitting there for? Walter says you don't want any cooked breakfast. And you haven't even touched your cereal. That's absurd. You must have something to eat.

[*He stares now at her, puts paper on bench.*]

What's the matter? Did you have too much to drink last night or something?

[*He rises and goes to french window.*]

Stanley . . .

[*Abruptly he goes into the garden.* LOUISE *stares after him in astonishment. She sits down at the table.* PAMELA *emerges on the landing with* STANLEY's *lumber jacket.*]

PAMELA [*knocks on his door*]: Walter!

WALTER [*coming from his room*]: Yes?

PAMELA: I wasn't really rude just now, was I?

WALTER: Rude? No, of course not. As a matter of fact, I was a waiter once, for a short time in Berlin. But they threw me out.

PAMELA: Why?

WALTER: They said I had no dignity.

PAMELA: How ridiculous. You're the most dignified man I ever met. [*Running off into the hall and knocking on* CLIVE's *door.*] Clive! Wake up, wake up, whoever you are! Get into your slippers, go down for your kippers . . .! Wake up, wake up . . .

[*She reappears and goes to the schoolroom, then to her bedroom.* CLIVE *follows in a jacket and trousers, with a slight hangover.*]

WALTER [*at his door*]: Good morning.

CLIVE: Good morning.

WALTER: Excuse me. I think I'll do a little work. [*He exits into his room.* CLIVE *goes up to the schoolroom.* PAMELA *reappears with riding-cap and riding-crop.*]

PAMELA: Salaams. A thousand welcomes, my handsome slave boy. Mine eyes rejoice in the sight of you! [*She whirls* CLIVE *around.*] Dance with me, my little pomegranate! Madden me with desire!

CLIVE: Drop dead! Where is everybody?

PAMELA: Downstairs. You'd better go down. You look a bit green. Do you want a fizzy?

CLIVE: No.

PAMELA: Well, salaams.

[*She runs off into her room.* CLIVE *goes slowly downstairs, where* LOUISE *still sits at the table. He is clearly reluctant to go.*]

LOUISE: You slept late. Perhaps you had a little too much to drink last night, too.

CLIVE: What do you mean?

LOUISE [*at window seat*]: There's kippers or eggs.

CLIVE [*crossing left*]: No, thank you. Is there any coffee?

LOUISE: Now what is this? First your father and now you.

CLIVE: Where is he?

LOUISE: Outside.

CLIVE [*perplexed. Crosses to the french window*]: Where?

LOUISE: In the garden. [*Pouring* CLIVE's *coffee.*] Well – isn't he?

CLIVE [*looking out*]: Yes. He's sitting down under the apple tree.

LOUISE: *Sitting?* In this weather! Without an overcoat? He'll catch his death. Tell him to come in at once.

CLIVE: Perhaps he prefers it outside.

LOUISE: Don't be ridiculous, Clive. The man must be mad, sitting out there on a freezing morning like this. [*Advancing to the french window.*] What on earth he thinks he's doing, I can't imagine.

CLIVE [*sharply*]: Leave him alone!

LOUISE [*amazed*]: Are you talking to me?

CLIVE [*firmly; almost surprised at himself*]: Leave him alone.

LOUISE: Are you sure you're feeling all right?

CLIVE: I – I'm sorry.

LOUISE: So you should be. That was very, very ill bred.

CLIVE [*whispering*]: Not really done.

LOUISE [*crosses above and to the right of table*]: Clive, I don't understand you this morning. I really don't.

CLIVE [*French accent*]: *Votre Majesté* should not worry 'erself about eet. It makes, as the French say, no nevaire mind. Your *Majesté.*

  [*He extends his hand in salutation. At the same moment the slow movement of the Brahms Third Symphony is heard from* WALTER'S *room. Suddenly she draws him to her – he allows himself to be drawn – and embraces him. A brief instant of great intimacy recurs, as it happened in the first scene.*]

LOUISE [*sits right of table*]: Jou-Jou . . .!

CLIVE [*kneels to her*]: Maman . . . !

LOUISE: *Mon petit Cossack.* . . . Silly boy. [*She holds him tenderly, in the position of subservience he took up before his Empress – only now very close to her. His back is to the audience, and from his inclined posture she can fondle his head.*] D'you think I'm so stupid that I don't know what's wrong? D'you think I can't see for myself . . .? We're a little bit jealous, aren't we? As if you didn't always come first. You know that. Don't you?

[*He nods, stiff now with reluctance.*]

Then it's ridiculous, isn't it, to be jealous? And of whom? A poor lonely boy with no people of his own to care for him, all by himself in a foreign country. Really, Jou-Jou, you ought to be ashamed. Let's say no more about it. I want you always to be happy – remember? Very, very happy.

[*He nods again.*]

There. [*She kisses his forehead.*] Now, let me cook you some breakfast. You could eat an egg, couldn't you? [*She rises.*]

CLIVE [*sits on bench below table*]: I suppose so.

LOUISE: You finish your coffee while I get started. [*She looks at him tenderly.*] Silly boy . . . [*She goes out into the kitchen.*]

CLIVE [*with a sort of bitter digust; to himself. Rises and crosses U.C.*]: On waves of sympathy. On waves . . . !

[*STANLEY comes in from the garden. He crosses the stage, goes out, and leaves the house through the front door, which he bangs behind him.*]

[*The door of PAMELA's bedroom opens after a moment and she comes into the schoolroom. She goes out of the schoolroom wearing the lumber jacket as a cape, and her riding-cap, and starts downstairs with her picnic basket and riding-crop. She misses her footing and falls in an undignified heap on the landing.*]

PAMELA: Damn! Damn! Damn!

[*Music stops. WALTER comes rushing out, startled by the great crash.*]

WALTER: What's the matter? . . . I'll help you. Are you hurt?

PAMELA: Of course not. Walter, put me down. Walter, put me down.

CLIVE [*who has reached the landing*]: Pam, are you all right?

[*LOUISE enters from the kitchen.*]

PAMELA: Yes, of course I am all right.

[CLIVE *goes back downstairs and into the kitchen.*]

LOUISE: What happened? What on earth was that noise?

PAMELA: It's all right, Mother. Don't fuss. Anyone would think I was dying. [*Feeling her head.*] Ow!

[WALTER *picks up* PAM's *jacket, cap, crop, and basket.*]

WALTER: See? You bumped your head.

PAMELA [*witheringly*]: When you fall down, you must bump something.

LOUISE: What happened, Walter?

WALTER [*concerned*]: She fell. I think you should look on her head, Mrs Harrington.

LOUISE [*with a faint touch of hauteur*]: Thank you, Walter. You can leave her to me now. [*She takes* PAMELA's *things from* WALTER.]

WALTER: Yes, Mrs Harrington. Of course. [*He gives his half bow and goes back into his own room.*]

LOUISE: Go on upstairs. . . .

[*They both go up to the schoolroom.*]

PAMELA: Fuss, fuss, fuss.

LOUISE [PAMELA *sits in chair left of the schoolroom table.* LOUISE *puts the clothes on the table. Examining her daughter's head*]: Let me look. Does it hurt?

PAMELA: No, it doesn't.

LOUISE: You say that as if you wanted it to. What on earth were you doing?

PAMELA [*exasperated*]: Nothing. I just tripped. And that stupid Walter has to come in and pick me up as if I was a chandelier or something. Holding me that way.

LOUISE [*carefully*]: What way, darling?

PAMELA [*crossing above* LOUISE *to her left*]: Well, trying to carry me as if I was a baby.

LOUISE: But wasn't he only trying to help?

PAMELA [*angrily*]: I think he's just plain soppy.

65

LOUISE: Because he was worried about you?

PAMELA: Oh, Mother. [*She rises and crosses to the chair right of the table. Puts her foot on the chair and rubs her ankle.*] You don't understand anything . . . It's just so *undignified*, can't you see? It shows no *respect* for you. I mean, if you're two years old it's all right to pick you off floors that way, and even then it's an invasion of your privacy. If children of two could speak, you know what they'd say? 'Why can't you keep your filthy hands to yourself?'

LOUISE [*picks up lumber jacket*]: You'd better be off on your ride before you get into any more trouble. [*Gives the lumber jacket to* PAMELA *who puts it over her shoulders.*] Here, take this. [*Picks up* PAMELA's *riding-crop and basket from the table; the brown sweater from the back of the left chair.*]

PAMELA [*crossing to the door*]: Oh, it's one of those days.

[*They leave schoolroom. The Symphony starts again in* WALTER's *room.* PAMELA *crosses to his door and listens.* LOUISE *closes the schoolroom door.*]

I bet you anything the horse breaks its legs. D'you think Walter heard me just now?

LOUISE: Well, you weren't exactly whispering, were you?

[*Both go downstairs and into sitting-room. While they are on their way, the record off-stage sticks. The passage is repeated several times, then the needle is moved on.*]

PAMELA: I think I'm the most impossible person I know . . . But then I suppose wonderful people always make you feel like that. Sort of ashamed all the time.

LOUISE: He makes you feel ashamed?

PAMELA [*takes cap from her mother*]: Not exactly ashamed but, well, like in those advertisements. I always feel like the grubby shirt next to the dazzling white one. [*Puts on cap.*] He's so fresh! Fresh and beautiful . . . [*Brightly.*] Don't you think he's beautiful?

LOUISE [*confused*]: I hadn't thought.

PAMELA [*takes basket and riding-crop from* LOUISE]: It's just exactly what he is. [*Crosses left to the right end of the bench.*] He should wear a frock coat and have consumption.

LOUISE: What nonsense.

PAMELA: Why? There *are* people like that.

LOUISE [*with sudden irritation*]: Well, Walter certainly isn't one of them. He's obviously quite a happy, normal young man. [*Crosses to* PAM.] There's simply no reason for you to weave any romantic ideas about him being tragic or different in any way.

PAMELA [*grandly*]: I'm afraid it's obvious you don't know him very well.

[*But* LOUISE *is unamused. Instead, she is making an effort at self-control.*]

LOUISE: If you're going, you'd better go. You'd better put on a sweater.

PAMELA: Oh, phooey.

LOUISE: Darling, it's cold out.

PAMELA: It isn't really.

LOUISE: Pam, it's very cold. Now do be sensible.

PAMELA: But Mother, I've got Daddy's big jacket on.

LOUISE [*snapping*]: Do as I say! Put on your sweater!

[*She leaves the room abruptly and goes up into the schoolroom.* PAMELA *looks after her in surprise.*]

PAMELA [*puzzled*]: 'Bye.

CLIVE [*off in the kitchen*]: Pam, is that you?

PAMELA: Yes, I'm just off.

[CLIVE *comes in, carrying a plate of eggs.*]

CLIVE [*sits above table*]: What were you playing at just now? Being the walls of Jericho?

PAMELA: Oh, shut up!

CLIVE: Have a nice time.

PAMELA: You should come with me.

CLIVE: I know. It does you good to get in the air.

[LOUISE *exits into* PAM's *bedroom with the clean bedclothes which were on the school desk.*]

PAMELA [*in a wildly affected, cheerful voice*]: Well then, bye-bye, darling. You're sure there's nothing I can get you from the village? A barrel of beer? Harris tweed?

CLIVE [*matching her accent*]: No, thanks, old girl. Just bring back the usual papers. The *Hunting Gazette* and the *Shooting Gazette*.

PAMELA: Righty-ho!

CLIVE: And the *Fishing Gazette* – and some wax for the old moustache.

PAMELA: Certainly, dear.

CLIVE: I say, Pamela – you are a brick!

PAMELA: Then I'll say ... [*Blowing him a kiss.*] Cheeribye, darling.
[*She shimmies out through the french window.* WALTER *emerges from his room with a book of piano pieces. He comes downstairs.*]

CLIVE: Hullo.

WALTER: Hullo.

CLIVE: What's the matter with your record?

WALTER: It's not the record. The needle keeps jumping. I think the table's not quite level.

CLIVE: Oh, really? It must be one of Father's.
[WALTER *gets a cigarette from the table next to the centre armchair.*]
Do you know that a judge trying a copyright case in this country once asked learned counsel: 'What exactly *are* Brahms ...?'
[WALTER *smiles in appreciation, sits on back of armchair.*]
Well, how are you? Clearly unwell, I should say. Only the sick and corrupt would spend a bright Sunday morning listening to music. In all decent English homes this time is reserved for sport. Staying still is the absolute proof of decadence.

WALTER: Yes. This is familiar to me. Where I was born – to sit reading was an offence too.

CLIVE: Why? You had to be out playing games?

WALTER: Games. Yes, but in small uniforms.

CLIVE [*scenting difficulty*]: I suppose every kid wants to be a soldier?

WALTER: Oh yes. [*Pause.*] But in England they are not told it is a good thing to be.

CLIVE: Why? Did your uncle believe it was?
[WALTER *does not reply.*]
Parents and guardians are desperately unreliable.

WALTER [*turning, smiling*]: Maybe we expect too much of them. After all, they are only us, a little older.

CLIVE: A little older and a little more depended on.

WALTER: Exactly.

CLIVE: So not a bit like us.

WALTER [*mischievously*]: Do you think *you're* going to make a very good father?

CLIVE [*takes plate to window-seat*]: I don't see why not. I was a complete success as a baby. [*Crosses to right of dining-table.*] I was so demanding, I gave my parents the idea they were indispensable.

WALTER: I wish I had known you then.

CLIVE: What on earth for?

WALTER: It would have been nice when I was a child.

CLIVE: Sometimes you make me wonder if you ever were ... But you're such an excluded person. It's the thing about you.

WALTER [*softly*]: No, not any more ... Clive, I'm sorry I ran out on you last night.

CLIVE [*stiffly. Crosses to bench – sits*]: Oh, let's forget it.

WALTER: It was kind of you to suggest a holiday together.

[CLIVE *looks at him woodenly.*]

I know you're not happy here ... I would be most honoured if you could talk to me about it. If there were things you want to say – like last night I felt there were things.

CLIVE [*darker*]: Look, I think we'll forget it.

[*In difficulty.*]

Walter, don't take me wrong ... but are you sure you did the right thing when you left Germany?

WALTER [*in amazement*]: You sound as if you wanted me to go back.

CLIVE [*very quiet*]: Yes.

WALTER: Why? ...

[CLIVE *does not reply.*]

Last night you did not want it.

CLIVE [*with sudden desperate anger*]: Last night ... ! I want it now. I want you to go. [*Modifying his tone with effort.*] For your sake.

Only for your sake, believe me ... You've got a crush on our family that's almost pathetic. Can't you see how lucky you are to be on your own? Just because you never had a family you think they're the most wonderful things in the world.

WALTER: Clive ...

CLIVE: Why have you got to depend all the time? It's so damned weak!

WALTER: You know nothing!

CLIVE: I can see.

WALTER: What can you see? My parents? My father – can you see him, in his Nazi uniform?

CLIVE: But – you told me your parents were dead.

WALTER [crosses up to commode]: Yes, I know. They are alive. In Muhlbach. Alive. There was no uncle.

CLIVE: Your father was a Nazi?

WALTER [crosses to back of armchair]: Oh, yes. He was a great man in the town. Everybody was afraid of him, so was I ... When war broke out he went off to fight and we did not see him for almost six years. When he came back, he was still a Nazi. Everybody else was saying, 'We never liked them. We never supported them.' But not him! 'I've supported them,' he said. 'Hitler was the greatest man our country has seen since Bismarck. Even now we are defeated, we are the greatest country in Europe. And one day we will win, because we have to win ...' [He crosses and sits in the chair right of dining-table.] Every night he used to make me recite the old slogans against Jews and Catholics and the Liberals. When I forgot, he would hit me – so many mistakes, so many hits.

CLIVE: But your mother?

WALTER: My mother ... she worshipped him. Even after we found out.

CLIVE: What?

WALTER: That during the war ... he worked at Auschwitz concentration camp ... He was one of their most efficient officers. [A slight pause.] Once he told me how many ... [He stops in distress. His voice was dead with loathing.] I could have killed him. I could have killed him till he was dead. And she worshipped him – my mother. She used to smile at him, stare at him – as though he owned her. And when he used to hit me, she would just – just look away as though what he was doing was difficult, yes – but unavoidable, like training a puppy. That was my mother.

CLIVE: I'm sorry.

WALTER [*recovering*]: So you see, Clive, I do know what it is like to have a family. And what I look for is somewhere . . . where now and then good spirits can sit on the roof.

CLIVE: And you think you've found it here? Do you?

[WALTER *does not answer.*]

[*Rises – cross right a few steps.*] You're fooling yourself every minute.

WALTER [*gravely*]: Don't you think I should find that out for myself?

CLIVE: Oh, for God's sake! If that horrible story was meant to change my mind, it didn't.

WALTER: I did not tell it for that.

CLIVE: Then go. Just get the hell away from here.

WALTER [*rises*]: Clive . . .

CLIVE: For my sake – I want it.

WALTER: But why?

CLIVE: Because I can't bear to watch.

WALTER: Watch? I don't understand you.

CLIVE: Well, then, just *because*.

[LOUISE *comes out of* PAMELA's *bedroom, goes through the school-room and on to the landing.*]

LOUISE [*calling downstairs*]: Walter . . .?

[WALTER *looks at* CLIVE *inquiringly, unwilling to court interruption.*]

CLIVE [*hard*]: Go on. Answer her. It's your duty, isn't it?

WALTER [*low, appealing*]: Clive . . .

LOUISE: Walter!

CLIVE [*turning on him ferociously*]: Answer her!

[*As* WALTER *stands irresolutely,* CLIVE *turns again and goes out abruptly through the front door.* LOUISE *descends the stairs.*]

LOUISE [*coming into the living-room*]: Ah, there you are, my dear

71

boy, all alone . . .? [*Going to coffee-table.*] Come and talk to me, it's not good for you to be on your own too much.

WALTER: I was not alone, Clive was here. He's just gone out.

LOUISE [*takes cigarette and holder*]: Where?

WALTER: I don't know – Mrs Harrington, I'm most worried for him.

LOUISE [*smiling*]: Poor Hibou, you worry about everybody, don't you? But you mustn't about Clive, really. It's just a tiny case of old-fashioned jealousy, that's all.

[WALTER *lights her cigarette.*]

Well, it's only to be expected, isn't it? [*Crosses to armchair.*] We've always been so wonderfully close, he and I.

WALTER [*courteously*]: Of course.

LOUISE: He'll get over it. One day he'll understand about women. At the moment, of course, he thinks there must only be room in my heart for one boy. So silly . . . [*She sits. Warmly.*] I don't believe you can ration love, do you?

WALTER [*sits, sofa. Admiringly*]: With someone like you it is not possible.

LOUISE: Nor with you, my dear. You know, last night held the most beautiful moments I've known for many years. I felt – well, that you and I could have a really warm friendship. Even with the difference . . . I mean in – in our ages.

WALTER: Between friends there are no ages, I think.

LOUISE [*tenderly*]: I like to think that, too.

WALTER: Oh, it's true. Like in a family – you don't notice how old people are, because you keep growing together.

LOUISE: Yes. Dear little owl . . . What's the matter . . . Are you embarrassed?

[*He shakes his head 'No'.*]

It's the last thing you must ever be with me.

[WALTER *smiles.*]

What are you thinking? Come on: tell me.

WALTER: Some things grow more when they are not talked about.

LOUISE: Try, anyway. I want you to.

WALTER [*looking away from her*]: It is only that you have made me wonder –

LOUISE [*prompting eagerly*]: Tell me.

WALTER [*lowering his voice still more as he walks towards* LOUISE]: Mrs Harrington, forgive me for asking this, but do you think it's possible for someone to find a new mother?

[LOUISE *sits very still. The expression of eagerness fades, and its remnant hardens on her face. She stares at him.*]

Have I offended you?

LOUISE [*smiles, without joy*]: Of course not. I am . . . very touched.

WALTER [*moved. Kneels*]: I'm so glad. [*Eagerly.*] That is why I feel I can talk to you about Clive, for example. I am most worried for him. He is not happy now. And I do not think it is jealousy. It is something else – more deep in him – trying to explode. Like the beginning of an earthquake or so.

LOUISE [*with increasing coolness. Rises. Crosses to coffee-table*]: Really, my dear, don't you think you're being a little over-dramatic?

WALTER [*dogged. Rises*]: No, I mean exactly this. You see . . . that boy . . . It is very difficult for me to explain.

LOUISE [*wryly*]: I appreciate your attempt . . . [*crosses to centre table.*] But really, I'm sure I know my children a little better than you.

WALTER [*persisting*]: Of course. But just in this case – with Clive – I feel something which frightens me – I don't know why –

LOUISE [*her temper breaking*]: Oh, for heaven's sake!

[WALTER *recoils.*]

[*Recovering quickly. Crosses to dining-table with dirty ashtray.*] I mean . . . after all, as you admit yourself, you *are* only a newcomer to the family, remember. [*Sweetly.*] Now why don't you go and play me some of your nice music?

[WALTER *looks confused, and lowers his eyes before her strained smile. He exits into kitchen.* LOUISE *starts to pick up dishes and silverware, but puts them down with a big crash.*]

SCENE 2

The same night, after supper.

The living-room is empty. Up in the schoolroom, WALTER *is hearing* PAMELA *in her irregular verbs. They are sitting in their usual position at the table.*

PAMELA: *Je meurs, tu meurs, il meurt, nous meurons* –

WALTER: No.

PAMELA: It must be.

WALTER: It's not. It's *mourons*.

PAMELA: *Mourons*. Oh, phooey ... you know, this is the perfect way to end today. It's been a stinker, hasn't it?

WALTER: Has it? I thought you had a good ride this morning.

PAMELA: Oh, that ... I mean the atmosphere since I got back. What Mother calls the *aura*. And Clive not coming in for lunch or dinner. D'you think he's run away?

WALTER: I think we'll do more French.

PAMELA: Mother was livid tonight when he didn't turn up. That's funny, too. I'd have thought Daddy would have been the one to explode, but he didn't say a word ... Do you think Clive's lost his memory or something?

WALTER: What is the future of '*mourir*'?

PAMELA: Perhaps he's been kidnapped. Just think of Daddy paying ransom. I wonder if he would.

WALTER: I think Clive can take care of himself. Now, *please*, Pamela –

PAMELA: Oh, I'm sick of French! Anyway, it's Sunday and that's supposed to be a Day of Rest.

WALTER: Yesterday you said you felt Jewish and Saturday was your day of rest.

PAMELA: That was Saturday – not Sunday. Tonight I'm going to

74

have a hot bath and go straight to bed and read. Mary gave me a most important scientific book last week and I just haven't had a moment to glance at it.

WALTER [*suspiciously*]: What kind of science?

PAMELA: Actually it's a kind of story.

WALTER [*resigned*]: Ah-ha.

PAMELA: But completely scientific. It tells what would happen if the earth got invaded by Venus. The people are just sweeties. They're all ten foot high and covered with blue jelly.

WALTER: Very educational.

[LOUISE *comes from the hall wearing a light blue sweater over her shoulders. She turns the lights on in the landing. We can now see that she is very strained and anxious.*]

LOUISE: Pamela –

PAMELA: There you are. You can't even have a scientific discussion any more without being interrupted by the world of triviality.

[LOUISE *comes into the schoolroom and goes to the right of* PAMELA. WALTER *rises.*]

LOUISE: How's the bruise, darling?

PAMELA: It's all right, thank you.

LOUISE: I've turned on your bath.

PAMELA: Has Clive turned up yet?

LOUISE [*wearily, but with a vestige of deep anger*]: No. Not yet ... [*Softening.*] Now get into your bath and don't dawdle, will you? [*She goes to the door. Having virtually ignored* WALTER, *who has stood uncomfortably by the table, she just notices him on the way out.*] Good night, Walter.

WALTER: Good night, Mrs Harrington.

PAMELA [*whispering*]: She looks as if she needs a fizzy.

WALTER: Pamela, that's very naughty.

PAMELA: Well, she does. Mother always looks like that when she's lost an argument. It's meant to mean she's been misunderstood.

WALTER: I think she's worried about Clive.

PAMELA [*rises*]: Phooey! Anyone would think he was still a child the way she goes on. [*Wickedly.*] I hope he stays out all night.

75

Wouldn't it be wonderful if he was giving babies to all the school-girls in Ipswich . . . ?

[PAMELA *goes to her bedroom for her robe and slippers. Re-enters.* LOUISE *enters through front door. She turns on the living-room lamps at the switch on the pillar.*]

[*Affected voice again*] Well, I'd better go and have my bath, dear boy. Oh Lord, Sunday night. London tomorrow. Breakfast at half past seven for that rotten train. I think Mondays stink . . .

[LOUISE *exits through french window – left.*]

Is there any religion with its Day of Rest on Mondays?

WALTER: Yes. There is the religion of Lazy Girls.

PAMELA: Oh, you are brutish!

[PAMELA *goes down the stairs, turns off the landing-lights and exits into the hall. Presently the front door opens.* STANLEY *comes in and walks into the living-room, taking off his overcoat.* LOUISE *enters through french window.*]

LOUISE [*hearing the noise of his entry*]: Clive? Oh, it's you . . .

STANLEY [*coming in*]: Isn't he back yet?

LOUISE: No.

STANLEY: Well, no one's seen him in the village. He hasn't been in any of the pubs.

LOUISE [*bitterly*]: The pubs. Always the pubs.

STANLEY [*goes to left end of sofa*]: Well, where else would he be likely to go? You know what the trouble is? Your son's turning into a drunkard.

LOUISE: . . . The way you've been behaving lately's enough to make anyone drink. No one would think he's your son. You treat him abominably. [*Takes off sweater, leaves it on chair above dining-table.*]

STANLEY [*sits on sofa*]: Do I?

LOUISE: You haven't the faintest idea how to deal with sensitive people. If I was Clive, I'd have run away from home long ago.

STANLEY [*bitterly*]: If it weren't for the saving grace of his mother. His sensitive mother.

LOUISE [*crosses to armchair*]: At least I understand him. I make an effort. Just because you can't see beyond the end of your stupid, commonplace nose – [*Sits.*]

STANLEY [*savage. Rises. Crosses to commode. Pours himself a drink*]: Shut up!

LOUISE: Charming.

STANLEY [*his pain also becoming rage*]: And what have you ever done for him that's so wonderful, may I ask? I'll tell you. Turned him into a snivelling little neurotic. A mother's boy.

LOUISE [*trying to recover her poise*]: That's not true.

STANLEY [*crosses down stage – left of chair*]: And I'll tell you something else. He's going peculiar. Yes: looney, if you want to know. He talked to me last night and I didn't understand one word he said.

LOUISE [*loftily*]: That doesn't surprise me.

STANLEY: It was like listening to a lunatic.

LOUISE: And that's my fault too? Just because I take an interest in our son, which you've never bothered to do in all these years, I'm driving him insane.

STANLEY [*with wild demand in his tone. Crosses above chair to her right*]: And when I tried to teach him things, what happened?

LOUISE: What things?

STANLEY [*crosses to sofa*]: Golf – swimming – I don't know, I can't remember. Who was it said, 'Clive's too delicate'? 'Clive can't waste his time on silly games. He's got his reading to do ...' [*Sits.*]

LOUISE: So it was wrong of me to encourage his reading?

STANLEY: He was my son as much as yours!

LOUISE: Yes, and what did you want to do for him? Push him straight into your third-rate furniture business for the rest of his life. That's not good enough for me, Stanley.

STANLEY: Well, he was my son.

LOUISE: He still *is*, my dear.

STANLEY [*hard*]: No. Not any more. You've seen to that.

[LOUISE *looks away from him sharply.*]

LOUISE [*collected*]: That's the nastiest thing you've ever said to me.

STANLEY: I didn't mean it.

LOUISE: Yes, you did.

STANLEY [*wearily*]: I don't know what I mean any more . . . It's all so bloody mixed up.

LOUISE: Must you swear?

STANLEY: I don't know . . .

LOUISE: I can't stand much more. I just can't.

STANLEY [*dead*]: What?

LOUISE [*rises and crosses left of armchair*]: It's no good, Stanley. My life was never meant to be like this – limited in this way . . . I know I'm unpredictable sometimes. I say things I don't mean. But don't you see . . . I don't know what I'm doing half the time, I'm so frustrated. I'm sorry, but it's the only word, Stanley. There are times when I feel I'm being choked to death – suffocated under piles of English blankets. Yes, my dear, I'm not English at heart and never will be, no matter how I try. I've never been able to take your boring world of shops and business seriously. Can't you understand? Can't you understand anything? [*She sits in the armchair again.*]

STANLEY [*flat*]: What do you want me to do, Louise? Louise, I'm asking you a question. D'you want a divorce . . .? Well?

LOUISE: Oh, it's all so vulgar.

STANLEY [*tired*]: I'm a vulgar man.

LOUISE: Do *you*? Do *you* want one?

STANLEY [*plainly*]: I'm too old to start again. And, besides, there's Pam. It wouldn't do her any good.

LOUISE: I notice you don't mention Clive.

STANLEY: Clive's no longer a child. Much as it may upset you to think of it, my dear, he's nearly twenty years old.

LOUISE: I think it's you who haven't gathered that.

STANLEY: Don't start – just don't start.

LOUISE: I didn't begin it.

STANLEY: Louise . . . I know I'm not the easiest man in the world to live with . . . I don't know what it is you want: but anyway I don't seem to have been able to give it to you . . . [*After a moment, in an altered voice, rises and goes to her.*] Look here . . . suppose we

went away somewhere – alone together? Just the two of us. Do
you think it would help? We could go to Monte Carlo.

LOUISE: You know I can't stand the place.

[PAMELA *comes from the U.R. hall on the landing in her dressing-*
gown and goes downstairs into the living-room.]

STANLEY [*controlling himself*]: Well, somewhere else then ... anywhere ...

[PAMELA *enters the living-room.* STANLEY *goes up to commode and*
leaves his glass there.]

PAMELA: Mother, isn't Clive back yet?

LOUISE: Good night, dear. Sleep well and don't read too late.

PAMELA: No. [*She crosses to* STANLEY *and kisses him.*] Good night,
Daddy. [*She goes out and upstairs to the schoolroom.*]

STANLEY [*goes to sofa. Sits*]: Well ... it's worth a try, isn't it,
Louise?

PAMELA [*to* WALTER, *in the schoolroom*]: Good night.

WALTER: Sleep tight.

PAMELA: Mind the bugs don't bite.

[*She goes into her bedroom.*]

LOUISE [*after a pause*]: Stanley, I want to ask you to do something
for me – something rather difficult. [*She rises and crosses above*
sofa.]

STANLEY: What's that?

LOUISE: It's to do with Pamela. I feel it's something you can manage
better than I can.

STANLEY: Pam?

LOUISE [*crosses left to above armchair*]: Actually, it's about Walter.
I'm afraid he's having rather a bad effect on her. She's just at that
stage, you know – impressionable, romantic – long walks in the
moonlight. I'm afraid she's got a bit of a crush. Nothing serious
of course – she'll get over it.

STANLEY: You want me to talk to her?

LOUISE: No. Something rather more drastic, I'm afraid. I think we
must let Walter go. In the most tactful way, of course. Actually the
sooner the better.

STANLEY: I see.

LOUISE: I think he's upstairs now – shall I send him down to you? I'll make myself scarce and you will be tactful, won't you?

[*She starts up the stairs.* CLIVE *blunders in through the front door – leaves the door open. He is drunk, but, as on the previous evening, perfectly coherent.* LOUISE *comes back down the steps.*]

LOUISE: Clive!

CLIVE: Good evening all.

LOUISE [*closes the front door*]: Oh, Clive.

STANLEY: Would you mind telling me where you've been? You've been out since twelve.

CLIVE: Like the tide. But we're back, you see.

STANLEY: Answer me!

CLIVE: Why do we always have to ask expected questions?

STANLEY [*rises*]: Now listen, my boy . . .

LOUISE [*crossing down stage to the left of* STANLEY]: Why don't you go upstairs, dear, and do what I asked you to?

STANLEY: Very well. I'll leave you to take care of your sensitive son.

[*He looks at* CLIVE *angrily for a moment, then he goes out of the room and up the stairs. He knocks at* WALTER's *door, receives no answer, and less resolutely approaches schoolroom door.*]

LOUISE [*bitterly*]: Your father and I have been worried to death.

CLIVE [*insolently*]: Do I detect a new note in the air? Your father and I. How splendid.

[LOUISE *sits on sofa.*]

The birth of a new moral being. Your-father-and-I . . . When did you last see your-father-and-I? Or is it just a new alliance . . .? All the same, I congratulate you. I always thought you two ought to get married.

LOUISE [*rises*]: You're drunk! And disgusting! [*Crosses to kitchen.*] I'll get you something to eat.

CLIVE [*coldly*]: Your-father-and-I will now get your supper.

[LOUISE *goes into the kitchen. The lightness of the room troubles* CLIVE. *He shuffles clumsily across the room and turns off the lights so that only the glow from the fire remains in the sitting-room. He sinks wearily into the armchair and covers his eyes.* STANLEY *enters the schoolroom.*]

STANLEY: Are you busy?

WALTER [*standing up; as always, made nervous by his appearance*]: Of course not, Mr Harrington. Is Clive back yet?

STANLEY: He just came in – drunk. Do you drink? I don't remember seeing you.

WALTER: Not very much, no.

STANLEY: Sensible. [*Pause.*] My son drinks. A lot. Doesn't he?
[WALTER *says nothing.*]
Can you think of any good reason for it?

WALTER: I do not think people drink for good reasons.

STANLEY: Sit down.
[WALTER *sits uneasily.* STANLEY *stands left of table facing him.*]
You don't think much of me, do you? Why?

WALTER: Mr Harrington –

STANLEY: Because I'm not educated. Is that it?

WALTER: Of course not.

STANLEY: Then why? Because the children say things?

WALTER: Mr Harrington. please, I –

STANLEY [*crosses to window*]: And what do they know? People say parents are selfish. They've got nothing on children. [*Crosses back to table.*] Do they ever think about anything but themselves? *Their* troubles ...? As if nobody ever had 'em before. Well ...? You ought to know. You teach 'em.

WALTER [*softly*]: I think children are less able to deal with their own troubles.

STANLEY [*not really listening*]: I tell you, children are the most selfish things in the world ... So he drinks. Did you know it was my fault? I drive him to it. So I hear.
[WALTER *says nothing.*]
Well, have you lost your tongue?

WALTER [*very low*]: No.

STANLEY [*sits left of table*]: I'll tell you why he drinks. He drinks so he can get over being with me. Have you noticed how this family never gets together in this house? Are you afraid of me?

WALTER [*straight*]: No.

STANLEY: Well, that's a wonder. My son is. That's something else I hear. What do you think?

WALTER: I . . . I think . . . yes.

STANLEY [*blankly*]: Do you?

WALTER [*with difficulty*]: I think he feels you do not love him, and yet all the time you are expecting him to love you.

STANLEY: Rubbish.

WALTER [*retreating at once*]: I'm sorry. You did ask me.

STANLEY: He's my *son*. How can he think that?

WALTER: He feels that you are judging him. When you look at him, he feels you are thinking – 'How useless he is.'

STANLEY: And when he looks at me – what's *he* thinking? That's a different story, isn't it? [*Bitterly.*] 'How common he is.'

WALTER: Oh, no –

STANLEY: Don't tell me. I've seen it too often. Common.

WALTER [*gently*]: You are wrong about him. With you always he feels that he has to justify his life. His Greek, maybe, or because he loves an opera. When a boy must apologize for ears and eyes, it is very bad.

STANLEY: Apologize? When have I asked him to apologize?

WALTER: That's not what I meant.

STANLEY: Then why use such ridiculous words? I can see where he gets them from.

WALTER [*gravely*]: Your son has got nothing from me, Mr Harrington. I wish he had. Look, sir. Clive needs help. Will he get it?

STANLEY: He can always come to me. He knows that.

WALTER [*raising his voice slightly*]: And will he come? *Does* he come?

STANLEY [*gathering dignity about him*]: As a matter of fact, we had a very frank talk last night. You didn't know that, did you?

[WALTER *shakes his head.*]

What are you thinking?

WALTER: I was thinking that you are very like your son, Mr Harrington.

STANLEY [*sarcastic*]: Oh yes. In education, I suppose.

WALTER: I say too much always . . .

STANLEY [*he shrugs. Suddenly he begins to talk more or less to himself*]: You needn't apologize . . . What's it matter? You start a family, work and plan. Suddenly you turn round and there's nothing there. Probably never was. What's a family anyway? Just kids with your blood in them. There's no reason why they should like you. You go on expecting it, of course, but it's silly really. There's just nothing. Bloody nothing . . .

   [*Unseen by him,* WALTER *gestures towards him in a futile attempt at communication. He goes on staring into space, not heeding the tutor at all.*] All the time you're saying: It'll be better next year. Next year it'll be all right. The children going to prep school, leaving it. Short trousers, long trousers. Perhaps he'll make the rugger fifteen or the cricket team or something – anything – and then his first girl friend and bringing her home – or perhaps just keeping her to himself till he's sure . . . [*Frankly.*] But nothing . . . Nothing . . . and now he hates me.

WALTER: No . . .

STANLEY: D'you think I don't know? How sensitive do you have to be for that? Tell me, because I don't know too much about that sort of thing . . . [*His bitterness rises again.*] I'm always too busy making money. [*Violently.*] Go on, tell me. Sensitive people have deep feelings, don't they? They suffer a lot.

WALTER: Please, Mr Harrington.

STANLEY [*violently*]: I don't want to hear.

WALTER: Excuse me.

   [*He rises, goes to the door, opens it, and goes down the stairs.* STANLEY *is left staring into space. He then goes to the bedroom door, opens it a little to see if* PAMELA *is asleep. Convinced that she has heard nothing, he closes the door, reaches down, and turns off the gas fire. He turns off the schoolroom lights, closes the door, and exits down the stairs, into the hall.* WALTER *reaches the living-room where* CLIVE *has been lying*

83

inert in the armchair in a strange awkward position suggesting acute depression.]

WALTER: Clive? Are you all right? What are you doing sitting here in the dark? [*He goes to the commode and turns on the lamp.*] I've been talking to your father. He thinks you hate him.

[CLIVE *does not appear to hear.*]

Clive . . . The kings of Egypt were gods. Everything they did was right; everything they said was true; everyone they loved became important. When they died, they were given faces of gold. [*Pause.*]

You must learn to forgive your parents for being average and wrong when you worshipped them once . . . [*Crosses right to the edge of the sofa.*] Why are you so afraid? Is it – because you have no girl friend? Oh, you are so silly. Do you think sex will change you? Put you into a different world where everything will mean more to you? [*Sits – sofa.*] I thought so too once. I thought it would change me into a man so my father could never touch me again. I didn't know what it would be like, but I thought it would burn me and bring me terrible pain. But afterwards, I'd be strong and very wise . . . There was a girl in Muhlbach. She worked in her mother's grocery shop. One night I had a few drinks and just for a joke, I broke into her bedroom through the window. I stayed with her all night. And I entered heaven. I really did. Between her arms was the only place in the world that mattered. When daylight came, I felt I had changed for ever. A little later I got up. I looked around, but the room was exactly the same. This was incomprehensible. It should have been huge now and filled with air, but no, it was small and stuffy and outside it was raining . . . I remember I hated the soap for lying there in the dish just exactly as it had done the night before. I watched her putting on her clothes. I thought: 'We're tied together now by an invisible thread.' And then she said, 'It's nine o'clock; I must be off' – and went downstairs to open the shop. Then I looked into the mirror: at least my eyes would be different. [*Ironically.*] They were a little red, yes – but I was exactly the same – still a boy. The rain was still here and all the

84

problems of yesterday were still waiting. [WALTER *rises and crosses to the right of* CLIVE. *He kneels.*] Clive, sex by itself is nothing, believe me. Just like breathing – only important when it goes wrong, and this only happens if you're afraid of it. What's the matter, Clive? Why don't you talk to me?

CLIVE [*very low*]: Walter ... What's wrong with me?

WALTER: There's nothing wrong with you. Nothing.

CLIVE: Don't fool me. I know.

WALTER: There's nothing wrong but in your mind. What you think about.

CLIVE [*despairingly*]: What is it? What have they done to me?

WALTER: Clive, your parents love you. Everything they have done has been from love. I am sure of this.

CLIVE: Then God save me from love.

WALTER: He will not ... You have more in you than any man I've ever met.

CLIVE: Stop it ...

WALTER: Please, let me help you.

CLIVE: Cut that out!

WALTER: What?

CLIVE: Pity.

WALTER [*gently. Rises and crosses above chair to* CLIVE's *left*]: I don't pity you, Clive. And you mustn't pity yourself. You can end this and you must. You must go away from here. [*Crosses.*] You – not me. At the moment you are – [*Gestures.*] – on your family. I don't know the word. Like a butterfly on a pin.

CLIVE [*with distaste*]: Impaled.

WALTER: Yes, that's it ... and you must get off the pin. [*Sits on centre table.*] At the end of term in Cambridge, don't come back here. Go anywhere else you like. Join your friend singing. Go into a factory. The important thing is this – the moment you get out of here, people will start telling you who you are. Clive, what is it you want from life? I could tell you what *I* want. To live in England. To be happy teaching. One day to marry. To have children, and many English friends ... And what about you, Clive?

CLIVE [*intimately*]: I think I want . . . to achieve something that only *I* could do. I want to fall in love with just one person. To know what it is to bless and be blessed. And to serve a great cause with devotion. [*Appealing.*] I want to be *involved.*

WALTER: Then break the glass! Get out of the coffin! Trust everything, not because it's wise, but because not to trust will kill you. Trust me, for instance. I'll see you often. But you must go away from here. Now please, say yes – you will go.

[STANLEY *enters from the hall. He is stopped by the conversation in the living-room. He stands at the top of the stairs listening.*]

CLIVE [*nodding*]: Yes. I'll go.

WALTER: The next vacation?

CLIVE: The next vacation.

WALTER: Good!

[STANLEY *starts coming down the stairs.*]

CLIVE: Isn't it silly? We seem to spend all the time ordering each other out of the house!

WALTER: A very friendly way to spend the time.

[STANLEY *has reached the pillar. The light switch he turns on lights the lamp right of the sofa.*]

STANLEY: Clive – don't you think you'd better go to bed?

[CLIVE *rises and starts to the stairs.*]

WALTER [*gently to* CLIVE]: Are you all right now?

CLIVE: Yes, I'm all right. Good night, Father.

[CLIVE *goes upstairs and into the hall.* WALTER *gives his half-bow and crosses below the armchair. He is stopped by* STANLEY *before he reaches the hall area.*]

STANLEY [*raging*]: Just who the hell do you think you are? [*Breaks down stage.*] So the world owes you a living; is that it?

WALTER [*comes down stage*]: Mr Harrington –

STANLEY [*brutally*]: Don't 'Mr Harrington' me, with your smarmy voice and bowing from the waist. You had the gall to patronize me just now – tell me what's wrong with my home . . .

WALTER: You forget – you asked me for my opinion.

STANLEY: Oh, yes. And what else did I ask you to do? Turn my son into a sissy?

WALTER: Your son is a fine, intelligent boy.

STANLEY: He's a mess, that's what he is. And it's your fault.

WALTER: My fault –

STANLEY [*blindly*]: Yes. You, the arty boys. It's you who've taken him . . . [*Hurtling the names as if they were insults.*] Shakespeare! Beethoven . . . All the time, till I can't touch him . . . Who gave you the right to steal my boy?

WALTER [*with pity*]: You will believe what you please.

STANLEY: I'm not blind you know – and I'm not deaf. I heard you telling him just now. 'Get away from here. Get out of this house.'

WALTER: Yes, I did.

STANLEY: How dare you say a thing like that? What right have you got – in my house, working for me – to say a thing like that?

WALTER: My friendship for your son.

STANLEY: And your friendship with my daughter Pamela too, what about that?

WALTER: Pamela?

STANLEY [*crisply, with satisfaction*]: Your employer, Mrs Harrington, has asked me to dismiss you because she thinks you are having a bad effect upon our daughter.

WALTER: . . . Mrs Harrington said this?

STANLEY: Yes.

WALTER: But it's not true. Not true at all . . .

STANLEY [*carefully*]: No, I don't think it is.

[*Slight pause.* WALTER *looks in utter distress and bewilderment at* STANLEY.]

WALTER: Then – why . . .?

STANLEY [*crosses to* WALTER]: Could it be because you've been trying to make love to my wife?

[WALTER *reacts sharply to protest.* STANLEY *goes on in the same quiet tone.*]

You filthy German bastard.

[*The boy winces as if he has been slapped.*]

Once a German, always a German. Take what you want and the hell with everyone else.

[WALTER *stands rigid, with face averted.*]

You're a fool, too. Did you really think she would ever risk anything for you? Oh, I know it's very cultured to look down on money, but that's a very different thing from giving it up. Well, now you've had your chips, and she's sent me to give them to you.

[STANLEY *crosses to the commode . . . keeping his back to* WALTER. *A long pause. When* WALTER *speaks, it is very quietly, from the depth of his humiliation.*]

WALTER: You can't believe this . . .? It's not possible . . .

STANLEY [*turns to* WALTER]: Oh, yes – it's quite possible. We've got a perfect witness, 'unimpeachable' as we say in England.

[WALTER *looks at him.*]

Can't you guess . . .? No . . .? [*Hard.*] Your pal. Your good pal.

WALTER: Clive?

STANLEY: Of course Clive. Who else?

WALTER [*in disbelief*]: No!

STANLEY: He told me he saw you together last night in this room.

WALTER [*looks at sofa*]: No – no.

STANLEY: Do you know what we do with people like you in England? Chuck 'em out. [*Lowering his voice.*] I'm going to fix it so you never get your naturalization papers. I'm going to write to the immigration people. I'll write tonight. I'll say – let's see – 'Much as I dislike complaining about people behind their backs, I feel it is my duty in this case to warn you about this young German's standard of morality. Whilst under my roof, he tried to force his attentions on my young daughter, who is only fifteen.' Try and get your papers after that. They'll send you back to the place where you belong . . .

[LOUISE *enters the kitchen with tray holding a covered dish. She turns on the lamp on the window-seat.*]

LOUISE: Stanley, I thought you were upstairs – Walter! What's the matter? [*Puts tray on dining-table.*]

STANLEY: I did what you asked me.

LOUISE: Yes, but how did you do it? [*She crosses below* STANLEY *to* WALTER.] Was he very brutal, *mon cher*?

[WALTER *does not look at her.*]

But you know yourself it's for the best, don't you? So it's foolish to be upset ...

WALTER [*grasps her hands, on his knees*]: Don't ... I beg of you ...

LOUISE [*trying to free herself, extremely ruffled*]: Walter, really ...

WALTER: No ...

LOUISE: Really, Walter ... Get up at once.

WALTER: Please ... don't ...

[STANLEY *backs left a few steps not being able to take his eyes off the scene.*]

LOUISE: Do you hear me? Walter! You're being embarrassing and ridiculous. [*She breaks loose from him and backs to the commode. She moderates her tone.*] Now, get up at once and stop making an exhibition of yourself.

[*He does so. He leans on the sofa with his back to the couple.*]

I'm sorry, but I'm afraid you deserved to be spoken to like that. I'm really very disappointed in you ... Both our children have been considerably disturbed by your presence in our house and you know I could never allow that. They've always come first with me. I'm sure you understand.

[*No reply. A few steps towards* STANLEY.]

Now about the financial arrangements, we will make it as easy for you as possible. You could manage an extra month's wages, I think Stanley?

STANLEY: Oh ... yes.

LOUISE: There you are. A month's wages. I call that quite generous, don't you?

WALTER [*in a remote disinterested voice*]: Yes, I do.

LOUISE: Good. [*Seeing his distress. A few steps right.*] Oh, Hibou, don't look so stricken. It makes it so much more difficult for everybody.

[*A pause.* WALTER *leaves the room and goes up to the landing.*]

LOUISE [*goes to the stairs*]: Walter ...

CLIVE [*appears from hall as* WALTER *reaches the landing*]: What on earth's the matter?

[WALTER *shakes him off and rushes into his room.*]

LOUISE. Well, of all the embarrassing, hysterical scenes . . .! [*Rounding on* STANLEY.] You seem to have handled it brilliantly, I must say.

[CLIVE *comes down the stairs into the living-room.*]

CLIVE: What's the matter with Walter?

LOUISE [*crosses below* STANLEY. *Sits on bench below dining-table*]: He's a little upset. There's some supper here for you – you'd better eat it.

CLIVE: Why is he upset? What's been going on down here?

LOUISE: I think it's better if we don't talk about it.

CLIVE: Do you want to talk about it, Father? What have you done to Walter both of you? I'm only asking a simple question.

STANLEY: If you really want to know, I told him what you said last night about him and your mother.

LOUISE: Me?

STANLEY: You and your daughter's tutor, my dear – a pretty picture.

LOUISE: What did he tell you? Clive, what did you say?

STANLEY: Never mind – I didn't believe it.

LOUISE: I want to know what Clive said to you.

STANLEY: What's it matter? It never matters what he says.

CLIVE [*looks at* STANLEY]: So you didn't believe me?

STANLEY: Do you really think I would?

CLIVE: Then why did you pretend to Walter just now as if you did? – Well?

[STANLEY *goes upstairs.*]

LOUISE: Jou-Jou, you didn't suggest . . . but this is horrible. You couldn't have said such things about me, surely?

CLIVE: Yes – I said them.

LOUISE: But why?

CLIVE: I don't know.

LOUISE: Jou-Jou!

CLIVE [*crosses below sofa*]: I don't know why. I do something terrible that I'll remember all my life, that'll make me sick whenever I think of it – and I don't know why.

LOUISE [*crosses to above chair*]: You're ill. You must be.

CLIVE: Oh no. It just means that I can damage people too. I can dish it out just like everybody else.

LOUISE: But it's not true. It's not true what you said!

CLIVE: True? I told a lie, yes. But what I felt under that lie, about you and Walter – was that so untrue? No, don't answer me, because whatever you say just won't be real. You've forgotten what it is to be honest about feeling. True? [*Sits, sofa.*] The only true thing I know is what's happened to him – my father!

LOUISE: You're out of your mind.

CLIVE: And you're so worried about me, aren't you?

LOUISE: Clive, you frighten me. Why are you being so terrible? What have I done?

CLIVE: Don't you know? Can't you see what you've done? There isn't a Stanley Harrington any more. We've broken him in bits between us.

LOUISE: I don't know what you're talking about. I really don't.

CLIVE: No, you don't. Poor man.

LOUISE [*sits in armchair*]: Clive . . . You hate me.

CLIVE: I hate. Isn't that enough? Is the war in this house never going to end?

LOUISE: War?

CLIVE: The war you both declared when you married. The Culture War, with me as ammunition. 'Let's show him how small he is . . .' 'Let's show her where she gets off . . .' *And always through me!* He wasn't always a bully. You made him into one.

LOUISE [*rises. Crosses to right of dining-table*]: I won't go on with this conversation another moment. It's obscene. Your father's upset, that's all. Simply upset.

CLIVE: But *why* is he upset?

LOUISE: About something I asked him to do.

CLIVE [*rises. Crosses above armchair*]: It was something to do with Walter, wasn't it? What have you done to Walter?

LOUISE: If you must know – he's been dismissed.

CLIVE: Mother – no!

LOUISE: I assure you there were excellent reasons.

CLIVE: But you can't dismiss him. You *can't*. Not even you – [*In sudden despair.*] He can't go away from here.

[*She looks at him curiously.*]

LOUISE [*calmly*]: If you want to know, I did it for Pam. I'm afraid his influence over her was getting far stronger than I cared for.

[*A slight pause. She sits.*]

CLIVE [*also calm*]: I see.

[*The Third Movement of Mahler's Fourth Symphony is heard from* WALTER's *room.*]

LOUISE: Well, evidently the boy himself is not so shattered by the news as you are ... [*Sits right of table.*] Don't you think you'd better eat your supper?

CLIVE [*matter of fact*]: What was it? Jealousy? Shame, when you saw the innocent together? Or just the sheer vulgarity of competing with one's own daughter?

LOUISE [*turns to* CLIVE]: How dare you!

CLIVE: Dearest Mother, who are you trying to fool? I know your rules. Don't give sympathy to a man if others are giving it too – he'll never see how unique you are. Besides, doing what everyone else does is just too vulgar. Like going to Monte Carlo, or falling in love.

[LOUISE *bursts into tears. Puts her arms and head on table.*]

[*Anguished.*] Mother!

[*She sobs helplessly for a moment with a wild, hopeless grief.*] Oh, it goes on and on. No meeting ... Never ... Why can't we be important to each other? Why can't we ever come into the room and be new to each other? Why doesn't a night's sleep, lying all those dark hours with ourselves forgotten and then coming alive again, why doesn't it give us new things to see – new things to say too: not just 'Eat your eggs', or 'You were in late' – the old dreariness. [*Desperately, crossing to his mother.*] I want to *know* you.

But you wonderful – changed into yourself . . . Don't you understand? So that you can change me.

[*She sits unmoving, no longer crying, giving no indication of having
heard.* CLIVE *kneels to her and embraces her with desperate tenderness.*]

[*Tenderly.*] Maman . . . Maman, chérie . . .

[*For a moment she endures his embrace, then, with a gesture of
hysteria, shakes him off.*]

LOUISE: Don't!

CLIVE [*falling back*]: Maman . . .

LOUISE [*rounding on him, her face terrible*]: D'you think you're the
only one can ask terrible questions? Supposing I ask a few. Supposing I ask them . . .! You ought to be glad Walter's going, but
you're not. Why not? Why aren't you glad? You want him to
stay, don't you? You want him to stay very much. Why?

CLIVE [*in panic, he rises from the floor:* LOUISE *drives him to the sofa*]:
Maman!

LOUISE [*harsh, pitiless now*]: Why . . .? You said filthy things to your
father about me. Filth and lies. Why? Can you think of an answer?
. . . Why, Clive? Why about me and Walter? Why . . .? Why . . .?
Why?

[*The record in* WALTER'*s room has stuck.*]

CLIVE: Stop it! You're killing . . .

[*In the silence, they both become aware of a strange sound: the record
playing in* WALTER'*s room has stuck. The same phrase is being played
again and again. The needle is not moved on. The pause is held. A
dawning alarm expresses itself in* LOUISE'*s face. She runs up the
stairs to* WALTER'*s room. She tries to open his door, but can't.*]

LOUISE: Something's wrong! It's gas. [*Calling.*] Stanley. Stanley!
Come quickly. [*She switches on the landing lights.*]

[STANLEY *enters up right. He rushes to* WALTER'*s room and turns
the handle, but has to push the door hard to get it open.* WALTER'*s
jacket is stuffed under the door. Both go into the room. The music stops.*
STANLEY *drags out* WALTER *on to the landing.* LOUISE *follows,
handkerchief to her face.*]

STANLEY [*kneeling over* WALTER]: Louise, get a doctor.

[CLIVE *has moved slowly out of the living-room and is now on the landing.* LOUISE *goes down the stairs.*]

Oh God, let him live. Let him live!

CLIVE: Walter!

STANLEY [*to* CLIVE]: It's gas. Open the window.

[CLIVE *goes into the hall and opens the window.*]

LOUISE [*at the phone*]: 342 please.

WALTER: *Ich verlasse euch fur immer – immer.*

STANLEY: Thank God.

CLIVE: He's not going to die?

STANLEY: No . . . no . . . he's coming around.

[PAMELA, *hearing the noise, enters from her bedroom putting on her robe. She crosses to the schoolroom door, turns on the light, and opens the door.* CLIVE *rushes up to her.*]

LOUISE [*on the phone*]: The doctor, please. It's urgent.

PAMELA [*to* CLIVE]: What is it? What's the matter?

CLIVE [*closes the schoolroom door and takes* PAMELA *to the bedroom door*]: Nothing . . . it's all right. Walter fell down and hurt himself. Like you did. Now go back to bed . . . Go on.

[PAMELA *returns to her bedroom. Closes the door.* CLIVE *crosses to the schoolroom door. Almost to himself . . .*]

The courage . . . For all of us. Oh, God – give it.

[*He turns off the schoolroom light and opens the door. He starts down the stairs as*

THE CURTAIN FALLS

Shrivings

A Play in Three Acts

As of now, this play has never been acted.

It is a much re-written version of another play of mine called *The Battle of Shrivings*, which has never been printed.

This first version was presented at the Lyric Theatre, London, in February 1970, by five fine actors: John Gielgud, Patrick Magee, Wendy Hiller, ebullient young Dorothy Lyman and compelling young Martin Shaw. It was directed with cool precision by Peter Hall, and placed by John Bury in a set so bone-white that a bowl of green apples placed suddenly on a table – 'the buttons of original sin' – riveted every eye. The action of the play was lightly formalized throughout, so that it could make an austere gesture somewhat at variance with the aesthetic standards prevailing on Shaftesbury Avenue. I found this gesture beautiful, since my intention from the start had always been to stage a fairly abstract proceeding, and theatrically I am strongly drawn to the cold which burns. However, it is possible that the proceeding was not abstract enough, or not cold enough to burn effectively. At any rate the play fell somewhere between domesticity and grandeur – a bad kind of fall – and though some critics found it exciting, many more received it with an almost jubilant hostility.

For myself, the more I saw *The Battle of Shrivings* performed, the more I wanted to change it. I do not mean that I just wanted to make it work. 'Working', in the sense intended by many theatrical professionals, far too often simply means a certain effectiveness purchased at the price of any ambiguous insight, or of any qualifying perception not immediately accessible to a dozing audience sullenly suspicious of language. Other plays of mine had relied for their completion on elaborate stretches of physical action: in this one I wanted the electricity to be sparked almost exclusively from the spoken words –

though of course there was a physical set-piece as well in the shape of the Apple Game. My dissatisfaction with the piece, therefore, had nothing to do with its rhetoric, which if anything I wanted to intensify; nor with its verbal duelling, which if anything I wanted to extend. I desired only to make the play more purely *itself*.

Successful plays of large scope die for their authors with a pleasant expiration, wrapped in a sheet of public approval: unsuccessful ones are apt to be left naked to the sky – particularly plays of a turbulent nature – writhing under an obloquy which never quite covers them and so turns into oblivion. I remember how in the first hard weeks after its public maiming, I became obsessed with considering what further writing was needed to give the play its quietus in my mind. I had loved it a great deal, but had I allowed it to speak entirely in its own voice? I suspected that the intransigence of the argument had been blunted by an almost conventional turn it had taken, towards the end, into domestic bickering. Certain furious passages between the husband and the wife had been undeniably useful in humanizing action otherwise largely concerned with debate, but I wondered whether fundamentally they had not constituted an easy way around the rigorous path which the piece should properly have followed. The first thing I did, when I started to rewrite, was to remove altogether the character of Enid Petrie, the pacifist's unhappy wife, thereby changing a quintet into a quartet.

The creation of Lady Petrie in the first place had been largely due to some speculation I once entertained concerning the household of Mahatma Gandhi. I had read in a famous Life of the great man how at the age of forty he had summoned his wife and informed her of his irrevocable decision to give up all sexual activity, since he had come to recognize in it the source of aggression in himself. This startling act of renunciation certainly impressed me; but I could not stop wondering at the same time about the reaction to it of Mrs Gandhi. Her possible sufferings seemed so extremely relevant to my theme, and to the doings in the Petrie household. Indeed some years later I received a passionate letter from a woman psychiatrist, warmly congratulating me on perceiving how often idealism of the lofty Petrie kind is fed by the life-blood of humble domestic victims. However, despite my speculations about Gandhi's wife (and the encouraging letter from this doctor) I could not finally avoid the insistent conclusion that Enid Petrie was a dramatic cliché, and that the scene where she was finally struck by her husband was simply no fitting climax for the play.

Obviously the horror of this story, in any version of it, has to be Gideon's lapse into violence after so many years of self-restraint. But with Enid removed, a more dramatically interesting target for the pacifist's blow instantly appeared: Lois, his idealistic and worshipping young secretary. An assault on a committed girl seemed to me in this situation even more appalling than one on an aggrieved wife. The fact that the girl was also an American clinched the matter for me.

Shrivings has always been an 'American' play. I associate it most strongly with sojourns in New York City in 1968 and 1969. The encounter between Mark and Gideon naturally sprang out of a division of feeling in myself, but it was charged with the violence of this angry city during one of her angriest times, when streets were choked with raging protesters against the Vietnam War, newspapers were filled with the killings at Kent State University, and there drifted through our midst the fantastic army of Flower People, now already turned into ghosts. So quickly does time run on, their passionate confronting of public brutality with public gentleness now seems almost totally unreal. The savage alignments of those days had about them such a relieving simplicity. I am aware that to many people in England the excesses of the Peace Movement occasioned feelings of near-amusement; but then near-amusement of this kind is one of the more obvious symptoms of an English strangeness.

As a foreigner in America, I became too possessed by the fever of that time, and the baffling contradictions it set off in my head. Obsessively I wanted to set out on paper the conflicting ideas which sprang up everywhere I looked – often enough taking the form of elaborate interior duologues. Over and over I returned to the apparent truth that an absolute non-aggressive position seems unattainable by Man without tangible loss of warmth and cherishable humanity – (what warm man will spare the Ruffian With the Pistol threatening his beloved?) – and yet a relative, 'human' attitude which permits retaliating under extreme provocation inescapably leads to horrors unenvisaged and unintended at the start of it: witness Hiroshima at the end of the Second World War.

Man squeezed like a nut between an ideal choice and a practical one, and cracked in bits by either, is scarcely a novel image; yet the discovering of it for oneself, the coming to any sort of awareness of tragic ambiguity, must always be new and painful. I remember how angry I felt with my many opposed thoughts, and yet how also exciting I found the idea of Insoluble Situation. Walking around Manhattan, I was accompanied everywhere by the nagging exhilaration of irresolveable argument. As I contemplated the pop-eyed King of Sassania in the Metropolitan Museum, Mark Askelon contemplated him too over my shoulder, and voiced his mocking comments in my ear. (Mark himself, of course, has clear 'American' ancestors: brilliant Ezra Pound, or magnificent Orson Welles, living half-fulfilled and half-wasted by the Mediterranean Sea.) The actual figure of the young student with hair torn out of his head appeared to me suddenly one evening in the apartment of a friend, a few hours after a savage clash had occurred near Wall Street between a band of youngsters and a gang of construction workers. I can still see vividly the patch of white on his head.

I remember starting *The Battle of Shrivings* high up in a tiny workroom in the roof of the Dakota Building on West Seventy Second Street. For relief, I would walk out and breathe fresh air on a small gargoyle-bordered terrace overlooking glorious Central Park. If it has ever energized you at all, it is impossible to resist the anguish of this most urgent and beautiful of cities. Over me its spell has long been unbreakable. In those days of early work on the play, its concerns seemed to me so immense that flying from Kennedy to Heathrow Airport felt like flying out of the twentieth century back to the nineteenth. A truly multi-racial society would be receding, in all the torment of its birth; approaching would be one chiefly insular, condescending, and frigid. This impression was of course unfair, and confessing it makes one seem self-righteous, but I was never happy in swinging, satirical London; the constant drizzle of put-down and small-minded preoccupation tended to dampen my spirits far too often.

I recall this feeling now because only now do I realize how living so much out of the country at that time enabled me to become infected with the need to discuss on stage, with flourish and head-on explicitness, the idea of human improvability. English dramatic taste rather deplores the large theme, largely broached: it tends to prefer – sometimes with good sense, but often with a really dangerous fear of grossness – the minute fragment, minutely observed. I am not saying that I did the job (or have re-done it) well. I simply reflect that had I remained a constant Londoner during that period, I doubt if I would have done it at all.

This said, I must confess that this second version of the play – composed three years ago, and now simply called *Shrivings* as earnest of plain intent – is much nearer to my original goal than was the first. I would like to thank my publisher deeply for letting me see it in print, laid out between hard and handsome covers, even though not interred in public acclaim. It is, after all, a brave act for a man of business to bring out a play which has yet to be produced on the stage. May the Protective God of Dramatists rain benefits upon him! And may the play itself now give me at last some kind of peace.

P.S.

SHRIVINGS

Characters:

GIDEON PETRIE, *Philosopher and President of the World League of Peace*

LOIS NEAL, *his secretary*

MARK ASKELON, *Poet and former pupil of Gideon*

DAVID ASKELON, *his son*

The action takes place at Shrivings, the Cotswold home of Sir Gideon Petrie. The time is 1970.

ACT ONE

SCENE 1: *Friday evening*
SCENE 2: *Friday night*

ACT TWO

SCENE 1: *Saturday night*
SCENE 2: *Sunday morning*

ACT THREE

Sunday night

THE SETTING

(All Directions are given from the viewpoint of the audience.)

In the Middle Ages, Shrivings was a House of Retreat. Now it shows a wide, austere, light-filled interior of white-washed wall and crude timber, divided into two levels.

Below: the main living area of the house.

Two huge arches, left and right. That to the left frames the door to Gideon's study; that to the right frames the staircase. Between them, the room goes back under the lip of Mark's bedroom, to the back wall of the house, which contains a window. The front door is assumed to be off-stage right, in this same wall.

Two doors, downstage, left and right. That to the left leads to the garden; that to the right, to the kitchen.

Two tables, left and right. That to the left – standing diagonally to the audience – serves as a desk: a chair, behind it; two stools before it, a telephone on it and a pile of letters, half opened. That to the right, a long refectory table for dining: a bench on the upstage side of it.

All the furniture has been made by David, which gives to the place an original look: cool, and beautiful.

At the head of the stairs, one can either turn right, to the other bedrooms, or left to Mark's.

Above: this room hangs over the playing area below, framed by the top half of the two large arches. It contains a bed and a table. Its window is assumed to be out front. The bathroom is off, to the left.

The whole atmosphere of this place is one of tranquillity and dedication.

ACT ONE

SCENE 1

Friday evening.

Five o'clock. DAVID, *a boy of nineteen, sits in the middle of the room, carving the leg of a small table, which is upside down on a sheet. He wears a frayed blue shirt and frayed blue jeans; his hair is long, and there are woodshavings in it. He concentrates very hard on the work.*

The telephone rings. He pays no attention. Finally LOIS *comes in calmly, carrying a cup of tea. She is a pretty American girl of twenty-five; tidy, efficient, and cheerful. She too wears her hair long and is dressed informally.*

LOIS [*picking up the phone*]: Sir Gideon Petrie's Secretary . . . No, I'm afraid he always spends this hour after tea completely alone. Beg pardon? Yes, sir; the vigil will go ahead exactly as announced. Sir Gideon will sit in Parliament Square from two o'clock till eight, tomorrow and Sunday. All who care to join him we welcome. Peace.

[*She hangs up and sits at the table, opening the letters.*]
Why didn't you answer the phone?

DAVID: It didn't sound interesting. It had that ring to it which said 'World Organization'.

LOIS: It's one of the neurotic symptoms of our time, you know, an inability to live in the real world.

DAVID: And where's that?

LOIS: O.K.

DAVID: No; where is it?

LOIS [*pointing to the desk*]: This is the real world, David.

DAVID: Letters?

LOIS: *These* letters, yes.

DAVID: This is the real world. Here.

[*He throws up a handful of shavings over his head.*]

LOIS: Ha, ha, ha. [*She turns to the desk.*]

DAVID: Hey!

LOIS [*impatiently*]: What?

DAVID: Hey!

LOIS: Hay is for horses.

[*The phone rings. She answers it.*]

Sir Gideon Petrie's Secretary. Beg pardon? . . . No, sir, there is no conflict in any way. The vigil ends on Sunday night. The Award will take place on Monday morning. Sir Gideon receives it for his twenty-fifth book *Explorations* – and Mr Askelon to mark the appearance of his *Collected Poems* . . . Well, I would have thought the award of a world-famous prize to two world-famous figures was Human Interest enough . . . No, I'm sorry. Shrivings is a place of quiet, and we like to keep it that way. Peace.

[*She hangs up, gently.*]

DAVID: You're beautiful.

LOIS: Me?

DAVID: You're so firm. It's marvellous to be firm like that.

LOIS: It sounds awful. 'Firm' 's a disgusting word for a girl.

DAVID: It's great when applied to breasts. And even greater when applied to moral outline. That's what you've got. Moral outline.

LOIS [*amused*]: Yeah, well why don't you just tidy all that away now, before your dad comes?

DAVID: Why? It creates an impression of industry, and dedication.

LOIS: It makes a grundgy impression.

DAVID: What a beautiful word!

LOIS: You know, I really can't believe I'm finally going to meet him. The great Mark Askelon! Do you think I should tell him I've been in love with him ever since I read *Wafers of Death* in Doubleday's Bookshop, the first day I arrived in New York?

DAVID: 'Grundgy!' That's perfect!

LOIS: He wrote about Catholicism like it was a disease. If my dad read any one of those poems, they'd have to take him straight to the hospital . . . What about your mother? She must have hated them.

DAVID: I bet she just laughed.

LOIS: But she was a believer?

DAVID: Giulia laughed about everything.

LOIS: Why do you call her that?

DAVID: Why not?

LOIS: She was your mother.

DAVID: Once. Since then, Father immortalized her in poetry. Now she belongs wholly to Penguin Books.

LOIS: She must have been incredible. I mean, to make a great poet give up writing revolutionary poems, and do all his writing about love!

DAVID: That's bad?

LOIS: Of course not. It's just irrelevant. Do you realize that some parts of this world are actually getting poorer? When you're faced with a fact like that, people's sex lives come to look a bit trivial, don't they?

DAVID: Absolutely.

[*He tries to kiss her. She turns away very coolly, slits open another letter with great dexterity.* DAVID *shrugs.*

The door opens. SIR GIDEON PETRIE *comes in. He is a gentle, noble man of over sixty. One senses a great toughness, both of intellect and staying-power. His manners show a charm composed of clarity, courtesy, and gaiety of spirit.*

There is about him a sort of sparkling serenity: a delicate earnestness, through which one glimpses a deep and passionate involvement. He contemplates the youngsters lovingly.]

GIDEON: Peace, my fliers.

LOIS: Peace, Giddy.

DAVID: Peace, Giddy.

LOIS: You're out early. It's not six yet.

GIDEON: I'm too excited to settle. When I think he'll be here any time now! My goodness! [*To* DAVID.] Are you up to it?

DAVID: No.

GIDEON: Nor me. He sets such standards, your father. Everything has to be so memorable.

DAVID: Yes.

GIDEON: How's the afternoon post?

LOIS: I've laid them out. [*Indicating piles of letters.*] Requests to speak. Requests to write.

GIDEON [*sitting at the desk*]: Yes, yes, yes to all requests today! I can't refuse anybody on the day Mark Askelon first comes to Shrivings! Do you think we did right in closing it this weekend? It's been bothering me.

LOIS: Why not? We've all got to be selfish sometimes.

GIDEON: Have we?

LOIS: You're too hard on yourself, Giddy!

GIDEON: You know, I haven't been working in there at all. Just lying on my bed, remembering him. Seeing him on his terrace in the sunshine. The Sage of Corfu, under his trellis of vines! Like a Roman pugilist gone to seed.

LOIS: You mean fat?

GIDEON: Of course.

LOIS: Oh, no!

GIDEON: He was always a mountain! A *sacred* mountain, of course. Everybody came from miles to sit round the foothills and listen!

    [*Louis laughs.*]

And what wonderful talk it was, my goodness!

LOIS: What kind?

GIDEON: Well, the last thing I remember him discussing – and it was all of eleven years ago, mind you – was whether the heart's blood the Furies dropped on Athens in the *Oresteia* was really their menstrual fluid.

LOIS [*a little shocked: trying not to show it*]: Gee! Oh, my!

DAVID: He really put a spell on you, didn't he?

GIDEON [*glancing through the letters and ticking some*]: From the first day he became my student at Cambridge! You know, the summer we met we went for our first walking tour. Even then, he moved through the Mediterranean as if he owned it.

DAVID: Do you see Giulia there too, under the trellis?

GIDEON: Whenever I picture your mother, it's always in movement.

DAVID: Me, too. She used to dance me to sleep, like other mothers sing. She'd light a candle and I'd have to watch her shadow on the wall. Up and down, up and down, till I went off.

GIDEON: How exquisite.

LOIS: D'you know the last thing *I'd* see at night when I was a kid? A beautiful plastic Jesus, like the ones they have in taxis to prevent crashes, only bigger. It had these great ruby tears on its face, and I'd have to pray to it before turning out the light: 'Dear Lord, make me a Good Catholic and a Good American. Amen!' We all have different backgrounds, I guess.

GIDEON [*laughing*]: And yours made you the fierce Falcon you are today!

LOIS [*smiling*]: Oh sure! [*Scooping up the letter.*] I'll do these now. While I've got the energy. [*She looks fondly at* GIDEON.] You're looking just great, d'you know that?

GIDEON: I feel just great; thank you. So are you, I may say.

LOIS: Really?

GIDEON: Prettier each day.

LOIS [*flattered*]: Ha, ha, ha!

[*Smiling, she takes the letters into* GIDEON's *study, shutting the door.*]

GIDEON: You know, you two are absolutely complementary. A Falcon and an Owl. She can give you the gifts of the day. You can give her the gifts of the night.

DAVID: Oh, Giddy!

GIDEON: What, my dear?

DAVID: I can't give anybody anything. Sometimes I think all the opposite things I feel should just cancel me out, and make me invisible. Like all colours make up white.

GIDEON: You know, your father's going to be very impressed with you.

DAVID: Why not? I'm very impressive. It's not everyone who can drop out of two public schools, and Cambridge University, all in the space of five years.

GIDEON: Do you think Mark cares a fig about academic conformity?

DAVID: I don't know. I don't even know what he feels about me being here.

GIDEON: If *I* had a son, there's nowhere in the world I'd rather think of him than in your father's villa.

DAVID: Six years' silence, punctuated by telegrams. 'Regret still not convenient you return. Father.'

GIDEON: We've talked about this a great deal, my dear. Perhaps he did not feel able to write. It happens.

DAVID: And why does he come now? Certainly not just to get a prize. He's had hundreds offered, and never accepted one.

GIDEON: Perhaps he needs us. Have you thought of that?

DAVID [*startled*]: Needs?

GIDEON: Yes.

[*Suddenly* DAVID *shudders violently.*]

David! What's the matter?

DAVID: Nothing.

GIDEON: But there is. Tell me.

DAVID: Nothing. Why do you listen to me? It's all nonsense!

GIDEON: Listen to me, then. Life hasn't been so easy for him these past years. People say hard things of him, I know. How heartless to forbid you the house all the time your mother was so ill. Was it so heartless to want to spare you the horror of watching her go? The paralysis claiming more of her each day?

DAVID: And afterwards? Staying there quite alone?

GIDEON: Your mother's death was the end of a world for Mark. I wonder if even you can quite conceive the end of a world ... [*Warmly.*] My dear, let's offer him this house these few days to be his home. Let's offer him Shrivings, with all its tradition of Peace. What d'you say? Oh my goodness; isn't that lovely work?

DAVID: Your goodness. [*Abruptly.*] I'll take this back to the stables.

[*He picks up the table.*]

GIDEON: What are you trying to tell me?

[*Pause. Then the boy shrugs.* LOIS *comes in.*]

LOIS: I've just typed the two for your personal signature.

GIDEON: I'll sign them.

[*With a look at* DAVID, GIDEON *retires to his study.*]

LOIS [*tidying up*]: Dinner's at eight. I've decided to make Roman eggs in honour of your father. Do you think he'll appreciate the subtle compliment?

DAVID: I don't know.

[*He goes out into the garden with the unfinished table. She looks after him, puzzled, then sits at the desk and starts sorting out some more papers.*

Pause. A voice is heard calling wooingly.]

MARK [*off*]: Gideon! ... Gideon! ...

[LOIS *looks up.* MARK *appears from the back, carrying a large package done up in sacking and a small parcel in brown paper. In his early fifties, he is the relic of an enormous man. A mass of hair falls from a massive head; eyes stare from an eroded face. He wears a Greek shepherd's cloak with a hood. His voice is still powerful.*]

LOIS: Peace.

MARK: What?

LOIS: Peace.

MARK: If possible.

[*He moves into the room, looking about him.*]

Stupendous!

LOIS: Can I help you?

MARK: Is that Lyssop Ridge up there behind the house?

LOIS: I'm afraid I don't know.

MARK: Those woods lie on it like a silver fox on a nigger's shoulder.

LOIS [*offended*]: May I ask who you are, please?

MARK: A shepherd, as my cloak proclaims. I suspect permanently without a flock. The name is Mark.

LOIS [*amazed*]: Not Mark *Askelon*!

MARK: Exactly so.

LOIS: How did you get here?

MARK: A hired Humber car in leatherette. It's just gone away.

LOIS [*excited and suddenly nervous*]: Oh Gee! I didn't expect you to
... well to ... look exactly like that! I didn't know what you'd
look like really! ... Where's your luggage?

MARK: In the hall. The maid can fetch it in later.

LOIS: We have no maids at Shrivings, sir. Sir Gideon does not
approve of servants. Here everybody has to do his own room. I do
this and the kitchen. Of course you won't have to – I'll do yours,
of course!

MARK: How many people stay here, then?

LOIS: Oh, it's just like a hotel. We've got fifteen bedrooms, and we
hope they'll be all filled every night. They're mostly kids on their
way someplace. We try not to turn anyone away who genuinely
wants a place to sleep.

MARK: You mean it's a sort of Commune for Transients?

LOIS [*laughing*]: Oh now, don't get scared! There's no one coming
this weekend. Giddy asked me to accept nobody for the three days
you're here. He figured you'd like some quiet.

MARK: And you do all the supervising?

LOIS: Sure! Giddy calls me a general factota! ... My actual name's
Lois. Lois Neal ... I'll get your case.

[*She runs off, and returns with a battered suitcase.*]

MARK: Where did he find you?

LOIS [*proudly*]: In jail, after a march! Two years ago. We talked all
night. In the morning he asked me to work for him. I was terribly
proud. I could type some, but I didn't know any shorthand at all.
So I took one of those Courses in Speedwriting for With-It Girls.
Do you know, after four weeks I could do a hundred words a
minute?

MARK: But surely there was a secretary here already?

LOIS: Oh, there was a grundgy old woman called Miss Crawford.
She looked like one of those Feminists from the 1910s. You know –
white cuffs, and tits like dried apples. She was going to retire anyway. One look at me, and she fled.

MARK: I bet she did.

LOIS: I think Giddy was glad to see her go – but of course he'd never say.

MARK: You admire him very much, don't you?

LOIS: He's a saint. [*Pause.*] Well, let me show you your room.

[*She turns and picks up the package wrapped in sacking.*]

MARK [*with a hint of sharpness*]: Please – let me carry that.

LOIS [*pleasantly*]: O.K.!

[*She picks up the case instead, and goes upstairs.* MARK *follows, leaving the small parcel behind on the table. They enter the bedroom above.*]

In here.

MARK: Thank you.

[*He puts his package on the table, down front.*]

LOIS: It's nice, isn't it?

MARK: Excellent.

[*He takes off his cloak. Underneath he is wearing a baggy old suit and a cheap cotton shirt.*]

LOIS: The bathroom's through there. I hope you like lemon soap. I put in a great cake of it.

[*He throws his cloak on the bed.*]

MARK: What's a saint?

LOIS: A man who doesn't know what it is to reject people.

MARK: And that's Gideon?

LOIS: He has no hostility left in him for anyone in the world.

MARK: Do you really believe that?

LOIS: Absolutely. He's proved it can be done.

MARK: You have American eyes.

LOIS: Is that good?

MARK: Eyes are inherited. Who gave you yours?

LOIS: I don't know. My father, I guess. He's a doctor in Chicago.

MARK: Does he approve your working for the President of The World League of Peace?

LOIS: God, no! All he thinks about is how to get me home, away from the enemies of the American way of life! ... [*Gleefully.*] Oh, gee, it's so great you're here! I'm making a special dinner in your honour. We're vegetarian here, you know.

MARK: We?

LOIS: Well, it's me really, I'm afraid. I'm a health food nut. Since I've come, Shrivings does without meat. Giddy entirely endorses this, I may say. I hope you don't mind. It's much better for you . . . I'm going to try and make a cream cheese soufflé for dessert. It can be spectacular, but it's a bastard to get right.

MARK: You do all the cooking here?

LOIS: Sure. I enjoy it.

MARK: Yes, but do the diners?

LOIS [*laughing*]: Well, they say they do!

[GIDEON *comes out of the study, and walks to the foot of the stairs.*] Giddy says I should publish my recipes altogether and call it *The Protester's Cookbook*. I think that sounds just a little pompous, don't you?

GIDEON [*calling upstairs*]: Mark?

[MARK *comes out of the room. He looks down the stairs, and sees* GIDEON. *He descends.*]

MARK: Gideon.

[*They embrace, very warmly.*]

GIDEON: My dear, you look marvellous!

MARK [*coming into the living room*]: You mean slimmer? It's true. God knows how, with my alcoholic constitution. Behold! [*He swirls across the room.*] Man is a reed – but a drinking reed!

[GIDEON *laughs delightedly.* LOIS *comes down also.*]

As for you – you haven't changed a hair. Not one hair since last I saw you – eleven years ago, in Corfu harbour!

GIDEON: I wish that were true. Alas, my dear, at my age the last hairs fall even quicker than the last illusions. You've met Miss Neal, I see. More than a secretary – she's a conscience.

LOIS: Nonsense, Giddy!

MARK: Oh, I sensed that right away. My moral hazel twig pointed straight at her!

GIDEON [*embarrassed for* LOIS]: You had a good flight, I hope?

MARK: Did I? We annihilated the Appenines, the Alps and the Dordogne in less than three hours. Is that good? . . . No matter. This room is compensation for anything!

GIDEON: It used to be a House of Retreat, you know.

MARK: Of confession, surely? Is that not what Shriving means? Confession and penance?

GIDEON: Oh well, I hope it won't be found too inappropriate for a thorough-going atheist.

MARK: I daresay a thorough-going rationalist has exorcized its spirit not a little.

[*They bow to each other.*]

Coming up your drive is an unforgettable experience. That long tunnel of elm trees, and at the end a great stone porch shouting 'Stop!'

GIDEON: Shouting 'Come!' my dear. 'Come.'

MARK: Is it?

[*Slight pause. Then abruptly indicating the parcel.*]

Please open that. My present to your house.

GIDEON: My goodness! Whatever can it be?

MARK [*to* LOIS]: Do you have wine?

LOIS: I've got a little for cooking. It's not very good, I guess.

MARK: So much the better. Household gods cherish the ordinary.

LOIS [*admiringly*]: Out of sight!

MARK: Please fetch it.

LOIS: Right!

[*She darts out to the kitchen.* GIDEON *lifts from the smaller package an ancient Greek drinking cup of clay.*]

GIDEON: Oh, my dear! How exquisite!

MARK: A libation cup from the sixth century Before Cant!

GIDEON: I'm overwhelmed.

MARK: Wine was poured into that to toast the Gods.

GIDEON: I'm afraid it's been years since I drank wine.

MARK: What do you need with it? Your spirit is the last of the wine.

After you, all is vinegar! . . . I shall put that into my speech about you.

GIDEON: Speech?

MARK: At the Prize Giving. I assume you are preparing one about me.

GIDEON: No. Surely that isn't part of the ceremony, that we eulogize each other?

MARK: If it isn't, I shall make it so.

GIDEON: Oh my goodness, I hope not!

[LOIS *returns with an open wine bottle.*]

LOIS: Here!

MARK: Splendid! Giddy, you pour. [*Extending the cup.*] Fill it to the brim.

GIDEON: Very well, my dear. [*He takes the bottle.*] I can always rely on you to make a delicious ceremony out of everything! [*He pours the wine into the cup.*]

MARK: There now. Thank you . . . Attention, please! [*He raises the cup.*] I lift this cup of many consecrations! I drink to your house!

LOIS: Wow!

MARK: To Shrivings – in whose cool chambers the dangling soul was once tied to the trellis of confession, and so helped to flower.

[DAVID *comes in from the garden, carrying a great object wrapped in a white sheet.*]

Here was sheath in a time of swords! Silence in a time of muskets! And now, in a time of bombs –

DAVID: Peace.

[*All look at him. A pause. He sets the object down. Then abruptly,* MARK *turns away and thrusts the cup at* GIDEON.]

MARK: Complete the toast.

GIDEON: I couldn't, my dear. I'm afraid it would make my head swim.

MARK: You must – or there will be perturbation in the house.

DAVID: I'll drink for him.

[MARK *contemplates him, then hands him the cup.* DAVID *drinks, wincing.*]

LOIS: I guess it's been open a few days.

MARK: Haven't we all? Well, not him perhaps ... Well, I did not expect to see you so soon. It's charming of you to come all this way over from Cambridge.

DAVID [*avoiding his eyes*]: I ... live here.

MARK: Live?

DAVID: I wrote to you.

MARK: I don't read letters.

DAVID [*embarrassed*]: I gave up Cambridge. And then Giddy – Gideon – suggested I move in here. So I did. I've been here since November.

MARK: You gave up?

DAVID: Well, it would have given me up. I just got in first ...

GIDEON: Philosophy is not David's metier. He prefers at the moment to make furniture for philosophers. A decision I selfishly encourage.

MARK: I don't understand.

GIDEON: All the furniture in this room was made by David.

[*Pause.* MARK *looks about him. He has difficulty in digesting this news.*]

MARK: Extraordinary. Where did you learn?

DAVID [*darting glances at his father, but unable to look him fully in the face*]: I took woodwork at my last school. Then Giddy has an old stables here. I felt I wanted ...

MARK: What?

DAVID: To do something with my hands.

MARK: Well, why not? ... It's a noble profession, carpentry. The only one with an indisputable patron saint!

[DAVID *laughs.*]

What's that you've got there? Something for my arrival?

GIDEON [*confidently to* MARK]: It's something special, I'm sure! He's been rather secretive lately. Are you going to show it to us?

DAVID [*embarrassed*]: Not now.

GIDEON: Of course now. Why ever not?

DAVID: Later. Tomorrow. I'll take it back. [*He moves to pick the object up again.*]

117

GIDEON [*in great surprise*]: David! . . . Please show us. We're all dying of curiosity.

[DAVID *stands staring at the ground.*]

LOIS: Come on, David, don't be so dopey!

[*He still stands not replying.*]

O.K. – *I'll* do it!

DAVID: No! [*To* GIDEON.] You! [*He smiles at* GIDEON.]

GIDEON [*smiling back, intimately*]: Me? I'm honoured.

[GIDEON *approaches the object.*]

Hey presto! One – two – three!

[*He takes off the sheet. Underneath stands a throne of marvellous austerity. A pause.*]

GIDEON: How beautiful! Oh, how beautiful, David! It's the most lovely thing you've done yet.

DAVID [*pleased*]: Really?

LOIS: Wow!

DAVID [*eagerly to her*]: D'you like it?

LOIS: It's out of sight! . . . Honest!

GIDEON: What do you say, Mark? Isn't it fine?

MARK: I say felicitations to my son on his sense of things. He obviously sees what is lacking here. A true Cathedral needs a true Cathe*dra*!

LOIS: Cathedral?

MARK: That's where we are, isn't it? Shrivings, the Cathedral of Humanism.

GIDEON: Don't be naughty, Mark!

MARK [*to* DAVID]: I'm right, aren't I? It is a throne?

DAVID [*low*]: Yes.

MARK: And for Giddy?

DAVID: Yes.

MARK [*to* GIDEON]: Exactly so! All for *you*! The Chair of Paternal Wisdom. I would hope to earn one myself in time. Such objects have to be earned, eh, David?

[DAVID *shrugs haplessly.*]

GIDEON: You sit on it. It would become you far better, a throne.

MARK: Maybe – but it hasn't been offered! We're here to witness *your* coronation. So please get up there and sit down as impressively as you can manage!

GIDEON [*grimacing modestly*]: Very well. Thank you, David. [*He sits on the throne.*]

[MARK *claps.*]

MARK: Hail, Gideon! First Pope of Reason! Hail!

GIDEON [*embarrassed*]: Stop it now, Mark, really!

LOIS: Hail, Giddy! Hail, Giddy! Hail, Giddy!

GIDEON: Now, please! Really! Really!

LOIS: You look absolutely wonderful there! Doesn't he, Mr Askelon?

MARK: Exactly in place!

GIDEON: Perhaps I should take it with me on the vigil. Set it up in Parliament Square. It would evoke irreverent comparisons with the one in Westminster Abbey!

MARK: Vigil? What vigil?

LOIS: We're all sitting, tomorrow and Sunday afternoon.

MARK [*alarmed*]: You mean a demonstration?

LOIS: Yes. It's been in all the papers!

MARK: I don't read newspapers. In the end, that is the only truly obscene four-letter word: NEWS!

LOIS: We're hoping for at least ten thousand people. Why don't you come too? It'd be the most tremendous help to the Cause!

GIDEON: She's right. I'm known as a crank – but you would really be a catch.

MARK: Oh no, I don't think so.

LOIS: Oh why not, Mr Askelon? It would be so *great* having you!

MARK [*lightly*]: Let's say, I hate to be old-fashioned.

LOIS [*bewildered*]: Old-fashioned?

MARK: Peaceful protest is absolutely Out, my dear. The really modern young have quite abandoned vigils. Especially in your fair country.

GIDEON: Which is why she left it, Mark; for the moment. Until there's another real peace movement, and not just Young Violence joining with Old.

LOIS: Which will be never.

GIDEON: Oh, come now. All revolutionaries idealize their Movement's early days. Don't fall into the same trap. The Flower Children shouted some simple truths. Home has to be found: it's not the place you're born in. Country can be a mental prison, and patriotism an ape's adrenalin. Do you think that'll be forgotten?

LOIS [*warmly*]: Not when you speak, no!

MARK [*ironic*]: And what did the flowers shout?

LOIS: Beg pardon?

MARK: If those daffodils could speak, which the flower boys handed out to policemen – if they could tell about their birth, through layers of icy spring soil, d'you know what they'd say? They'd open their yellow mouths and yell 'Violence! Violence!' at the top of their stalks.

LOIS [*laughing*]: No, they would not! They'd shout 'Effort!' That's not the same thing at all.

GIDEON: Well said, Lois!

MARK: *Touché!* . . . What would I have to do at your vigil? Sit in front of the House of Commons and chant Down With The Bomb!?

LOIS: We're concerned to ban all weapons, you know. Not just the bomb.

MARK [*playfully*]: Even penknives?

LOIS: Beg pardon?

MARK: Even vegetable knives? Those clever little knives which dice carrots for your joy-giving, life-enchanting salads?

LOIS: Well, that would be a dreadful idea!

MARK: What is not a weapon? The tongue, Miss Neal, can be a dreadful weapon. Should we have them all cut out?

LOIS [*becoming a little confused*]: I mean, here at Shrivings we think it is wrong to fight in any circumstances.

MARK: Any whatever?

LOIS: Any whatever!

[*She looks at* GIDEON *for approval.*]

MARK: Even Hitler?

LOIS: Well, it is hard to adjust to that particular concept, I admit. But once you start fighting, you become as guilty as your enemy.

MARK [*blandly*]: You mean, the men who freed Belsen were as guilty as the men who made it?

LOIS: No, of course not.

MARK: Then what? The evil you don't fight, you enlarge.

GIDEON [*softly*]: No, my dear. The evil you do fight you enlarge. That's surely the point. You arm yourself to destroy gas chambers in Poland. Five years later, you are melting the eyeballs of fishermen on the Yellow Sea. We've had centuries of fighting back for Freedom and Justice. It doesn't work. We've had centuries of trying to *limit* fighting back: battle by mercenaries; truces on Christmas Eve. It doesn't work either. So long as boys can continue to hose each other down with fire on Boxing Day, their Christmas Day truce is an obscenity; a sop to the unseeing.

[*Pause. Reassuringly he squeezes* LOIS*'s hand.*]

MARK [*brusquely*]: If a ruffian with a pistol entered this room, and was definitely going to kill Miss Neal – assuming you had a pistol too, would you use it on him?

GIDEON: No.

MARK: You would let him kill her?

GIDEON: I have no choice, unless I wish to become him.

MARK [*to* LOIS]: Same situation. Would you let him kill Giddy?

LOIS: Yes.

MARK: Touching loyalty you have for each other here at Shrivings!

LOIS: We *do*!

MARK: Apparently.

LOIS: Shrivings *is* the loyalty!

MARK [*to* DAVID]: What would you do, my son?

[*Pause.*]

DAVID: Is it a girl ruffian or a man?

LOIS: What difference does *that* make?

DAVID: I think I'd use the gun.

MARK: Why?

DAVID: Because I'd rather have Lois alive than somebody I didn't know.

MARK: Unreasonable boy! And she's not even flattered, are you?

LOIS [to DAVID]: How can you be so subjective about everything? It's like you can't grasp the simplest general idea!

MARK: Don't blame him too harshly, Miss Neal. Beauty, after all, confuses the best of us!

LOIS [embarrassed]: Oh! Well! Gee! ...

MARK: I must confess that I myself, seeing you threatened by this ruffian, would have a hard time leaving you to your fate.

LOIS: Thank you!

MARK: But I would, of course. Out of deference to your principles.

LOIS [nervously]: Oh, of course!

MARK [his tone darkening]: I would – with the utmost regret – abandon you to his pistol. Or to his razor. Or to the dungeons of the Inquisition. Or the locomotives of Chiang Kai-Shek, who, I have been told, fed his prisoners into their furnaces in order to keep them running. Or for that matter, to the hands of New York Construction workers ... [He stops suddenly.]

GIDEON [puzzled]: Mark?

MARK [his tone totally changed]: Have you seen the Ruffian at work? Really seen him? Have you, Giddy? You sit here so calmly ... Have you seen a boy scalped? I have. Last year – in the civilized city of Manhattan ... [Pause.] I'd gone there after Giulia died, to keep busy, as they say.

GIDEON: Yes, I heard that you went.

MARK: To declaim poems to college students, written twenty years before they were born ... They were in fact swarming all over the city the day I arrived: yet again protesting the Vietnam War – in this instance, the invasion of Cambodia. Isn't it amazing the way the Young simply won't give up? There they all were, in their velvets and zippy boots – hair-cuts like so many liberty bells – still handing out pamphlets, still squeaking 'Stop Killing' in desperate little voices. And the next day their elders – as if the murder of four children in Ohio that week had not been enough – decided to punish their impertinence in New York. [*Pause.*] I was sitting with my lawyer in his office in Wall Street. Suddenly we heard this roar outside – it was about noon: a sort of sea of approaching fury. We walked to the window. Four floors below us, a terrified group of youngsters was standing quite still. On both sides of them stood massed ranks of workers from the building trade – men whose present affluence has apparently compelled them into the right wing. Dreadful-looking thugs, with faces like huge steaks, wearing hard yellow hats. And then we watched *their* protest: *their* statement of human dignity. For fifteen minutes, they beat the children into pulp. They bashed them with their fists. They kicked them in the balls and the breasts with steel toes. They tore cheeks from faces. They danced on vomiting girls. And then they swept on, shouting 'America! America!' – round the corner, to the next gang-bang. And all the while, not moving, not doing anything, stood policemen – their Irish potato faces barely concealing smiles. [*Pause.*] My lawyer, a fellow of infinite social conscience, had dashed into the street, leaving me alone. Suddenly the place was quiet again, and there was only one figure visible. A boy, sitting on the kerb, wearing a sort of eiderdown. Lumps of hair had been torn from his head. Can you imagine the force that needed? – and he was moaning in unspeakable pain. But with some kind of instinct for city tidiness, he was carefully dropping what blood he could into a drain. I stood in the window watching him, a dry martini in my hand. It was a day of April. Clouds of pollen were streaming down the street between us. Golden dust tumbling through the air. It seemed to be settling over him, like dandruff ... And then he raised his head and looked at me.

LOIS: What did you do?

MARK [*brutally*]: I raised my glass.

LOIS [*confused*]: But ... but couldn't you have? –

MARK: What?

LOIS: Well, gotten him an ambulance?

MARK: I could. But I wanted another drink.

[*A shocked pause.*

Abruptly he goes upstairs into his bedroom, and bangs the door. GIDEON *moves after him, but suddenly the door is loudly locked from the inside.* MARK *sits on the bed, his face in his hands.*]

LOIS: He's nuts! He's completely *nuts!*

GIDEON: Lois, please.

LOIS: What's that supposed to mean? What's he *talking* about?

GIDEON: He was always addicted to drama. You know that.

LOIS: Drama?

GIDEON: Why don't you just start dinner?

LOIS: Jesus! . . . [*Regaining control.*] O.K.!

[*She goes out to the kitchen.* DAVID *stands unmoving, staring at the stairs.*]

GIDEON: It's just fatigue. That's all. He'll be down for dinner . . . Why don't we take a walk in the garden? What do you say? . . . David . . . He's simply tired –

[DAVID *turns and goes abruptly into the garden. Puzzled,* GIDEON *follows him. Above,* MARK *springs up from the bed. He opens his case and takes out two bottles of brandy, which he places on the shelf. Then he returns and extracts another two, which he also puts on the shelf. Then he takes out one shirt, closes the case, and kicks it under the bed. He turns to the package in its sacking on the table. He places his hands on it.*]

MARK: *Proteggimi. Proteggimi. Proteggimi!* . . . And him. Keep him safe from me. By your limbs, I beg you. By your murdered limbs, keep them all out of harm from me: Gideon – David our son – that silly girl.

[*He unties the string and stuffs it into his pocket. Then he lowers the sacking to reveal a black wooden box with doors. On the top is a little pediment in pink wood: this he erects, with a deliberate delicacy.*]

My wife. My own true wife. *Santissima, Beatissima* Giulia!

[*Standing behind it, he opens the doors of the box to reveal, staring straight at us, the head in effigy of a young woman painted in naive style. The whole shrine is coloured in the gay, crude manner of peasant*

work from Southern Italy: on the inside flaps of the doors are bright,
little gilded saints. Mark moves round and kneels to it, reverently.]
MARK: I'll not go down there again. I'll keep in here till the prize-
giving. Then straight back to Corfu – hurting no one. I swear it,
my darling. *Te lo juro! Te lo juro, mia moglie! Santa Giulia Paralytica!*

SLOW BLACKOUT

SCENE 2

Friday night.

Ten-thirty. As the lights come up, LOIS *is clearing the dinner table.* DAVID
sits cross-legged on the floor, rolling a joint. Upstairs, MARK *lies on his bed.*
One hand holds a half-empty bottle.

DAVID: I saw an armoured car today.
LOIS: What?
DAVID: In Trister village, just before dinner. Well, it was one of
those converted ones. At first I thought it was full of chrysan-
themums. Then just as they passed me, they all separated, and
turned out to be four shaggy male heads and four shaggy female,
all the same colour bronze. If I'd chosen the next street, there'd have
been no car. If I'd seen them at the next corner, they'd already have
separated.
LOIS: Are you stoned?
    [*He does not reply.*
    She gives him a bewildered face, and goes into the kitchen with her tray.
    DAVID *lights his joint.* MARK *stirs on the bed.*]
MARK: Brilliant. Absolutely brilliant! Not ten minutes in the house,
go off like that – bang! Just for one pretentious American slit . . .
    [*He sits up and looks at the shrine.*] No, it was his fault, the boy.
Coming in like that – your eyes in his head! . . . Who knew he was

125

here?... Standing there like some medieval half-wit, all shrugs and shavings in the hair. Who the hell is he? Master carpenter to Gideon Petrie. I sent him to England for *that*? – to carve his throne! 'Hail to my new daddy – Lord of the twenty-five books!' My old daddy only wrote four, and they were just poetry! That doesn't count...

[LOIS *returns with a bowl containing four green apples. She piles the remaining plates on the tray.* DAVID *watches her.*]

And what about his eyes, eh? Gideon's? Did you see all that white gum in the corners? My God, he's aged!

[*He lifts the bottle to his lips, and drinks.*]

DAVID: Smash one.

LOIS: Huh?

DAVID: Say Let this Plate be Dad, and smash it. Banish the Demon Uptight.

LOIS: It wouldn't.

[*She goes on piling the plates.*]

MARK [*half to himself*]: 'Peace!' 'Peace!' What's that supposed to mean? Well, of course, you could hear it – defiance. 'I'm Giddy's boy now. Let's not mistake ... Son and heir of Shrivings ...' Sagging Jesus!

DAVID [*warmly*]: I'm sorry.

LOIS: I mean, O.K., I just wish you'd warned me in advance. I wish you'd told me; please overlook my Dad's behaviour, because he's clinically insane. I'd have been prepared.

DAVID: He's not.

LOIS: Yeah, well, like what's he doing up there now, locked in his room all night? No dinner – nothing.

DAVID: Your elbows are very upset.

LOIS: What?

DAVID: They're up in arms.

LOIS: Ha, ha, ha. [*She picks up the full tray.*]

DAVID: Hey.

LOIS: Hay is for horses. [*She goes into the kitchen.*]

MARK [*to the shrine*]: Alright, dance for him. You dance for him. [*He gets off the bed, and stands glaring at the shrine.*] You go in there and dance him to sleep *now*! Try it, why don't you? Get out of bed, and try it! ...

[*He begins a drunk parody 'dance', singing to himself. Sitting below,* DAVID *looks upwards. The dance stops.*]

[*Shouting at the shrine.*] All right, stop it! Just stop ... Sad looks. Reproach ... Well, well! Can't you ever cry? Can't you ever fight me like a woman, not fucking saint? ...

[*He starts pacing about.* DAVID *rises anxiously to his feet.*]

That damn book. Always that prayer book! Can't you see it's disgusting? Filthy coloured pictures – Christ the Shepherdess! Have you got no dignity at all, praying to a Bearded Lady? Signora Gesù, Little Bo-Peep of Souls!

[*He starts to laugh – snatches up a large white towel, and lurches off to the bathroom.*

Below, DAVID *shudders.* LOIS *comes in with a cloth to wipe the table.*]

LOIS: What's the matter?

DAVID [*not looking at her*]: On the terrace.

LOIS: What?

DAVID: He'd sit and watch me for hours. Straw hat – eyes ...

LOIS: What are you talking about?

DAVID: When I used to play ... I'd go la-la-la, pretending to sing.

LOIS: I thought you adored him. You sort of said ... [*He turns and shrugs, hopelessly.*] Look, why don't you go up there now? It's obviously what he'd like.

DAVID: It isn't.

LOIS: Of course it is. It must be.

DAVID: It isn't.

LOIS: How do you know?

[*He shrugs again.*]

Well then what does he *want*?

DAVID: I'll whisper it. Here.

[*She approaches, puzzled. He kisses her abruptly. She lets herself be kissed, but remains inert.*]

Thank you.

LOIS: You're welcome.

DAVID: You know something? You're so uptight, it's a joke.

LOIS: A person is not uptight, my dear, just because she doesn't happen to want that.

DAVID: I think she is. I think that's exactly what she is.

LOIS [*gently*]: Or because she respects somebody else's opinions. I know it's me being pompous again. O.K. But we've talked about this one hundred times. This is Giddy's place. His whole meaning. Don't you realize this is where he did it? Probably in this very room.

DAVID [*sarcastic*]: Wow! . . .

LOIS: Do you think it was easy for a normal man to go to his wife on his forty-fifth birthday and tell her he can't have sex anymore?

DAVID: It certainly wasn't easy for her, was it? She buggered off, and maybe that's exactly what I should do too.

LOIS [*alarmed*]: What d'you mean?

DAVID: Piss off, that's what I mean. Exit. Is that what you want? Come on, tell me. Is that what you'd like – for me to go, as she did?

LOIS: Don't be silly. You know I'd hate it.

DAVID [*warmly*]: Would you?

LOIS: I'm simply asking you to respect the spirit of a great man in his own house, that's all.

DAVID [*playfully*]: Because he's a vegetarian, we all have to be?

LOIS: Yes.

DAVID: Even though he doesn't mind?

LOIS: Yes. Because I do. On his behalf.

DAVID: You know what you are? You are a Disciple.

LOIS: And proud of it.

DAVID: I don't know a word that means so many boring things.

LOIS: O.K.: I'm boring. I know it. You're not saying anything new.

DAVID: I didn't mean that.

LOIS: It doesn't matter.

DAVID: I don't know what I mean. Not from one second to the next!

LOIS: If you could ever get involved, you might just find out. Till then you're like a sort of ghost, tapping on the window. Do you know?

[*He pulls 'ghost faces' at her.*]

I'm serious David. I mean it! . . . [*She breaks up laughing.*] Oh cut it out!

[*She returns the faces. They are both playing, when* GIDEON *comes out of his study.*]

GIDEON: I suppose Mark hasn't been down?

LOIS: No sign of him.

GIDEON: Then I'd better go up.

DAVID: D'you think you should?

GIDEON: We're starting a Vigil of Peace tomorrow. We can't leave distress at home . . . Are you coming with us?

LOIS: Of course he is! Oh, Giddy, it's going to be wild! I heard on the radio they're expecting twenty-five thousand people. Isn't that crazy? You'll have to address them.

GIDEON: Will I?

LOIS: Well, of course. The eyes of England will be upon you!

GIDEON: Oh, my goodness.

LOIS: You'll have to say something witty and profound.

DAVID: And very loud; the open air.

GIDEON: Very well. I shall say – 'Go home, the lot of you! What the devil do you think you're doing here, parading the streets in fancy dress, and annoying the police who have far more important things to do than take care of you lot!'

[*Both the youngsters laugh.* GIDEON *ascends his throne with an air.*]

'What is it you want? We have educated you, at vast expense, in all the wisdom at our disposal. You've been given expert courses in all the right subjects. Mangerism, or worship of Family; Flaggism, or worship of Tribe; Thingism, or worship of Money. In our theatres and on our screens, we have taught you to find the act of killing men exciting, and the act of creating them obscene. You can go to Church, and respect the stopped mind. You can go to the war memorials, and respect the stopped body. What more do you want?'

[*Both youngsters laugh and clap.*]

LOIS: Oh, Giddy, that's great! You've got to say it – just like that!

GIDEON: And then, perhaps I'll ask them what they *really* want. If they are honest, they'll reply: 'A point to our lives. A meaning.' 'Very well, then,' I'll say: 'ask yourselves who you are. Look at each other. What do you see there? A crowd of weird beings, standing half-in, half-out of Nature. Animals possessed of powers completely non-animal. Powers to symbolize, to imagine, to laugh with self-ridicule. What could they be, these powers, if not tools to help free you from the violent, circular force which dominates all other life? [*He sits.*] Scientists go about the world looking for the Missing Link. It is staring them in the face. [*Pointing to* DAVID.] *You* are the Missing Link. [*Pointing to* LOIS.] *You* are the link between animals and what must appear if we are not to be sucked back into annihilation. Remember, as animals we are failures, and as aggressive beings also. We have to come at last to see Ego in a new way. As a pod, evolved for our protection during our years through pre-history, but which has now become our prison. If we are not to suffocate in it, we have to burst it open.'

LOIS: Wow!

GIDEON: We know more and more about our aggressions. We can't ever hope to remove them by reason alone; but if we don't make the attempt, not merely to concentrate their fury on to ever-lessening objects, but absolutely to starve them to death, we are doomed. Let me simplify it for you to the point of a crazy imperative. The Drug Children of today cry: "Unite with Nature!" I say: Resist her. Spit out the anger in your daddy's sperm! The bile in your mother's milk! The more you starve out aggression, the more you will begin yourselves!'

DAVID: Oh, that's beautiful!

GIDEON: 'Fight your instinctive dislike of other people. Fight the clinging to possession. Fight the need to invent enemies. If you want fights, I have them for you in plenty! I tell you, you must fight all the preserving mechanisms which you have inherited from evolution. Only so can you fulfil your Destiny. I detest that word. It is fascist, and Siegfriedish and faintly embarrassing. But I can't think of another. Man *has* a Destiny: to be a loving creator, or a dead duck!' . . . How about that?

DAVID [*laughing*]: You're a mad old ham, aren't you?

LOIS: David!

GIDEON: Not too mad, I hope.

DAVID: I don't know.

GIDEON: Anyway, I've made a huge decision. I'm going to fast, all week-end!

LOIS: Fast? Whatever for?

GIDEON [*getting up*]: I've been thinking what his father was saying: how vigils and protests are out of date. Well, there's really nothing I can do about that, since war and violence are even more out of date. But the least I can do is pep things up a bit. Inject a little show business into proceedings! Hence the fast. If I were to faint from hunger on the pavement, the effect could be sensational.

DAVID: I don't like it.

GIDEON: Oh, come. Pathos still remains the best way of influencing the middle classes.

LOIS: I think it's out of sight! Why don't we ask everyone who comes to fast too?

DAVID: And pass out too, all at the same time! You could blow your nose as a signal, and twenty-five thousand people could collapse, holding their tummies.

LOIS: Ha, ha, ha!

GIDEON: No, she's got a good idea, David. [*To* LOIS.] Look, why don't you ring the newspapers? We can make the first editions if we hurry. Say I'm announcing a two-day hunger protest and would like everyone who's coming tomorrow to stay hungry as well. The Press will love it. It's so delightfully vulgar.

LOIS [*getting up*]: Great!

GIDEON: They always say my head's in the clouds. They'll have to admit this is pretty nifty.

131

LOIS: I'll get started right away. And you two go to bed. You'll need your strength. Both of you, now. [*She goes out into the study.*]

GIDEON: What's the matter?

[*Pause.*]

DAVID: Starving people aren't protected.

GIDEON [*puzzled*]: Protected? Against what? . . . Why should I need protection?

[*Pause.* DAVID *shrugs, looking at the floor.*]

GIDEON: Are you being fanciful again? . . . I'll go and see your Father. You go to bed. Things will look fine in the morning.

[*He goes to the stairs.* DAVID *rises anxiously.* GIDEON *turns, aware of this.*]

[*Amusedly.*] I should think pot is allowed on a fast, wouldn't you? Does that make you any happier?

DAVID: Peace.

[*The boy walks rapidly past him, and runs upstairs, out of sight. To the right* GIDEON *ascends after him. He knocks on* MARK'*s door.*]

GIDEON: Mark! . . . Mark!

[MARK *appears slowly from the bathroom.*]

Let me see you, please. Just for a moment.

[MARK *moves into the room, without replying.*]

I beg you. Please let me in.

[MARK *stands before the shrine.*]

Mark . . .

MARK [*whispering to the shrine*]: *Se viene, non ne sono responsabile!*

GIDEON: I'll not go away till I've seen you. There. What do you think of that? I'll stay here all night. It'll be the start of my vigil.

[MARK *laughs aloud.*]

Come on, now! Let me in! [*He rattles the door-handle.*]

MARK: *Non ne sono.*

[*He moves to shut the doors of the shrine – then pauses and mischievously opens them again. Then he goes to the door, unlocks it and retreats to the bed, where he sits.* GIDEON *enters.*]

GIDEON: Peace.

MARK: I am surprised.

GIDEON: By what?

MARK: To find locks at Shrivings.

GIDEON: People require privacy at times.

MARK [*sarcastically*]: You mean for love-making?

GIDEON [*imperturbably*]: Among other things.

MARK: And who makes love here?

GIDEON: Youngsters stay every night. I imagine they're at it all the time.

MARK: How does Miss Neal regard that? Is she delighted by all that hippy coition?

GIDEON [*smiling*]: I think she tends to turn a blind eye.

MARK: Yes, I've seen that blind eye. It's magnificent. A great improvement on your ex-wife's, to be honest.

GIDEON: Really?

MARK: Enid's eyes were like two pebbles in a January stream. I can say that now.

GIDEON: You've lost none of your naughtiness, my dear!

[*He turns and sees the shrine.*]

MARK: Giulia's of course, you remember. Around them flared that corona. Invisible there, of course. But quite detectable in David.

GIDEON: Yes.

MARK: I had her made by a craftsman in Corfu, from an old photograph. As a souvenir, she works well. Also as a reliquary.

GIDEON: Reliquary?

MARK: For her ashes.

[*Pause.*]

GIDEON: How beautiful.

MARK: Yes, well there we are. Two old men with two dead wives.

GIDEON: To be pedantic – you are still young, and Enid is still alive.

MARK: Married to an accountant I believe.

GIDEON: Yes. In Berkshire.

MARK: Isn't that death?

GIDEON [*laughing*]: You really are outrageous!

133

MARK: Do you miss her?

GIDEON: Very much.

MARK: Still?

GIDEON: Yes.

MARK: I leave tomorrow.

GIDEON: Leave?

MARK: For Corfu.

GIDEON: I won't hear of it. Why?

MARK: I'm out of practice at being a guest.

GIDEON [gently]: There are no guests at Shrivings. You're part of a family, and have to work at it.

MARK: Is my son part of this family?

GIDEON: Everybody is who stays here.

MARK: And he's stayed six months. He must enjoy it. Naturally. The more unreal the place, the more he would thrive.

GIDEON: Unreal?

MARK: We are not Place People, David or I. My father was not called Askelon, but Ashkenazy. Israel Ashkenazy, of the ghetto face. He bequeathed me no home on earth; only envy of home in others. That boy will never walk a Dorset lane like an Englishman – rock a Vermont porch like a Yankee – doze under a Corfu cypress like a Greek. He's a mongrel! Russo–Jewish–English–Neapolitan! Whelped in one island, weaned in another.

GIDEON [with energy]: Then lucky him! He at least has no chance to fool himself with illusion! We are all mongrels, Mark. Don't hunt for your home in the bloodstream! Home is an act of will.

MARK: Do you imagine?

GIDEON: Make no mistake: Shrivings is real. It would still be real if it were a tent or a set of shacks. Ask the people who come here, the hopeful young, who flood in every night. It's not a family, as so many people know it – a box of boredom for man and wife – a torture chamber for the children. That idea of family must soon be obsolete, surely? – a miserable little group, marked off by a flat door, or a garden fence! . . . [Ardently.] No, my dear. Here is a new place of love. Stay with us, not just till Monday. See it for yourself

. . . This one weekend, for your sake, I broke all rules and closed it
– just to give us time alone. I believe I was wrong.

[*He extends his hand.*]

MARK [*coldly*]: I leave tomorrow. No more questions.

GIDEON [*very gently*]: We simply will not allow it.

MARK: Please go.

GIDEON: I can't believe you mean this.

MARK: Go!

[*Pause.*]

GIDEON: Peace.

[GIDEON *leaves the room.* MARK *sits on for a moment, takes a swig
from his bottle – then suddenly rushes downstairs after him. Startled,*
GIDEON *turns.*]

MARK [*blurting it out*]: All right! *Save me!*

[*Pause.*

LOIS *comes out of the study.* MARK *immediately turns away.*]

LOIS: Oh, excuse me.

GIDEON: It's all right, my dear.

LOIS: I talked with six papers. They're all printing something in their
first editions.

GIDEON: Good girl. [*He silently signs for her to go upstairs.*]

LOIS: Don't stay up too late. Goodnight, Mr Askelon. [*Tenderly.*]
Peace.

[*He nods. She goes upstairs. Pause.*]

GIDEON: Save you from what?

MARK: Dust.

GIDEON: Dust?

MARK: Pollen.

GIDEON: That morning you spoke of. In New York. The riot in New
York.

MARK: Yes?

GIDEON: There was pollen in the streets.

MARK: Yes.

GIDEON: Well? What of it?

MARK: It's hard.

GIDEON: Yes?

[*A long pause.*]

MARK: It was there between us. Me and that student. Between us in a long stream. I remained at my lawyer's window, looking down at him. He sat there on the kerb looking up at me, through that curtain of pollen. We lasted like that forever. I mean, five minutes. Five centuries in another sense, until I saw him transformed to an earlier time, five hundred years at least, when Wall Street was just a granite ledge padded by Redskin feet, and he another human sack, holding its scalped head . . . Five hundred years and no change. Five thousand, and still the identical horror. The tearers and the torn. The orderers. The Penalizers. The Joyless, returning and returning like the spring – Unalterable . . . Do you know the taste of Unalterable? That boy sat glued to the earth, with the pollen twirling round his red scalp – clouds of glinting dust – round and round the blood patch, like flies . . . I leant out, and it flew up to my mouth. I breathed it. I chewed it – It entered my stomach like powdered drug: dead spring – round, dead, unalterable spring, with its meaningless glints of hope! On and on we glared at each other, and on and on his blood dripped into the drain, and the pollen twirled inside me, and the years turned, till I was sick. Till I vomited down the side of that smart new building. I saw my sick running down the glass walls, and the boy began to laugh.

GIDEON: Oh, my dear Mark! My poor man!

MARK: There he sat – blond puppet, in his eiderdown! There he sat on the kerb – my wife, in her canvas jacket, staring at me, those fixed eyes, '*Gesù! Gesù!*'

GIDEON: Your wife?

MARK: Yes! . . . YES! . . .

[*Pause.*]

Public murder or private; it's all the same.

GIDEON [*bewildered*]: Murder?

MARK: Pull the hair out – pull the life. It's all the same. Takes longer, of course. Ten years longer. But it's all the same.

GIDEON: What do you mean, Mark? Murder?

MARK [*drily*]: Killing. Taking the life of.

GIDEON: What are you saying?

MARK: I'm saying I killed my wife. Is that hard to understand?

GIDEON: Oh, look – my dear . . .

MARK: Yes?

GIDEON: This is entirely my fault. I should never have left you alone in that villa! I should have come out myself and brought you back here. I ask you to forgive my selfishness . . . Sometimes one makes the most terrible mistakes; just for fear of intruding on grief.

MARK: Grief? Is that all you see, then? *Grief?!*

GIDEON: It is the most warping emotion in the world.

MARK: The great poet, grieving for his love! Sagging Jesus! . . . Look at you. What can you see? [*Viciously.*] Gummy worried old eyes. What can you really see, Giddy, through all that white gum?
  [*Pause.*]

GIDEON [*imperturbably*]: I like to think of it as spirit gum.
  [*Pause.*]

MARK [*lower*]: Twelve years ago, you couldn't see. Even when you were in Corfu, I'd already started to kill her. You couldn't see it.

GIDEON [*distressed*]: My dear – my dear, dear man . . .

MARK: Even if I told you every detail. If I described to you exactly how I finished her off – what I actually *did* to her on her last night on earth . . . you wouldn't believe me. I'm your darling. Your first flier.

GIDEON: Of course you are.

MARK: Your eagle.

GIDEON: Yes.

MARK: No, Giddy.

GIDEON [*passionately*]: Yes, my eagle! The most marvellous pupil I ever had. The most marvellous friend!

MARK [*quietly*]: Stop it.

GIDEON: That's what you could never quite believe: that everything you did was a *marvel* to me.

MARK: Please stop it, Giddy.

GIDEON: Now I've found you again I'm not going to let you go until I've mended those damaged wings and sent you soaring up again into the sky of action – your proper element – your *real place*!

MARK: *Stop it! Will you stop it?*

[*Pause. He draws* GIDEON *gently to him, and stares into his face.*]

[*Softly.*] Believe me, old master, I could tear the faith out of your head, as easy as they tore the hair out of that boy.

GIDEON [*levelly*]: My goodness.

[GIDEON *smiles. They remain unmoving, very close together, staring at each other.*]

MARK: Poor Mark. Grief has made him quite dotty, hasn't it?

GIDEON: A little unfair on himself, I think.

MARK [*quietly*]: Is there no way of convincing you of your danger?

GIDEON: From you? . . .

MARK [*intensely*]: It isn't grief, Giddy! Be warned.

GIDEON: Then what, my dear?

MARK: The dust. It seeks converts . . . Do you know how long it took me to fall finally from your faith? The time it takes vomit to slide down a wall. Now I know – and have to make others know.

GIDEON: What do you know?

MARK: That the Gospel According to Saint Gideon is a lie. That we as men cannot alter for the better in any particular that matters. That we are totally and forever unimprovable.

GIDEON: No.

MARK: We will kill forever. We will persecute forever. We will break our lust forever on enemies we invent for the purpose.

GIDEON: No.

MARK: We are made of hostility as the spring is made of pollen. And each birth renews it, as the spring renews the year.

GIDEON: No.

MARK: Prove it.

GIDEON: Impossible. It is a faith, like others.

MARK [*ironically*]: Faith! Saint Gideon Petrie on his peacock throne of Reason, ringed by the irises of adolescence! Do you know what they say about you? Your discipline alone can save the world – because you alone have withered out of yourself entirely the roots

of hate. Is it possible? [*Slyly.*] How if I showed them their delusion
– Miss Neal, and my doting son? . . . 'Stay with us', you say, 'in
this Commune of Love.' I say, if I chose, they would see you drive
me out of it with hate.

GIDEON: Never.

MARK: Within one week.

GIDEON: Never.

MARK: Within one week-end.

GIDEON [*serenely*]: Never. Never. Never.

    [*Pause.*]

MARK [*hard*]: Very well. Let's see? . . . I propose a battle. It is now
Friday night. I say by Monday morning – day of our joining award
of Humane Letters – you will have thrown me out of Shrivings.
How about that?

GIDEON: You would lose.

MARK: *I want to lose!* Because, if you lose, it'll be an end for both of
us . . . If you can survive me with all your gentleness intact, I will
stay here and work as your disciple. But you succumb – order me
out of here, for whatever reason – and you will not again be able to
preach Improvability. As for me, once you slam that door upon
me, I will stagger down your tunnel of elm trees into the arms of
Mother Church. Whether Roman or Greek to be later determined.
So. I give you The Battle of Shrivings. [*He drinks.*]

GIDEON: You know, my dear, you really are the naughtiest man in
the world!

MARK: Aren't I?

GIDEON: I think you'd say anything for the sake of drama!

MARK: I come out of the dust. Into the Church of Man. Do I join it,
or pull it down? . . . You're right. I'm ridiculous. Goodbye. [*He
strides to the door.*]

GIDEON: Mark!

    [MARK *pauses; turns.*]

Stay in this house as long as you wish. Shrivings will never reject
you.

MARK: So be it.

GIDEON: Now it's very late. We can resume this tomorrow, surely?

MARK: You have no choice, now.

GIDEON [amused]: Oh my goodness.

[MARK goes to the stairs, then turns.]

MARK: Don't you know who I am?

GIDEON: Who?

MARK: The Ruffian with the pistol. Shoot me, and *you're* dead.

GIDEON: Peace, my friend.

MARK: Impossible. Battle has begun.

[He goes upstairs. GIDEON stares after him, then goes into his bedroom. The light fades.]

CURTAIN

ACT TWO

SCENE 1

Saturday night.

Eleven o'clock. MARK *sits alone at the desk, listening to a large transistor radio.*

B.B.C. ANNOUNCER: In the debate which followed, Mr Lucas Brangwyn, the Member for Bloomsbury, called the wholesale destruction of Devonshire Square 'nothing less than a national scandal'. In his reply the Minister of Housing said nobody regretted the passing of old London more than he, but he sincerely believed the demolition had been carried out in what would ultimately be the best interests of the British public.

    [*Pause.*]

This afternoon at two o'clock, Sir Gideon Petrie sat down in Parliament Square, Westminster, to begin the first of his two six-hour vigils outside the House of Commons in protest against the manufacture of all arms in the United Kingdom. He was accompanied by members of the World League of Peace, of which Sir Gideon is president: as well as many students and well-wishers. Minor outbreaks of violence occurred when a group representing the League of Empire Loyalists threw bags of refuse over the sitting figures. They were moved on by the police.

    [MARK *smiles.*]

Sir Gideon, who is also on a two-day fast, appeared composed and smiling throughout.

    [*Pause.*]

The forecasters say that the easterly winds sweeping the country are dying down and it will become warmer tomorrow, but with a chance of showers –

[MARK *twiddles the dial. Loud rock music comes out of the radio. He turns it off contemptuously. The front door slams.* MARK *rises, hearing the voices of the returning protesters. He tip-toes out into the kitchen. Into the room come* GIDEON, LOIS *and* DAVID, *flushed and excited, taking off their thick outdoor clothes.*

Chattering, they peel off scarves and boots. DAVID *relieves* GIDEON *of his overcoat and beret, and hangs it up on the peg by the garden door.*

LOIS: Yeah, that was great! *That* was the best!

DAVID: No, the old man in the top hat was the best!

LOIS: Yeah, but did you see the old woman in the fur coat dancing the Hare Krishna with those kids? I acted dumb, you know – pretending not to know, and I asked her what she was doing. Do you know what she said? [*Cockney accent.*] 'I don't know, love. It's a new religion. Ride-a-Christian!'

GIDEON [*laughing*]: That's delightful! I wish I'd heard that.

LOIS: Isn't it great?

DAVID: D'you know who I really liked best? You probably didn't notice him. A short, fat man carrying a pork pie with a flag in it, saying 'Peace for all Pigs!' It turned out he was from the Society of Vegetarians.

[LOIS *laughs.*]

GIDEON: Oh, that's marvellous! Yes, that's really the best!

LOIS: They were all fasting, you know. Everyone in that square, I bet you.

DAVID: That girl in the string mini looked like she'd been fasting for a month.

LOIS: What's that smell?

[*Pause. They sniff.*]

DAVID: Cooking.

LOIS: It can't be.

GIDEON: Oh, I think it can. [*Slight pause. He calls.*] Mark!

[MARK *enters from the kitchen, wearing an apron, a chef's hat made out of newspaper, and carrying a cooking-slice.*]

142

MARK: You called for me, sir?

GIDEON: Peace.

MARK: How are you? Rumour reached me that people threw things at you.

GIDEON [*calmly*]: Only a few. It's not the first time the League of Empire loyalists has emptied its rubbish over the British public. Besides, I was in wonderful hands. These two looked after me all day, like the brave fliers they are!

LOIS: Nonsense, Giddy. He was just great, Mr Askelon! You should have seen him! His head was like the still centre of that whole huge crowd!

GIDEON: Well, it didn't feel very still, or very central, come to that!

MARK: Why? Did you fast badly?

GIDEON: Not at all. I saw two members of Parliament, who had obviously just left the dining room of the House of Commons. I thought they looked at me with envy.

LOIS: You should have a good hot bath and go straight to bed. I'll run it for you.

GIDEON [*staring at* MARK]: In a moment. You appear to be cooking something.

MARK: Yes. I'm a weak brother, I regret to say. I held out all day, out of sympathy. But just fifteen minutes ago, I yielded. I'm afraid I started to make myself the very smallest repast. Of course, I'll eat it out of sight, in there.

[*He makes to go back to the kitchen.*]

GIDEON: Mark.

MARK: Yes?

GIDEON: Bring your very small repast in here. Please.

MARK [*grinning*]: Certainly.

[*He goes out. They all watch the kitchen.* DAVID *squats on the floor.* MARK *re-appears, without his hat and apron, and carrying a laden tray.*]

Here we are.

[*He seats himself at the table, shakes out a white napkin, and tucks it under his chin.*]

A couple of lamb chops. What could be more sustaining?

LOIS [*shocked*]: Lamb?

MARK: Bought in the village, this afternoon! [*He uncovers them.*] Behold them – beautifully crisped in the English manner. With them, one salad of watercress prepared in the French. One hot roll, leaking butter into a sympathetic napkin. One bottle of Corton, 1964. Your bin is woefully spartan, Giddy. I took the liberty of replenishing it by telephone. [*He raises the Greek cup.*] Well, here's to famine! Self-willed famine, of course.

  [*He drinks.* DAVID *laughs.* LOIS *throws him a look of outrage.*]
  [*To* GIDEON.] So. Were you impressive? Did you change hearts and collect minds?

  [GIDEON *comes and sits next to him.*]

GIDEON: I hope so. In one way or another.

LOIS: He was cheered all day.

MARK: Were you?

GIDEON: Well, it was more people cheering up themselves, really. It keeps out the damp.

LOIS [*smiling*]: That's not true. When he got up to go, it was just deafening. Tomorrow they say there's going to be an even bigger crowd.

MARK: Are you going tomorrow, David?

LOIS: Of course he is! Why don't you change your mind and come too?

MARK: Were you fasting, David?

DAVID: I don't know. I didn't get anything to eat, anyway.

LOIS: What do you mean? Of course you were fasting. You agreed to it.

DAVID: I didn't say anything, actually. You told me I was.

MARK [*blandly*]: Well, would you like something now? There's this other chop here.

LOIS [*indignantly*]: He certainly would not! ... [*To* GIDEON.] I saw this man from the *Observer* taking pictures like crazy. He was trying to get you to turn your head for half an hour. He'll be there again tomorrow.

GIDEON: Perhaps I should faint for him.

LOIS: Into my arms!

GIDEON: Excellent idea. It should make a brilliant poster. A Pietà, with the ages reversed!

[DAVID *rises*.]

DAVID [*to* MARK]: Thanks. I'll have it. [*Pause*.] The chop.

[*He goes to the table*.]

MARK: By all means. Here –

[*He forks one of the chops to* GIDEON, *who sniffs it, interestedly, and passes it to* DAVID.]

GIDEON [*imperturbably*]: *Bon appetit*.

DAVID: Thank you.

[*He sits*. LOIS *glares at him*.]

MARK: Have some wine.

DAVID: No, thanks. Actually, I don't like alcohol much.

LOIS: He prefers pot.

MARK: You do?

DAVID: Yes. I think it's better for you. Or anyway, it does you less harm.

MARK: I've heard that argument before, my dear boy. It's merely pot calling the bottle black.

[DAVID *laughs*.]

LOIS: I'll run your bath, Giddy. Please come upstairs.

[*She moves to the stairs*.]

GIDEON: Very well. [*To* DAVID.] You find that repulsive, don't you?

DAVID [*his mouth full*]: Yes.

LOIS: I hope it chokes you.

[*She goes upstairs*.]

MARK: Pacifism makes people so generous.

DAVID: She's alright.

GIDEON: She takes things very seriously, our Falcon.

MARK: Wisely.

[*He smiles at* GIDEON.]

GIDEON: Excuse me.

[*He goes upstairs*.]

MARK: Well. Alone at last.

DAVID: Yes.

MARK: Am I . . . as you remember me?

DAVID: You've lost weight a bit.

MARK: With whom? [*He laughs.*] It's well known, no one reads me any more. Mind you, there hasn't been that much to read recently. Unlike the productions from Shrivings. It's a veritable philosophy factory here! [*Raising the cup.*] To home!

[*He drinks and hands it to his son, who also drinks.*]

DAVID: Home.

MARK: You're happy here, aren't you?

DAVID: Yes.

MARK: That's good. All the same, of course, you can hardly intend to remain forever. I mean, sooner or later, Shrivings is going to be full of furniture. Unless you are intending to start a workshop, and supply the area.

DAVID [*smiling*]: I'm not going to be a carpenter all my life, you know.

MARK: I hadn't actually imagined you were. What do you really want to be?

DAVID: I don't know.

MARK: You must have some ideas.

DAVID: They keep changing.

MARK: Well, let's hear some of them.

DAVID: Last week I wanted to be an old woman.

MARK: Yes?

DAVID: Living near here. Its strange, but the Cotswolds mean more to me than the Mediterranean. I suppose green turns me on, and yellow doesn't . . . I'd gone for a walk the other side of Trister. And there was this brick house with a sign saying Jam for Sale. The door was open and the wireless was playing. I could see it through the window. It was a real wireless – one of those Gothic ones, with fretwork on the front. I rang the bell and this woman came. She had red knuckles and hair-grips – you know, the old-fashioned, wavy ones. She saw me and smiled. Just like that. A huge smile, all National Health teeth; the way you can only smile, I bet you, if you've been there four hundred years. She was absolutely *there*. She wore great carpet-slippers, cut out at the toe for her corns, and they were part of the corridor, like the flagging. She weighed everything very solid in her hand, the jar of jam, the money I gave her, the latch on the door, and, you know something – the only word she said the whole time was 'Thank you'. Over and over. 'Thank you'. It was like a little flat song. 'Thank you for shillings. Thank you for cold. Thank you for greengages and hair-grips and the wireless. Thank you for asking the way' . . . And suddenly I wanted to be her, more than anything else.

MARK: Good. I deserved it.

DAVID: What?

MARK: Mind your own business, father. You've forfeited the right to inquire.

DAVID: I didn't mean that!

MARK: I had no idea I had such a witty son. A charming way of telling me.

DAVID: That's not true!

MARK: Sssh! Not another word. I understand . . . Doubtless you find it easier to converse with Gideon. Well, naturally. Over a few months a giant intellect can learn anything, even the parlance of the young.

DAVID: You must know what I'm talking about. You *must*!

MARK: Well, I can learn. You'll have to teach me, of course. It's a new language – it always is – *young* English!

DAVID: *Don't!*

MARK: What?

DAVID: You said 'Home!'

MARK [*hard*]: And you've found it. Good!

[*Silence.* DAVID *looks away.* LOIS *comes downstairs and crosses to the study with* GIDEON'S *clothes.*]

MARK: Ah, Miss Neal. The sage is laving himself?

LOIS: Sir Gideon is having his bath, Mr Askelon.

MARK: Washing the fascist tomatoes out of his hair!

LOIS [coming out of the study]: I'm afraid I don't find that very funny, sir. The man is quite exhausted.

MARK: It's entirely his own fault. He is hardly of an age to sit about on wet pavements.

LOIS: There are some things more important than physical comfort, sir.

MARK: What things in particular? What exactly has been achieved by today's nonsense? One old man lying dizzy in the bath-tub, instead of sitting down here eating a nice Welsh rarebit.

LOIS: That's plain silly! Excuse me, but it is.

MARK: Then what did he really do today? Tell me that.

LOIS: He made a sign.

MARK: And that's sufficient?

LOIS: When the first monk set himself on fire in Saigon, everyone in the so-called civilized world was suddenly aware of Vietnam. That was a sign. O.K.? Well, in a small way that man, walking out of that square tonight, being touched by hundreds of people – that was a sign too.

MARK: I declare you believe in the People, Miss Neal. How moving. It has a sublime simplicity – like Doric pillars, of bread and jam!

LOIS: Huh?

MARK: The poor tormented People, who left to themselves would make such a loving world! Exquisite.

LOIS [with an attempt at calm]: It is very easy, Mr Askelon, to put a person down by calling her simple. O.K. I'm simple. I'm a naive, simple-minded American. I believe in the people, yes. And I believe that most of them don't want any part of the world they've been given. They don't want war. Or politics. Or organized religion. They've been taught to want these things by the ruling class, just desperate to keep its power. If they could ever get their heads straight, ordinary people would realize what history is all about. How it's just the story of a great big lie factory, where we've all been made to work every day, printing up labels: Serf.

Heretic. Catholic. Communist. Middle class. And when we're through, we're made to paste them over each other till the original person disappears, and nobody knows who the hell he is any more!

DAVID [*admiringly*]: Yes!

LOIS: Till we can't ever tear them off us again and just be the great thing you despise, Mr Askelon. People.

DAVID: Oh, when she talks like this I can listen all night.

MARK: I agree. It's better than the opera!

DAVID [*Yorkshire accent*]: Will ya marry me, Lois, lass?

LOIS [*upset*]: Oh, cut it out, David!

MARK: I'd take him up on it, if I were you. Not many girls get proposed to on the strength of their rhetoric.

LOIS: *Ha, ha, ha!* ... Why did you come here, Mr Askelon? What do you want? ... I used to admire you so much. I used to think you were one of the few real people in the world ...

MARK: Used to!

LOIS: Boy, can you ever be wrong!

MARK: *Used to!*

LOIS [*very near tears*]: I must have been out of my mind!

MARK: *Used to admire! Used to!*

LOIS: I don't care what suffering you've had in your life! It doesn't excuse a damn thing!

MARK: Sagging Jesus – *Once!* The crucifixion of Once! You *said!* You *wrote!* You did *once!* ... Nail a man to Once and cry when he drops, leaving his fingers on the wall! You arrogant little beast, do you imagine I live my life to be approved by *you?*

[LOIS *turns away, dabbing furiously at her eyes.*]

DAVID: Stop it. Please!

MARK [*hard*]: What?

DAVID [*embarrassed*]: I mean ... Well, that's not fair. Really.

LOIS [*suddenly turning back on* MARK]: Boy, oh boy, are you contemptible! The Grand Old Man, destroyed by suffering! When you're my age, you'll understand. Till then I can kick your head in all I like!

DAVID: Hey, hey!

LOIS [*to* DAVID]: I tell you I don't know one person over fifty –
except Giddy – who isn't full of shit!

[MARK *rises in apparent fury. She falls quiet. He approaches her.*
Pause.]

MARK [*gently*]: Who gave you those eyes?

LOIS: Huh? . . .

MARK: Blue as the jeans of innocence. Blue as fall sky above your
Elysian Field, where the unicorn masses crop the grass of Universal
love – till they're taken out by wicked keepers and shot . . . It's a
lovely vision, Miss Neal. Many of us dreamed it once. And then
woke.

LOIS: You didn't wake, Mr Askelon. You went to sleep for good.

[*Pause.*]

MARK [*still very calm*]: In 1920 the greatest psychiatrist in Europe
analysed the dreams of five hundred patients. From them, he
slowly made out – detail by detail – the appalling shape of the Nazi
beast. It was there, waiting to spring out of the black cave of the
Common Unconscious . . . Out of that deep pit, stinking of
orgasm, economical soup and the halitosis of mediocrity, have
risen all the terrors of the earth. All the kings who now sit in
museums, glaring at the tourists. The rulers of Assyria tearing lions
in half. The despots of Asia, with their cold lozenge faces, forever
denying forgiveness. The pop-eyed Lord of Sassania, primp.ng his
silver beard, saying 'Behold perfection! I have no petty thoughts.
No haemorrhoids. No moments when I fail to get erection. Long
live the King! The King *must* live forever!' . . . Who would make
such objects? God cannot make anything infallible. Who needs
Forever? Who raised these idols from the anonymous dust –
hysterical puppets of Nineveh or Nuremberg? Who linked the
wires? Started the sceptre arms flailing, the saluting arms of self-
abuse? Who opened their anthem-yelling metal mouths? Who if
not I? Him. You. [*Pause.*] You walk royal portrait galleries as if you
are attending identity parades for murderers. Start looking for

yourself there, Miss Neal. You might just begin to understand history better.

[LOIS *stares at him, fascinated.*]

DAVID: Oh hey! Thank you! Wow!

LOIS: What do you mean?

DAVID: The words.

LOIS: What do you mean, 'wow'?

DAVID: The words . . .

LOIS: So it's wow for Giddy and wow for him and wow for me and wow for everybody with you?

DAVID: Yes!

LOIS: No distinctions! No differences at all?

DAVID: Well, you screw up your mouth too much. It doesn't do a thing for your face.

LOIS: What?

DAVID: You don't have enough moments that only happen once. You should have more.

LOIS: I think you're mad.

DAVID: I mean, to turn tummies over.

LOIS: I really do! Life's just a set of pictures to you, isn't it? What we say here doesn't connect with you at all.

DAVID: Pictures connect.

LOIS: You know what that means?

DAVID: Pictures are real.

LOIS: It means you have a complete inability to feel anything not related to personal gratification.

DAVID: Really?

LOIS: Yes, really. I'm sorry for you, David.

DAVID: Thank you.

LOIS: I really am. Anyone who can't feel social injustice is sick. I mean it!

DAVID [*exploding*]: All right! You mean it! You really pity me! Poor me! Poor bloody me! [*He springs up and pulls a 'mad' face at her.*]

LOIS: David. Ssh!

151

DAVID: All right, I'm insane! [*He rushes to the table, stands on it, grabs some watercress out of the salad bowl, and puts it on his head. He flicks some watercress at her.*] Deficient Dan, the Insane Man!

LOIS: Stop it!

DAVID: Couldn't feel things, so away he ran!

LOIS: Stop it, David! Cut it out!

DAVID [*quietly*]: You stop it. Stop picking . . . Mad people shouldn't be picked on!

MARK: No, but heretics should. [*Standing up.*] And that's what you are, my boy. A raving, flagrant heretic, ripe for the burning. Don't you realize what you have just admitted?

DAVID [*shyly*]: No.

[MARK *moves to* DAVID.]

MARK: A sense of the Unalterable. Oh my poor, demented son: in this house that is enough to get you stoned to death and buried in the midden! [*Kindly.*] Give me some watercress too! Let me go down with you under the knives of optimism! [*He plunges in his hand, takes out some watercress and jams it on his head too.*] Acolytes of the unalterable: unite! Let's wear our green with courage! Green for Nature! For the returning cycles of our agony! The grazing green of God!

[DAVID *laughs.* MARK *begins to walk about, enjoying himself, crowned with greens.*]

Ssh! You'll upset Torquemada . . . Isn't it amusing how the fashions in Inquisition stay the same! They all have one thing in common. A passion for invisible Gods. First we had vengeful Daddy, wrapped in clouds. Then Mobile Mary, whizzing up to Heaven. Now it's Self-Raising Man, jumping himself out of Nature: what an astonishing sight! . . .

[GIDEON *appears on the stairs, dressed in a long white linen bathrobe. He halts, staring at the scene – then comes down into the room.*]

But perhaps I'm being unfair. No one ever saw Airborne Intacta on her jet flight to Jehovah – but with the God of Shrivings we may be luckier. Anytime now we might see something. Maybe today! Who knows? In a few hours the birds up there on Lyssop Ridge will be piping up a new morning. And the hands of perfectable Man will flutter out of sleep to begin again his wonderful work of self-creation. The hands of police will stir and pick up clubs. The hands of nuns will resume whipping fables into frightened children. The hands of patriots will tie some more electrodes on to partisan balls. The hands of the envious will load fresh guns, to assassinate hands more graceful than their own. And the delicate, nicotined hands of genius will continue to stuff all ages together – dark, middle, and decayed – into one metal sausage. Hail to Man! *Homo Improvabilis*!

GIDEON: Smug!

MARK: What?

GIDEON: Smugness! The endless smugness of pessimism! Under all that litany of woe I heard only one note: *relish*! Comfort in the idea of your own perpetual failure. How can you receive that, and still have anything to live for?

MARK [*grandly*]: I do not require anything to live for!

GIDEON: Then you are unique in the world.

MARK: On the contrary, like everybody else, I live NOT to understand!

GIDEON [*sharper*]: Then why demand of me a Faith you *can*? You want an Indefinable God, but *I* must produce a definable Man. Trot him out of a shed for your inspection, like one of your icons on a trolley! How unfair you are! . . . I offer you what you want. An indefinable mystery. This hand.

[*He extends it.*]

MARK: Offer me first one proof it can do better.

GIDEON: Its change of ownership.

MARK: What d'you mean?

GIDEON: Two thousand years ago, when it chained men all their lives to galley ships – one thousand, when it blinded an entire Byzantine army – five hundred, when it pushed men on to fires, and gutted whole towns to impose True Religion – it was the Gods' hand: plural or singular! Its crimes were accepted. They were God's will – God's scourge – God's anything, so long as they

kept its owners from shame. Since we started to abolish Independent
God, we have become measurably less callous.

MARK [*sarcastic*]: Oh, good!

GIDEON: It *is* good! Concern has its evolution. That's good.

MARK: Marvellous! We weep more – we war more. What a liberat-
ing equation! Agonize while you atomize!

GIDEON: We do not war more. It is only techniques that bring us to
holocaust.

MARK [*derisively*]: Only!

GIDEON [*bursting out*]: Yes, only! *Only!* . . . I say again: concern has
its evolution. Everything in *us* can have *unending* evolution. That is
our glory – our amazement! . . . [*Scornfully.*] How *can* you dish out
that gloating old rubbish about the Unalterable? You ought to be
ashamed! If we know *one thing* about Man, it is that he cannot *stop*
altering – that's his condition! He is unique on earth in that he has
no fixed behaviour patterns! Look at the world. At the differences
in families – in tribes and nations. Some are paternal: some are not.
Some are predatory: some are not. Some are aggressive, sustained
by the desire to dominate others. All right, but equally others are
not. Oh yes, they can be *made* to be. These differences are social –
but they are not inherent. They are not *biological*. Do you follow,
children? . . . [*He turns to them.*] There is no proof whatever that
man is born inherently aggressive.

MARK [*ironically*]: No proof?

GIDEON [*sternly*]: None. And I deny it, absolutely. Man is born free
to make himself . . .

[*He approaches* MARK, *again extending his hand.*]
[*Urgently.*] This hand – this is your proper focus for worship. Not
glaring idols, or ancestor poles, or mothy banners hanging in
cathedrals. This. This tool, for making . . . And soon to be extinct
if we pursue our blasphemies against ourselves much longer.

[*He is moved, and stands staring at* MARK *as if challenging him not to
agree.* MARK *takes* GIDEON's *hand, and inspects it closely.*]

MARK [*with disgusted interest*]: In the Middle West of America, I
watched this thing kill a man, seventeen times in succession.

GIDEON: You saw a man killed seventeen times?

MARK [*dropping the hand*]: Yes. What kind of evolution do you call that?

GIDEON: How?

MARK: In the psychology department of a major university, where they were working on aggression. The professor had set up a board with six buttons. These were allegedly controlled by electrical wires attached to an actor, sitting across the laboratory, bound and gagged. Members of the public, chosen off the street, completely at random, were admitted one by one and asked to assist at a scientific experiment of an undisclosed nature. They were told the first button would give the man a mild electric shock – the second more – and so on, up to the sixth, which was, in fact, a death button. It was clearly explained to all that if they pressed that button the man would die. They were then left alone for an hour each, to play . . . A simple scene: one helpless man at the mercy of a complete stranger who was his absolute master in the matter of the punishment given him.

GIDEON: And seventeen pressed the death button?

MARK: Exactly so.

GIDEON: Out of how many?

MARK: Seventeen.

LOIS: I don't believe it.

GIDEON [*patiently*]: My dear, there is a famous experiment of this sort; but it wasn't exactly as you described. There was no death button. And the people were not left alone. They had two pseudo-colleagues – fake scientists whose job it was to provoke them. The result was that more than half agreed to vote for painful shock. Depressing, I admit, but scarcely as final as you make it out.

MARK: That was one experiment. I watched another.

GIDEON [*dryly*]: I see.

LOIS: I don't believe you. Go on, admit it. You made it up. You're reduced to making up stupid lies! How incredible.

MARK: Am I?

LOIS: Yes, you are!

GIDEON: Lois, please!

MARK [*staring at her*]: It's easily proved.

LOIS: Proved? How?

MARK: Sit down. We'll play my game here.

GIDEON: Here?

MARK: Why not? These apples will do very well.

[*He takes them from the bowl on the table, and lays them out in a straight line, parallel to the audience.*]

The buttons of Original Sin! Ouch – oucher-oucher – Death! What do you say? Will you play? I'll be the victim.

LOIS: You mean you'll act?

MARK: Exactly so.

LOIS: You've got to be kidding.

MARK: Try me and see. David?

DAVID: I'd like to see you act.

MARK: Good. Giddy? I can devise a short version for you, if you are tired.

GIDEON: I don't see how you can devise *any* version, my dear. We know you will be acting – and those are apples. The illusion that we can actually kill you being destroyed, there seems little point in the exercise.

MARK: Well, I would have to claim a few rights in compensation, denied to the original victim.

GIDEON: Of what nature?

MARK: Speech.

GIDEON: That seems fair.

MARK: Free speech. Complete license, no matter how provoking. Strictly of course for the purpose of the game.

GIDEON: That could be interesting.

LOIS: I don't see how.

MARK: Shall we try?

LOIS: I think it's time Giddy was in bed.

GIDEON: All the same, I would like to see what Mark intends.

MARK: Of course you would ... All right, then.

[*He pulls from his pocket the string with which he had wrapped the shrine.*]

Ah now, this will do very well! Come, David; tie me to your throne of reason.

[*He sits in it, and offers the string.* DAVID *approaches.*]

Come on. Tie down the wrists.

[DAVID *takes the string. He begins to tie.*]

LOIS: I don't see the point of this. I don't see the point of it at all. It's just plain stupid.

MARK: The head of the house wishes it. As I understand things, what he wants, so want the rest of you. Isn't that true?

LOIS: Ha, ha, ha!

GIDEON: Come on now, you fierce Falcon; it's only a game. An after-fast entertainment!

MARK: Exactly; only a game. Whatever that word means ... Tighter, David; anyone can see I can get out of *that* ... You do allow me complete licence of speech, by the way, Gideon?

GIDEON: Yes.

MARK: Miss Neal?!

LOIS: Why not? I guess there won't be any difference from the sort of things you say normally.

MARK: David?

DAVID: Anything you want ... Can you move?

MARK [*wriggling about*]: No, that's fine. You might have made this chair especially for the purpose. To incapacitate your old dad! All right, join the others.

[DAVID *goes to the others, standing by the table.*]

You are, of course, all playing at once. The solo, masturbatory element has been eliminated. You must admit, I'm making it very difficult for myself.

GIDEON: I certainly admit that. Yes.

LOIS: What are you going to do? Just insult us till one of us bangs this last apple?

MARK: More or less.

LOIS: Jesus! I've never heard anything so stupid! Grown people standing up in the middle of the night, playing with apples.

GIDEON: Which is the mildest one?

MARK: The far one from me.

[GIDEON *goes to it and raises his hand to touch it.*]

LOIS [*with sudden alarm*]: Giddy – don't.

GIDEON: Why not?

LOIS: Well . . . it's just so childish. [*Pause.*] Goddam childish, that's all.

GIDEON: Let's oblige our guest. Don't you want to see how he acts?

[LOIS *shrugs her acquiescence.*]

LOIS: O.K. Go ahead.

[GIDEON *delicately presses the first apple.* MARK *writhes a little.*]

MARK: Ah! Ah! Stop it, please.

[GIDEON *stops pressing.*]

GIDEON: Excellent. Thank you.

[*The two men bow at each other.*]

LOIS: I don't think it's excellent! I think it's lousy. I've seen people under electric shock. It doesn't look at all like that.

MARK: Trust you to introduce a boring, factual note into the proceedings.

GIDEON: Really, Mark!

MARK [*apologetically*]: License, Giddy! License!

LOIS: What does the second button do?

MARK: Push it and see.

LOIS: I don't want to waste my money. What do you do? Twice as much?

MARK: Push it and see.

LOIS: Because that would only be twice nothing!

MARK: Push it and see.

LOIS: O.K. Just this next one. Just to see how you make out. Look everybody – Acting Class Number Two! Bang! [*She bangs the second apple.*]

[MARK *writhes more.*]

Presenting Mark Askelon, the greatest actor of our time, in – 'The
Electrified Man!' . . .

[MARK *stops writhing.*]

Why are you stopping, Mr Askelon? I haven't taken my hand off
the button!

[MARK *resumes writhing.*]

MARK: Ah! Ah! . . .

LOIS: There we go! Now you, Giddy! – you press number one again,
and let's watch the subtle way he changes!

[GIDEON *hesitates.*]

Go on, it's only a game. Like you said!

GIDEON: True.

LOIS: O.K., then!

[*He presses the first apple again, and she takes her hand off the second.*
MARK's *convulsions lessen.*]

Oh, beautiful! Beautiful! . . . Now mine again!

[GIDEON *stops pressing and she resumes.* MARK *writhes more
energetically, and his cries increase.*]

Now you, David! Press number three. He should really blow his
mind on number three! [*To* MARK.] Go on, keep it up! I'm still
pressing! . . . Come *on*, David!

[DAVID *hesitates.*]

What's the matter with you? We're just having fun!

[DAVID *shrugs, smiles, shakes his head.* LOIS *takes her hand off her
apple.* MARK *relaxes.*]

You really are a pain in the ass, aren't you?

MARK: You certainly are, David. For once I agree with Miss Neal. I
was enjoying myself hugely. And it is only a game, after all. That's
why Miss Neal could afford to reveal herself so completely.

LOIS: What do you mean?

MARK: For one moment there, when you realized that I had to keep
writhing for just so long as you kept pressing, you became interested.

LOIS: Sure, I did. The longer I did it, the bigger fool you looked.

159

MARK: That's not the reason you did it, Miss Neal. Not by any means.

LOIS: Well, what other reason could there be, Mr Askelon?

DAVID [*distressed*]: Oh stop it, Lois!

LOIS: What?

DAVID: Stop it.

LOIS: Thanks! Thanks very much. That's great. That really is great! ... You tell me I'm so serious, and I'm too serious, and when I play a game you say Stop it.

DAVID: You weren't playing a game.

LOIS: Well, what the hell else was I doing? ... I'm bored with this, Giddy. Why don't we go to bed?

MARK: Ah, that's sweet. 'Why don't we go to bed?' Can you really mean that seriously – to a man you've selected entirely because he can't?

GIDEON: Mark, really!

MARK: Well, it's true, isn't it? Look at her – Miss Lois Neal! What the hell is she doing in this house? Making the beds, making the eggs, making the laws round here like a sort of Earth Mother – or sorry: Earth Auntie. Unmarried, of course.

GIDEON: Mark, I must protest.

MARK: License, Giddy – license!

GIDEON: All the same! –

MARK: Who is she, this Illinois idiot, creaming her committed little panties every time you enter the room? [*American accent.*] 'Oh, Giddy you're so great! Gee, Giddy, you're so wonderful! You're a fuckin' saint, boy, honest!' ... Is that what you really want? A sticky little acolyte plunging after a man three times her age, just because he's safe?

[*All the others stay rigid:* DAVID, *head lowered,* LOIS *looking away*.] What's in your mind, Lois? His wife couldn't stand it, could she? Stuck it three years after his famous vow of chastity – then ups and bloody goes. But you're made of sterner stuff than that, aren't you? You're going to last forever! Forever deliciously unsatisfied! Forever a Vestal Virgin, waving the flag of Humanity high over your frozen Mount of Venus! Sagging Jesus, protect me from all Liberal American Virgins!

GIDEON: David, please untie your father. I find I am tireder than I thought.

MARK: You granted me license.

GIDEON: Yes, and now withdraw it. Goodnight.

MARK [sotto voce, to DAVID, *who is approaching the chair*]: Keep still.

GIDEON: Come, Lois.

MARK: Yes, come, Lois – before you hear any more. Before you hear, for example, why exactly Enid left! . . . Do you imagine it was because of that boring vow of chastity? You must, as they say, be joking! Enid Petrie never cared about sex. To her it was always 'nasties'! She's much happier now with her middle-aged accountant. One dry kiss at night before they skin the Ovaltine! She didn't leave Shrivings for *that*! . . . It was the hypocrisy she couldn't take. Poor old stick, in her own way she had a sort of maidenly integrity.

GIDEON [*facing him directly*]: What are you talking about?

MARK: Do you have to ask? . . . Why do you imagine, Miss Neal, that your employer gave up sex? Because he found you ladies such a block on his path to virtue? Don't you know the only sex Gideon ever really enjoyed was with boys? Slim brown boys with sloping shoulders. He used to chase them all over Italy on our walking tours. And then, of course, the guilt would chase him; and I'd have to endure boring vows of repentance all the next day – to be broken again, naturally, all the next night, in the very next piazza! In the end he gave everything up. Guilt, nothing but guilt! The world saw only a Great Renunciation on the grandest philosophic grounds: but not so Enid. All she saw was a self-accusing pederast, pretending to be Gandhi!

DAVID [*low*]: Stop it.

MARK: Mind you, old habits die hard. Once you grow accustomed to having Mediterranean boys, I suppose you get to need them. Send for them. Import them. Steal them, if necessary, from your friends!

DAVID [*in pain*]: Shut up.

MARK: Make my chairs! Make my tables! Make my bed, and we will lie on it together!

DAVID [*moving forward*]: Shut up!

MARK: Not, my dear boy – my flier! my owl! – that I would suspect *you* of anything so bizarre! Innocent to the last breath, I make no doubt!

> [DAVID *rushes to the table, picks up the 'death apple', and smashes it down over and over again. Pieces fly about the room.*

DAVID: SHUT UP! SHUT UP! SHUT UP! SHUT UP!

MARK [*triumphantly*]: *What?!* Oh! – AAAHHH!!!

> [*He 'dies' in elaborate convulsions. All freeze. Pause.*
> *Then, with a violent motion,* MARK *snaps the ropes from his wrists and rises from the throne. With a grin at* GIDEON, *he flaps like a great eagle up the stairs into his room. Pause again. Then* DAVID *drops the bit of apple still in his hand and walks very stiffly out of the house. The front door slams.* LOIS *turns round at this.* GIDEON *approaches her, his arms outstretched – but with a stifled cry, she avoids them, and runs into the garden.* GIDEON *is left standing alone. He bows his head over the table. The lights go down a little below, and come up above, where* MARK *is kneeling to the shrine.*]

MARK: I begged him! You heard. I *begged* him, over and over. 'Let me go. No questions.' He wouldn't believe me. Like you. You never saw me, either. I was literally invisible to you. [*Piteously.*] The two of you. *You can't see!* [*Pause.*] And then when it happens, you look at me with that stare of unbelievable pain. *He* will, too. Soon now.

> [*He stands up.* GIDEON *moves towards his study. He is upset and alarmed. He pauses at the throne, fingering the ropes that still hang from it.* MARK *pours himself a glass of brandy.*]

Thing is, I didn't believe me either, last night. I only half meant it, the battle. My usual half-meant, *you know* . . . And now it's here. The knife's in. Suddenly there's blood dripping in the house. Surprised blood . . . No return . . .

> [GIDEON *moves slowly to his study door, opens it – looks back at the room, and disappears.*]

[*Darkly, to the shrine.*] I begged you, too. '*Proteggimi*' – remember? Look after me. What does that mean? Look after? What language do you speak, then, Saint? ... [*Bitterly.*] Saint ... Saint ... SAINTS!

[*He throws the brandy in the face of the statue. It drips from the shrine as* MARK *turns away from it, and stands with head sharply averted.*]

SLOW BLACKOUT

SCENE 2

Sunday morning.

Ten o'clock. The telephone rings insistently. LOIS *is tidying the room – picking pieces of apple off the floor. She ignores the telephone. Finally it stops. Her whole manner is shocked and cold.*

GIDEON *comes in from his study and looks at her. He appears tired, and is dressed very casually; as if he has become involved with his clothes by accident.*

Above, MARK *lies inert on his bed.*

GIDEON: Peace.

LOIS: Sure.

GIDEON: Who was that on the phone?

LOIS: I don't know.

GIDEON: Oh. How are you feeling?

LOIS: Fine. You?

GIDEON: It hasn't been a very pleasant night for any of us, I imagine. Where's David?

LOIS: I don't know.

[*Pause.*]

I want you to do something for me.

GIDEON: Certainly. What?

163

LOIS [*hard*]: Tell that man to go.

GIDEON: I can't do that, my dear.

LOIS: You have to.

GIDEON: There is no have to. We can't throw people out of here. Least of all him. If this house can't overcome what's happened to Mark, then it's useless.

[*Pause. She dusts.*]

Look: he asked us all yesterday what would happen if a ruffian came in here with a pistol. We all said we wouldn't fire back, didn't we?

LOIS [*short*]: Yeah.

GIDEON: Well, it's as simple as that. As complex as that.

LOIS: Yeah.

GIDEON: What can we do, but try and disarm him another way? Aggression is like a fire: smother it in blankets, it dies for want of air. Our blanket is acceptance.

LOIS: Yeah. O.K.

GIDEON: I know it sounds hopelessly abstract, after last night – but what else are we here for? You left America for one reason; the Peace men were joining in the violence. Well, is that what you want me to do now?

[*She goes on dusting.*]

Or is it something else? What he said about me.

LOIS [*flat*]: Don't be ridiculous.

GIDEON: No, be honest now.

[DAVID *comes downstairs.*]

DAVID: Hallo. How are you feeling?

GIDEON: Peckish.

DAVID: Me too. [*To* LOIS.] Good morning.

[*No reply.*]

Peace.

LOIS [*to* GIDEON]: I've got some letters to do. Excuse me, please. The car will collect you at twelve, same as yesterday. The assembly point will again be the statue of Charles the Third.

GIDEON: First.

LOIS: Big deal.

GIDEON [*sympathetically*]: Lois!

DAVID: What the hell's the matter with you?

LOIS: If you don't know, I'm not telling.

DAVID: Well, I don't know.

[*She pauses a second, then marches across and picks up a piece of apple.*]

LOIS: This, then. This, David.

DAVID: The apple?

LOIS: You really think that was a smart, civilized thing you did last night?

DAVID: Well, it stopped the voice.

LOIS: Voice?

DAVID: That was supposed to be the point.

LOIS: The point, David, was not to touch the goddam thing. You deliberately played his game.

DAVID: It shut him up, didn't it?

LOIS: Ha, ha, ha!

DAVID: Well, didn't it?

LOIS: O.K. It shut him up! Well done! Great.

DAVID: So what's the matter? It was just an apple.

LOIS: 'Just' an apple!

DAVID: Yes! An apple is an apple is an apple.

LOIS: And an idiot is an idiot!

GIDEON [*mildly*]: Children, please. I beg you.

DAVID: I'm sorry, Giddy.

LOIS: I'll go answer letters. [*She moves to the study.*]

GIDEON [*calmly*]: Before you go, I would like to make a brief observation about homosexuality. I mean, my own.

[*Slight pause.*]

DAVID: I think that's a boring subject.

GIDEON: Nevertheless, since it's been raised.

LOIS: O.K. What about it?

[*Pause.*]

GIDEON: How to put it? . . . When I was young, I had, as they say, sex on the brain. I meant by that, that even when I worked on equations, or read Political Science, the impulse of my attention was somehow sexual. Sex was everywhere. A girl's hair bobbing down the street. The sudden fur of a boy's neck. The twitching lope of a red setter dog. In flowers, even – the smell of cow parsley in a field of poppies would almost make me faint. To say I was bisexual would have been a ludicrous understatement. I was trisexual. Quadri. Quinti. Sexi-sexual, you might say!

[DAVID *laughs and sits on the floor, to enjoy it.*]

I tell you this, just in case you've been wondering about the guilt attributed to me last night. So far was I from feeling that particular emotion, I confess throughout my twenties I cheerfully, and indeed gratefully, engaged in repeated encounters with both sexes.

DAVID [*gleefully*]: Which did you prefer?

GIDEON: Boys were physically more attractive to me; their lines are more economical. But for sex I preferred girls. In that department, at least, God got his mathematics right!

[DAVID *laughs again.* LOIS *does not laugh.*]

However – after fifteen years' abstinence, I find the whole area of experience somewhat remote. That is why, my Owl, though you are extremely attractive, I hope you won't find it unforgivable in me not to have responded more vigorously to your charms. You too, of course, my Falcon.

[DAVID *springs up happily.*]

DAVID: I'm not sure. I think we should both be very offended! [*Warmly.*] Oh, that's lovely! . . . You're lovely. You are! [*He hugs the old man.*]

LOIS: All the same, you stopped.

GIDEON: True.

LOIS: It couldn't have been that great, if you stopped.

GIDEON: I describe intensity, not joy. You might not conceive it of me, but in those days I knew great violence. It grew, I think, from what used to be called Despair. The great Myth of sex told of coitus and transfiguration. Co-mingling of spirits! I found the reality to be very different. This supreme experience of union appeared to me with more and more force each time, to be simply

166

a twin act of masturbation, accompanied by murmurs designed to disguise the fact. Out of that realization, slowly, came a sort of cruelty. Having and discarding. Searching ever more mechanically, in a savourless frenzy of disappointment. I grew to hate the very shape of desire. Its parody of closeness. Its separating climax. Finally, I came to know that for me, it was the main source of aggression. That before I could even start on my innocence, I would have to give it up . . . My wife left me for the reason I have always told you. The decision was too rigorous for her. I didn't blame her. How could I? I myself found it . . . very difficult . . . Almost unendurable, in fact.

[*Pause.*]

The youngsters who come here find this all absurd, no doubt. Sex is no problem to them. Or so they tell us, anyway, with their tulip heads like emblems for tenderness. Can it be true? I pray so. If they can really kiss without the taste of conquest, then they've done more than all generations before them: detached the whip at their belts, and hung a flower . . . So . . . Everyone has a struggle. That was something of mine.

DAVID: Thank you.

[*Pause.*]

DAVID [*enthusiastically*]: Let's go for a walk. All three of us!

[MARK *stirs on his bed.*]

GIDEON [*to* LOIS]: Yes! We have the time, my dear.

LOIS: You two go. There's too much I've got to do here.

DAVID: Well, leave it.

LOIS: I'm afraid I can't do that.

DAVID: Oh, balls!

LOIS: Shrivings does not run itself, David. Excuse me. [*She goes into the study.*]

GIDEON: What's wrong?

DAVID: She's shocked.

GIDEON: Impossible. By what? My language? But she's such a free girl. She couldn't be shocked just by words. Not a liberal girl like my Falcon! Do you really think she found me coarse?

DAVID: I love you. I wish I could keep you from harm.

GIDEON: Am I in danger?

DAVID: Don't you feel it?

GIDEON: I feel . . . a little unnerved. Perhaps it's the fast.

[MARK *gets off his bed and comes to the window. He stares out front.*]

DAVID: You didn't sleep last night.

GIDEON: No.

DAVID: You're changing.

GIDEON: What d'you mean?

DAVID: So's Lois.

[*Pause.*]

DAVID: That's the thing.

GIDEON: What?

[DAVID *shudders.*]

David!

DAVID: He changes you. But he can't change himself.

GIDEON: I don't think that's true. He's changed more than any of us. I never realized he had become so desperate.

DAVID: Become?

GIDEON: Well, yes, in the last few years. Was that what you were trying to tell me, before he arrived? You suspected this had happened?

DAVID: Not become.

GIDEON: What d'you mean? He was always like this? . . . That's nonsense, my dear. He was often trying – bombastic – egocentric – all of that. But never . . . never like this.

[DAVID *shrugs.*]

What did you mean before? You wanted to stop the voice?

DAVID: The thing in it.

GIDEON: What thing?

[DAVID *shrugs again.*]

I'm not sure I understand you.

DAVID [*fiercely*]: *The thing!*

[*Pause.*]

GIDEON [*perplexed*]: He would never hurt you. You know that.

DAVID: Let's go for our walk.

[*He goes abruptly over to the garden exit, where the coats hang, and takes* GIDEON'S *scarf and beret.*]

GIDEON: David . . .

DAVID [*handing him the beret*]: Here.

GIDEON: Thank you. [*He puts it on.*] If I asked him to leave Shrivings, would you like that?

DAVID: You can't.

GIDEON: You mean, I mustn't.

DAVID: I mean, you can't.

[GIDEON *stares at him.* DAVID *takes his hand.*]

[*Quietly.*] Come on.

[*They go out together. Above,* MARK *stares out front.*]

MARK: Well, there they go. Father and son – hand in hand up the meadow. Touching! The whole hippy dream in one frame: old and young, leaping the generation gap like mountain goats! . . . Look, he's dancing. Our boy!

[*He turns away.*]

[*Bitterly.*] Dances with Giddy, and I stay here with you. No, with myself. Alone. You'd be up there with them leading the dance. '*Venga, vengate!* Dance with me, San Marco!' [*Pompously.*] 'No, no, my dear Giulia, good heavens: – *dance*, with my girth? You must be mad! . . . *You* dance; I'll watch.' *You* laugh; I'll watch. You live; I'll watch and turn it all into Literature. Literature counts, after all! It's so much more important than life . . .

[*The telephone rings.* LOIS *comes in from the study and answers it.*]

LOIS: Look, mister: a Vigil *is* a public statement. What more do you want?

[*She hangs up and goes listlessly to the refectory table.*]

MARK: So who's left downstairs? The Innocent Abroad, savaging her typewriter! Bashing out manifestos of love, with hating little touch-type fingers!

[LOIS *sits at the table, staring miserably ahead.*]

I must say I'd like to give her some touch-typing myself. One hour could change her life. What's she ever known, after all, but student fumbling?

[*He sits on the bed.*]

Why not? Superb move! Life in Shrivings would hardly be the same ever after, that's for sure. How would the old man take it? How would David? –

[*He breaks the thought, snapping at the shrine.*]

Ah, don't be idiotic! I couldn't do it, anyway. Look at her! The odds are a thousand to one. Richard the Third had better with that dreary Lady Anne! ... [*Slyly.*] All the same. There she sits – tighter than a Labrador limpet. Here I sit, the well-known blade, not entirely rusted yet. One could always see. The most anyone can say in the end, to God or Man, is 'Let us see!'

[*He gets up. He smiles.*]

My move, I think.

[*He leaves the room and tiptoes down. At the bottom of the stairs he pauses, contemplating the girl.*]

All alone, with your Remingtone?

[*She ignores him. He advances into the room.*]

Are you still angry with me for last night? You shouldn't be. Truth hurts – but in a house of Shriving, one should tell nothing else. And then one should forgive. Isn't that the point of this house?

LOIS: Why don't you just get out of here?

MARK: Where? Back to Corfu?

LOIS: So long as it's away from me, I don't give a damn.

MARK: Now that, I'm afraid, is *untrue*. I think you lie in bed at night thinking a great deal about me.

LOIS: You're right. I do think a lot about you. Not necessarily in bed. Would you like to hear what I think about you, Mr Askelon?

MARK: Not at all. Mediocre descriptive powers are not necessarily improved by having a great subject to work on.

LOIS: You think you're the last representative of the Grand Manner, don't you? – all cooking and quotations! You wear your learning lightly. You got style. Well, let me tell you – most of the kids I know have more style in their assholes than you have in your whole drunken body.

MARK: And Gideon? Do they have more style than Gideon?

LOIS: Damn you, Mr Askelon! We were happy before you came.

MARK: Liar! I saw you the day I arrived, Anxious Annie clutching her nervous little fistful of attitudes. Happy? You haven't even been goosed by happy!

LOIS: Screw you!

MARK: What was my real crime? Showing your saint in a real light?

LOIS: Get out of here – that's all I want.

MARK: Look, stop hiding from it. Giddy is completely queer, for what that's worth. He never slept with a woman in his life.

LOIS: That's not true.

MARK: It's not in the least important. Who cares, after all?

LOIS: It's not true!

MARK: It's just a question of the facts. Boring, unilluminating facts.

LOIS: *It's not true!*

MARK: You have proof to the contrary?

LOIS: Yes.

[*Pause.*]

MARK: How beautiful. What a delicious discovery! Women can be as gallant as men. *More* gallant in this instance. I didn't exactly think Giddy displayed much last night. The way he came to your protection.

LOIS: You're not worthy to wipe his ass.

MARK: Or rather – didn't.

LOIS [*tight*]: I don't need any protection.

MARK: 'I find I'm tireder than I thought.'

LOIS: What?

MARK: That was the most he could manage to say. 'I find I'm tireder than I thought.' Hardly the last word in gallantry.

LOIS: You couldn't begin to understand him. You couldn't begin!

MARK [*admiringly*]: You really are remarkable.

LOIS: What d'you mean?

MARK: After a scene like that – to defend him like that. Eyes sparkling. Breasts heaving . . . You're a Valkyrie.

LOIS: Get fucked.

MARK: All right, I'm joking, a little. But it's true, when you say you don't need protection. You have an integrity that is absolutely scary. You know, you are the first person I've met – since I first met myself – who can really treat abstractions like lovers.

LOIS [drily]: Great.

MARK: I mean kiss them. Beat them for infidelity.

LOIS: Ha, ha, ha.

MARK: It's what my wife never dug. She couldn't cope with the simplest general idea.

LOIS: Her son has the same problem.

MARK: She would have adored you. Honesty excited her above everything. Her eyes would have widened on you. They were quite miraculous, you know. Round the pupils flared a sun-ring. In all other ways she was quite ordinary. A spindly, red-haired dancer from the Rome Opera, not actually very good. When she retired to live with me on pasta and poems, she grew less shapely – but her eyes never lost their light. God knows where she got them. Her father was a grey civil servant with eyes like a carp. Her mother's, two clams on a plate of spaghetti. I can only conclude, therefore, that Giulia's were miraculous. Like yours.

LOIS: Oh, sure.

MARK: Who gave you those eyes? Some baby-faced doctor from the plains of Illinois? Not on your mid-Western life! Eyes are the sequins of grace. The angel sews them, when she calls.

[Long pause.]

LOIS [calmly]: Giddy's eyes are disgusting.

MARK: What?

LOIS: That white stuff. It's really awful. Why doesn't he do something about it? And the way they're never really on you.

MARK [slyly]: As if they're . . . out of focus?

LOIS: You're really very clever, aren't you?

[He grins.]

MARK: I was.

LOIS: Yeah, sure.

MARK: You don't know how clever I was.

LOIS: 'Once,' you mean? Once?

MARK [*staring at her*]: Yes. Once. [*Pause.*]

LOIS [*softer*]: Will you go now, please?

MARK: I was someone amazing!

LOIS: Just leave me alone . . .

MARK: I was the world!

LOIS: Please! Get out of here! . . .

MARK: I knew an Encyclopedic Sympathy: there was nobody outside of *me*! I was the arriving lecturer – and the doorman who admits him, cringing. I was the Fabergé Prince – the traveller in undies – the teagirl who stands for eight repetitive hours between two steaming urns. I went to parade grounds, brisk in khaki. Returned at night, tired dandruff in an aching bus. I was the arch of the morning – Cream of Corelli – the indigestion of a wasted day! I was a replete, complete Man . . . but for one thing. I was never quite alive. [*Pause.*] Inside me, from my first day on earth, was a cancer. An incapacity for Immediate Life. When I was a boy, the crowd at football matches jumped to its feet, shouting. All I could see was a ball and legs. At student dances, I hopped in silence. They all said: isn't it exciting, the music? I grinned, but heard nothing. The only music I ever heard was words, and the clear thought of Gideon Petrie. When I yoked them, I became your admired Poet. I slew Generals. I drowned Presidents in spit. The insane Popes! The Rabbits of Repression! Oh, they kept me going for years, good hates – *the scapegoats for myself*. The only thing was, they ran out. Even atheism itself ran out, the moment I felt one poem as an act of worship. The next second – when I realized how worship demands the Present – then hell began. I was no longer a Revolutionary Poet. I was a self-ordained priest without a faith.

[*Pause.*]

Do you know what I'm saying? I have never lived *Now*. And that 'Never' makes crueller murderers, even than Christ or Country.

Look into my eyes. What do you see? The envy? The endless
living through others? Jealousy squinting through the glare of
commitment? ... There is where Vietnam starts. Don't sit on
pavements to ban armaments; sit, if you must, to ban these eyes.
They would kill Gideon, if they could, for his goodness. They
would kill David for his instinct. Yes, my own son – as they killed
his mother: Giulia. Poor girl, you are looking at a murderer. But
don't be afraid. You're quite safe. You have nothing I want, you
see.

[*She kisses him gently on the mouth. He draws back, then kisses her
passionately. She throws her arms round him.*]

CURTAIN

ACT THREE

Sunday night.

Eleven-thirty. Above, LOIS *lies in* MARK'*s bed, naked, under a sheet. Behind her, stands* MARK, *also naked and wrapped in a large white towel. He holds a bottle.*

MARK: Are you awake?

LOIS: Mmm.

MARK: Then listen, Miss America. Go home. Forget Europe. She's old, wicked, and useless – like me. Purge her. Get her right out of you, if you want to live. Believe me, everything bad started here. The pox. The subjugation of woolly heads. The social layer cake, which God's hand alone is allowed to crumble. Above all, the Police State. That's our main gift to the world. We've never been without it. The helmetted thugs of Prussia. Hohenstauffen – Hohenzollern. All those Bourbon nights. The shadows of agents everywhere – Fouché spies in the arcades – Metternich men – the soutanes of insane Priests slipping through the twilight – Rome, with her tinkling bells, summoning us to avoid ourselves. Giddy's quite right . . . [*Fiercer.*] Never forgive them. The kneelers! The followers of carriage axles. The motorcade boys. The smart saluters. The slow lookers through documents. The postillions of the state in dark glasses, now not even bobbing on cream horses, – just on mobikes! Not even in plumes, – just in perspex, crackling with transistors. Disembodied, uninteresting as the astronauts, their heroes. Assembled men! . . . We taught you the tricks, and you've made them shoddier. Get us out of you entirely! The hell with Europe. Get us out of you! . . . I'm pissed.

[*He hands her the bottle.*]

LOIS: You're fantastic. Do you know you've been talking all day?

MARK: And you keep sleeping. Well, naturally. Speeches of such preternatural tedium.

LOIS: Don't be silly. Hold my hand.

[*He moves to the bed, and holds it.*]

MARK: Look at your eyes. It's a joke.

LOIS: What is?

MARK: Your mouth all day long shouts Equality! But your eyes keep singing Uniqueness! You won't hear *them* demanding Equal Eyes For All Women!

[*She giggles, and drinks from the bottle.*]

If I could once make them in a poem, I'd never open my mouth again. Consider that.

LOIS: Sssh!

[DAVID *comes from his room, pauses a second on the landing, then runs down the stairs.* LOIS *freezes.*

The boy is naked, save for a white towel: he carries another. He goes straight to GIDEON's *study and knocks on the door.*]

GIDEON [*inside*]: Hallo?

MARK [*kissing* LOIS's *hand*]: Firm, typewriter-bashing little hand. I think I'd quite like to be that Remington.

LOIS: Oh, stop it now.

[MARK *laughs.* GIDEON *opens the door. He is wearing his white dressing-robe.*]

DAVID: You're still wet.

GIDEON [*coming out into the room*]: I am a bit.

DAVID: Sit down, I'll dry you.

GIDEON: No, it's all right.

DAVID: Sit!

[GIDEON *sits.* DAVID *starts to towel his head.*]

MARK: We'll have to go down in a minute.

LOIS: No.

MARK: We must.

LOIS: I don't want to.

MARK: You're just going to stay here?

LOIS: Yes.

[*She turns away from him and throws the sheet over her head.*]

GIDEON: It was noble of you to sit with me today.

DAVID: Don't be silly.

GIDEON: You got even wetter than I did. You looked like an otter.

DAVID: I enjoyed it.

GIDEON: Did you?

DAVID: I think because Lois wasn't there. I mean, yesterday she looked at me the whole time, like she was challenging me to find it boring.

GIDEON: Your opinion matters to her.

DAVID: Do you mean that?

GIDEON: Of course. Otherwise you wouldn't have such power to upset her.

DAVID: I really am naive, aren't I?

GIDEON: Yes, if you mean unconscious of your charm. Now, you will be more conscious, therefore less charming.

DAVID: Life's depressing, isn't it?

GIDEON: No denying it.

[MARK *stands up.*]

MARK: Come on, now. It's time you got up.

LOIS [*under the sheet*]: No.

MARK: They've been back fifteen minutes. Gideon will be wanting his dinner. He must be starving.

LOIS: He can get it himself.

MARK: That's not a very nice thing to say.

LOIS: Oh, leave me alone!

DAVID: Where the hell can she be?

GIDEON: I don't understand it.

DAVID: We held the car for ages.

GIDEON: She must have been walking, and not realized the time.

DAVID: I don't believe it.

GIDEON: Why not? It's a natural explanation. She wasn't exactly pleased with either of us.

DAVID: Lois would never forget a vigil.

MARK: Lois.

GIDEON: Then what? You mean, she did it deliberately?

MARK [*harder*]: Lois.

GIDEON: But why? Why on earth would she? . . .

    [DAVID *towels harder*.]

  Gently, my dear!

DAVID: What's going on, Giddy?

GIDEON: Going on?

DAVID: What is it? What has he said to you?

MARK: Here!

    [*He jabs her. She sits up.*]

LOIS: Cut it out!

    [*They glare at each other.*]

GIDEON [*gently*]: Trust me, my dear.

DAVID: What about? Trust you what about?

GIDEON: You know, they say there are seven meals between Man and Revolution. I've missed six already.

DAVID: Poor Giddy. I'm sorry . . . I'll get you something right now. Let's see what there is. [*He crosses to the kitchen.*]

GIDEON: She didn't even leave us any food ready. I can't think why.

DAVID: Because she's a selfish cow.

GIDEON: Sssh!

MARK: Get out of bed.

LOIS: No.

DAVID: You're all right, aren't you?

GIDEON: I think so. How about you! You haven't eaten either.

DAVID: I'll be better after a snack. Excuse me.

    [*He goes out.*

     MARK *comes over to* LOIS.]

MARK [*hard*]: Get up, Lois!

LOIS: What's the matter with you?

MARK: I need you downstairs.

LOIS: Need?

MARK: Exactly.

LOIS: What *is* this? What game are you playing?

MARK: My own. As always.

LOIS: But I figure in it, don't I? You want me downstairs very much. Why?

MARK: Press it and see.

LOIS [*realizing it*]: You're going to tell, aren't you? You're going to tell, right now! . . . You are, aren't you? Why? . . . *Why?*

MARK: Stop questioning me, you silly bitch! Put on your panties and get downstairs.

LOIS: You've *planned* it! . . . You've planned the whole thing!

MARK: Let's have no hysterics, please.

LOIS: Every bit of it . . .

MARK: Lois –

LOIS: Every bit!

MARK [*quietly*]: I'll open the door. You can scream again.
    [*He moves to the door.*]

LOIS: I'm not leaving this room. I'm staying right here.

MARK: As you please.
    [*He leaves the bedroom and comes downstairs.*]
    Good evening.

GIDEON: Peace.

MARK: How was your vigil? A smash-hit, I should imagine. You *are* clever, making that addition to the story. I mean the fast. Add the possibility that the leading actor might pass out at any minute, and you turn the inevitable anti-climax of a second-night performance into pure thriller. Congratulations.

GIDEON: I again missed you among the audience.

MARK: And Lois. You must have missed her too.

GIDEON: I did. Where is she?
    [DAVID *comes in, carrying a can of soup.*]

DAVID: I've found some lentil soup. It's only a tin –
    [*He stares at his father.*]

MARK: Would you lay a place for me also? After all, it's an occasion –

the breaking of the Great Man's fast. Perhaps we should call it the First Supper!

DAVID: It'll be five minutes, Giddy.

[*He starts to go back to the kitchen.*]

GIDEON: Lay a place for your father, too, please.

DAVID: Alright.

MARK: And for Lois too, please. She will be hungry also. [*He smiles.*] It's not only vigils that make man hungry.

DAVID: What?

MARK: Lay for your father, and he will lay for you.

[*Pause.*]

DAVID: Where is she?

[*They stare at one another. Intuitively,* DAVID *moves to the foot of the stairs.*]

[*Calling up.*] Lois? . . . *Lois!*

[*The girl starts up in bed.*]

MARK: Perhaps she's asleep.

DAVID: Lois!

[*The girl gets quickly out of bed, wrapping the sheet about her. Standing there, she drinks elaborately from the bottle.*]

GIDEON [*to* DAVID]: Gently, David, I beg you.

DAVID: Lois!!!

[*Carefully, she puts down the bottle, winds the sheet around her, and comes slowly downstairs: a white figure joining three others.*]

GIDEON: Peace.

LOIS: Good evening. [*To* DAVID.] Good evening. [*To* MARK.] Good evening. [*To* GIDEON.] You got wet.

GIDEON: I'm afraid I did.

LOIS: Well, that's all right. It was that kind of a day. Everybody got wet! . . .

[*She starts to wander round the room.*]

Actually, it was an ordinary day. Absolutely ordinary. Some people got chicken in their gut, and some people got a bullet, and some other people – the lucky ones they *say*, got something else. And it's all explicable only in the eyes of God. [*To* MARK.] Right? . . . [*To*

DAVID.] What are you doing with that? Are you going to give that to Giddy? Is that all he gets after two whole days' starvation – is that all he gets in *his* gut? – a lousy plate of canned soup? Ah, poor Giddy! I stop looking after you for one day, and see what happens. You see – you still need me!

[*She gives a strained laugh.*]

Well actually no one needs anyone. That's just a word – *needs*, one of those crazy words . . . mess up your head . . .

DAVID: Lois . . .

LOIS [*fiercely snatching the can of soup out of his hand*]: *Give me that!*

[*She turns and goes with it into the kitchen.*]

GIDEON [*to* MARK: *cold*]: What have you done?

MARK [*innocently*]: I?

GIDEON: I can't believe . . .

MARK: What?

GIDEON: Even . . . Even within the context . . . *No, Mark.*

MARK: What? What, Gideon?

GIDEON [*bursting out*]: That even you! –

MARK: 'Would stoop so low?'

[*He laughs.* DAVID *turns and stares at him.*]

MARK [*to his son*]: What are you gaping at? An old wreck still attractive to women? Disgusting, isn't it? Pleasure's for the young. Everyone knows that! . . . Portrait of a teenager discovering the world not made entirely in his own image!

[*Pause.* MARK *sits on the throne.*]

Don't worry, boy! You didn't miss much. It wasn't exactly the sex act of the era. She's as cold as haddock, you must know that. Deep Freeze Dora, the Tundra Gash!

GIDEON: Be quiet!

MARK: Still, I gave her *something*. What do you think she wanted from you, eh? Drugs and shrugs, and a pleady kiss once a week. D'you think that satisfies a girl? I know you pot babies. It's all wow and wee-wee, with you, isn't it? You can't get it up to save your stoned lives!

GIDEON: Be quiet! Be quiet, this instant!

MARK [*ignoring him*]: No wonder she couldn't stand you – your mother. Even in her, deep down, was the natural Italian horror of the Unmale.

GIDEON: Mark, I beg you!

[MARK *gets up again. He approaches his son, and puts his arm intimately around his neck.*]

MARK: Now don't fret, boy. We're two of a kind, you and I. I could never dominate a woman either. You don't want to believe all that stuff about me, the Great Lover. It was all rubbish. I failed just as early with Giulia. Well, of course. All she wanted was the ancestral Roman pattern. Smashed fist; smashed plate. How else do you know you are loved? I was hopeless at it! – her 'big shy Englishman'! It was my fault, really, she had to turn elsewhere for comfort.

[DAVID *turns to him sharply.* GIDEON *rises, appalled.*]

Oh well, yes! What's so new about that? What's the big surprise? You must have realized! No? . . . You mustn't be too hard on her. After all, what else was she going to do? She was a hot lady, your mum. What I couldn't supply, she had to get somewhere. So she found it in Corfu harbour. A vulgar choice, but there you are.

GIDEON [*in pain*]: *Mark!*

MARK [*roughly*]: Oh come on now, Giddy. Stop play-acting! It's time we told him.

GIDEON: 'We'?

MARK: My snot son, who claims no kinship with the Mediterranean! It's time he knew our little secret.

GIDEON: Secret? . . . What secret? . . . There's no – no – no secret! . . .

DAVID [*soft: dead*]: Stop it.

GIDEON [*desperate and confused*]: I know no secret, David!

[DAVID *stands rigid, looking at neither of them.*]

DAVID: Just stop it, Giddy.

GIDEON: I know nothing, David. Believe me: nothing. He's inventing every scrap of this!

MARK: Oh, come now: you can do better than that! You don't have to resort to lies, Gideon. Protect him, if you want – but don't lie! It's shocking when *you* do it!

GIDEON [*urgently*]: David? . . .

MARK: It's really obscene!

GIDEON: Dear boy?

DAVID [*low: stiffly*]: Just stop it. Just stop the voice. The voice . . . The voice . . . *Please!* . . .

MARK: Look at you! Is that my face? Dirty olive out of the standard wop jar! Is that my body? Slack-waisted camel-walk; the harbour hump! Get with it, you lump of Italy – it took a lot of pasta to make you!

GIDEON [*breaking out*]: Be silent! Abominable – abominable man! Close your mouth!

MARK: You know it's true.

GIDEON: I know nothing of the sort. There's not one word of truth in any of this, and you know it. Believe me, David, not one!

MARK: Why, what's the tragedy? Some matelot lowered his flap to his mum under the arcade. So what? We're all God's bambini, aren't we?

GIDEON: Liar!

MARK: I forgave her. Gave you my name!

GIDEON: Liar!

MARK: My glorious *name* – which some girls still conjure with! . . . All right, when you were young. But come thirteen, when she saw her little Corsican stoker or whatever he was, start to slouch round the villa, memory-sized – ah, then she got the Gods! Suddenly she couldn't bear to look at you any more! Started calling you her punishment. God's retribution on a Catholic girl who had strayed! You had to go, and I had to do it. Send you to England for your education. Keep you away from Corfu. Telegrams every few months – 'Still not convenient you return. Your loving father.'

[DAVID *looks at him in horror.*]

GIDEON: Listen to me, David. All of this is part of a game. A hideous,

183

disgusting game. Your father is simply trying to provoke me, that's all. That is all it's about.

DAVID [*in anguish*]: Just stop the voice, Giddy! Stop it, that's all I want!

MARK [*raising his voice*]: Why else should I keep you away from Corfu all those years? Answer me that! Why else should I keep you away for six whole years – if she hadn't begged me to? Why else would I do that, Giddy? Perhaps you can tell!?

GIDEON: I don't know. I don't care!

MARK: Why else?

GIDEON: Hold your tongue.

MARK [*to* DAVID]: Why else? Why else? Give me one reason, my dear little bastard!

GIDEON [*exploding*]: No! . . . I order you! – I order you – YES! . . .

MARK [*jeeringly*]: What?
   [*Pause.*]

GIDEON [*controlling himself with great effort*]: To be quiet.
   [*Suddenly* DAVID *runs to the garden exit, snatches up his boots, and shoves his feet into them.*]
David! . . . Where are you going?

DAVID: Away.

GIDEON: Where?

DAVID: Out of the voice.

GIDEON: No!
   [DAVID *runs towards the front door.*]
Stay here.

DAVID: I can't.

GIDEON: Please, David. *Please!*

DAVID: I can't, Giddy. No more!

GIDEON: All of this is lies. Every bit of it. Everything he says is a lie!

DAVID [*in great anguish*]: I KNOW! I KNOW! *I KNOW!* . . .
   [*Slight pause.*]

GIDEON [*with desperate quietness*]: *Then why?*

DAVID: I've got to get out. That's all.

GIDEON: No. Not you! . . . Not *you!*

184

MARK: Then who? Who's got to get out, then, Giddy? . . . *Who?*
 [*A pause.* GIDEON *wrings his hands.*]
GIDEON: No one. Everyone must stay. No one must leave this
 house. No one.
 [*He stands, looking straight ahead.*]
DAVID [*dead*]: That's right. No one. In the end, there's no one. 'Be
 silent. Hold your tongue.' That's all you can do. You can't stop it.
 The voice goes on and on – and all you've got against it is words.
 Lovely words. And theories – lovely theories. And fasts!
GIDEON: Owl!
DAVID: Theories and hopes and vigils and fasts! And *nothing! Lovely
 nothing!*
GIDEON: David! . . .
DAVID [*savagely*]: No one and Nothing!
 [*He turns on his heel and moves to the stairs.* GIDEON *pursues him.*]
GIDEON: David! . . . Listen to me, I beg you. Please, David, – look at
 me, at least. My dear, dear boy – look at me. Please . . . Won't you
 look?
 [DAVID *turns.*]
DAVID [*howling*]: FUCK OFF!
 [*He dashes upstairs. A pause.* GIDEON *begins to move slowly down-
 stage.* MARK *comes up to him.*]
MARK: Congratulations. The battle's over. You win. I see there is
 nothing I can do will make Shrivings reject me. You will even help
 torture a boy to maintain its foundations.
 [*He opens his arms wide.*]
 Master – Receive your Disciple!
 [GIDEON *stares at him, then crumples in a faint on to the floor.* MARK
 crouches over him in horror.]
MARK [*in a whisper*]: Giulia! . . .
 [*He looks wildly about him, then retreats in panic to the stairs, calling
 aloud.*]
 Lois! . . . LOIS!
LOIS [*off*]: What is it? [*She rushes in.*] Giddy!
MARK [*moving to the table*]: Water . . .

LOIS [*kneeling*]: Giddy! . . . Jesus! . . . Giddy! . . .
> [*She pulls him to a sitting position.*]
> . . . Giddy!

MARK [*approaching with the water*]: Give him this.

LOIS: No!

MARK: It's only water.

LOIS [*ferociously*]: Get away! Don't you touch him! Get away!
> [MARK *scrambles to the foot of the stairs where he watches her revive* GIDEON.]

Hey . . . Hey now . . . Hey now, Giddy . . . Hey now . . . Open your eyes. Open your eyes for me, Giddy. Come on now: be good. Be good with me, Giddy . . . Be good . . .
> [*She starts to rock him to and fro in her arms.*]

LOIS: Come on, now, be my Giddy; my own Giddy; my darling! Come on, now, be my Giddy; my own Giddy; my darling! Come on, now, be my Giddy; my own Giddy; my darling!
> [GIDEON *opens his eyes, and stirs.*]

Hi! You fell. It's all right. I'm here. Try and stand. Come on. Lean on me. Up we go . . . That's it . . .
> [*She helps him to rise.* MARK *moves up the stairs into his bedroom, leaving the door open.*]

Now we'll sit over there. Come on. It's only a few steps . . . There we are . . . Come along now . . . That's it.
> [*She leads him tenderly across the room to the table, and helps him sit behind it, facing front.*]

Now I'll make you some soup. It won't take a minute.

GIDEON [*faintly*]: No.

LOIS: Of course, my dear. You're very hungry. That's why you fell.

GIDEON: No.

LOIS: I'll bring you some bread, first. Just while I heat it.

GIDEON: Please leave me alone.
> [MARK *suddenly raises his head and calls out:*]

MARK: David!
> [GIDEON *half rises.*]

LOIS: Giddy, please sit down. You haven't any strength at all. Go on, now.

[*He obeys her.*]

LOIS: You just sit there. I'll be right back.

[*She goes into the kitchen.*]

MARK [*roaring*]: David!

[GIDEON *lowers his head and puts his hands over his ears. Suddenly* DAVID *dashes out of his bedroom, crosses violently into* MARK'*s room, and slams the door behind him. He glares.*]

[*Throwing out his arms.*] All right – I'm here. Look. Look. *Look!* Keep them on me, your eyes – your mother's – yes! Ruined by me! Who the hell else could I be but your dad? Keep looking. This is it. The last time. You'll hear the voice just once more – then never again. I'll go back to Corfu for life!

[*Father and son stare at each other, each dressed in white towels.*]

Now. Now – I'll tell you why I kept you out of your home.

[*He raises a bottle to his lips – then suddenly chucks it on the bed instead.* DAVID *keeps looking at him.*]

Your first week on earth you stared at me like that. Before you could even see properly, you heard the voice. The dead man's voice, singing a lullaby. Your face wrinkled in fear.

[*Pause.*]

When you were six, I watched you race your bike through the olive trees. Your mother was standing beside me. Your mouth opened with glee. Hers too. All I got were the mouths opening and shutting. No glee. Just physical movements. I stood there hating you both. Filling up with hate. And you, twisting the handlebars, turned and caught my eye, you shook – and fell off. Giulia screamed and ran to you. I didn't . . . Do you still shake?

[DAVID *stands unmoving.* MARK *turns away. Below,* LOIS *comes in with a board of bread and a dish of butter.*]

LOIS: Here now. Have a slice of this.

[GIDEON *does not move.*]

Don't give me a hard time now, Giddy. Sit up.

GIDEON [*raising himself*]: Please go away.

[*Determinedly, she cuts the bread and butters it.*]

LOIS: There. I want you to finish that by the time I bring the soup. O.K.?

[GIDEON *does not move. She goes back into the kitchen.*]

MARK: Do you know what it's like to be worshipped by a saint? She truly believed that I – this object in front of you – because a writer, was actually *better*, actually superior to her, mere creature of instinct! What could I do? I encouraged her. I got her to regard herself as entirely frivolous. Trivial! Unworthy of her important husband! . . . And the more she cringed in awe, the more I hated her . . . Well, naturally . . .

[*He goes to the bed, snatches up the bottle, and drinks.*]

My Son–Confessor. You were never fooled. You saw him only too clear: the killer in me. It's why I had to get rid of you. You knew how he'd finish the brandy alone at night in the villa – then stand in the bathroom, sticking pins of seconal into his face, saying: 'Let this be the Young! The hateful Young!' How he'd tear his own hair in front of the mirror – hit himself with his own construction worker's hand, screaming inside: 'Why was I born without joy? Why do others have it, and not me?' [*Softer.*] And later, lying beside her in morning light, watching her wake. The only girl I ever knew who smiled first thing on waking. Watching the smile come, a second before the eyes open. Spill over me their bright love . . . Watching her in such anger.

[*Pause.*]

Till one morning, she doesn't smile. She groans instead. One morning – after one particular night.

[*He turns away.* GIDEON *begins to murmur below. He is very disturbed.*]

GIDEON [*low*]: No one.

MARK: And I've got to . . . tell you . . .

[*He sits on the bed.*]

GIDEON: No one and nothing . . . Just words . . . Words and nothing.

MARK: How does a dancer die, who doesn't want to live?

GIDEON: No! . . .

MARK: I watched my hate creep up her legs. It was as if I was needling it into her veins.

GIDEON: Theories . . . Lovely theories . . .

MARK: She goes to bed. The hips suddenly won't move. Don't want to any more.

GIDEON [*agitated: half to himself*]: Well, what else could I *do*? Join in? Bang, bang! 'Get out. Shrivings can't cope with you!' – is that what you want? . . . 'Stop it,' you say. 'Stop the voice!' All right! That's easy to say. The hard thing is *not to*! Let it go on! Let it die of itself. Can't you see that? *It must die of itself!*

[*He springs up and starts pacing the room, speaking feverishly.*]

The hard thing is to do nothing. Almost impossible . . . Well, we've spoken of it often enough . . . Answer me this! How could we throw him out, and live here afterwards ourselves? Doesn't it – in the end – doesn't it just – *just* – come down to *that*? To the sheer impossibility of that? . . . In the end, to shift at all – make any change that *is* a change – to *shove*, if you like, evolution on – and that's the task: no less! – *there have to be priorities!* . . . All right. Abstraction! That's just another bogey word! . . . I'm talking about a new kind of honour. Holding on to priorities. Do you see? . . .

[*He continues to walk up and down the room, hands clasped, caged in pain.*]

MARK: Finally, nothing moves. Except her mouth, praying. Just sits there in a canvas jacket, praying.

GIDEON: Yes . . . *Exactly!* . . . That's what's needed . . . A new kind of *honour* . . .

MARK: Shoving the book under the pillow whenever she hears me coming. 'Sorry, Gesù! Must go now! *He* won't understand!'

GIDEON: When we say Faith, it's *that* . . . What is worth honouring? Really worth it? . . . Really? . . . *Really?*

[*He stops short.*]

You real people, what will you really honour?

MARK [*shouting at the shrine*]: Oh you martyrs! You martyrs!

[*He springs to his feet and over to the shrine.*]

Why couldn't you ever fight me like a woman?

GIDEON [*rapidly*]: You speak of love all the time. But what will you honour?... Everyone says Love: you've got to fight for your love. All right! But what does that mean? Do you think silence can't be fight? Do you judge a love only by the *bashing* you do for it? [*Bitterly.*] Oh yes! Stand up! Square up! Come outside! Come on the battlefield! History of the World! Put your fists where your faith is! Marvellous!... [*Harshly.*] And that's what you want too, with all your long hair, sweet looks!... All of you, just the same...

[*Pause. He stands for a moment, with eyes closed.*]

[*Quieter: very calm.*] To let go. Just to let go that *indulgence*. Fill up instead with true passiveness. A feeling so total, it's *like* violence. An immense Nothing inside you. A sledgehammer Nothing which alone can break that crust of Ego ... Fasts – Vigils – all those tricks: what are they about, except this? – to fill up in a new way!

[*Pause. He stands very still, like a statue.*]

You have to stand there, my dear, and take it. Bang – and no reply. None. [*Dead.*] None. None ...

[*He starts to tremble. Suddenly he begins to imitate himself, in a new and bitter, spinsterish voice.*]

'Be quiet, Mark, please. Be silent, Mark. Mark, I forbid you. Mark, I beg you.' [*Savagely.*] Words! Words and nothing! Lovely nothing! [*Crying out.*] Oh, David!

MARK [*standing before the shrine: low*]: Giulia!

GIDEON: *David!*

MARK: My dancer!

GIDEON: *David! My David! ... My owl ...*

[*LOIS comes in with a bowl of steaming soup. She stares at* GIDEON. *He becomes aware of her. Slowly he sits again at the table. She places the soup in front of him.*]

LOIS: Eat.

[*He does not move, or look at her.*]

Eat, Giddy. [*Pause.*] Look, if you're mad at me, O.K. let me have it. Anything but the noble act. Sitting there all wounded. That's just shit, Giddy.

[*He remains motionless, as do father and son above.*]

O.K., I did it! So what does that make me? A Scarlet Woman? . . . O.K., say it, if that's what you think. And it is exactly what you think! Only it's too aggressive to say it right out, isn't it? . . . Wow!

[*Pause.*]

Gee, I'm disappointed in you. Who'd have thought that you, of all people in the world, would be jealous? Anything so *ordinary*! . . . Sagging Jesus, as my lover would say! . . . Well, you live and learn. Or do you? I don't learn a damn thing, except that everyone's full of shit, and that's not much to learn. Every classroom cynic you meet in college tells you that. It's funny to find out they're right. That's funny . . .

[*Pause.*]

Say something, for Christ's sake! Who d'you think you are, some kind of a priest or something? Mark's right – he's absolutely right! It's the Pope! I've offended the Pope! The lowly acolyte has displeased the Pope of Reason! [*Mock humble.*] All right, I did it, Your Holiness. I have sinned. I did it, Your Holiness. I have sinned. I did it. So what? [*Angry.*] Sex, sex, sex! So what? Supposed to be so great! What's great? *He's* the famous lover – he didn't find it great. It took him forever! Just a fat old man, dropping his sweat on me! And that's supposed to be beautiful! . . . *What are they all lying about?*

[*Pause. Still* GIDEON *does not move.*]

MARK [*softly*]: Perdonna. Perdonna me. Perdonna.

[LOIS *laughs.*]

LOIS: No, that's not why you're angry, is it? It's not the fuck, is it? It's him! The Enemy! I went off with the Opposition! [*False English accent.*] 'Isn't that the end, my deah? She doesn't do it for two whole years, and when she *does*, who does she choose? A nice Progressive fuck with an approved young boy? Oh no. She has to have a beastly, reactionary fuck with his old man!' [*She laughs: then coolly.*] You don't care at all, do you? I'm kidding. I know it's not jealousy. It's nothing. It's absolutely nothing – right? You don't give a damn who I go to bed with! As far as you are concerned, I could go to bed with Hitler! . . . [*She laughs.*] Boy, you really are a mess! I mean it. Like you sit there with your nose up in the air, preaching all the time – Non-attachment – Get Beyond the Possessive Scene – all that beautiful new humanist shit! – and all there is *you*, making a great Cause out of not caring. A way of life, yeah, a whole religion – out of not feeling anything personal at all! [*She comes closer.*] I saw you last night, when he attacked me. Oh, you were distressed, all right. It was a distressing scene. Difficult to handle, even for a saint. But you managed. You managed, Giddy. You handled it O.K.! [*Grandly.*] 'Come, Lois. I am tireder than I thought.' [*Pause: coldly.*] You bastard.

[*He looks at her in amazement. She speaks with deep hostility.*] I think you actually enjoyed it. Like it was a test of your virtue. 'Poor Lois. Horrid for her, of course; but good for her too. You gotta be tested, after all. Everyone's got to be tested?' Right? Just stand there and take it. Right . . .? [*Leaning into his face.*] Isn't that right?

[GIDEON *puts his hands over his ears and turns away from her. For a second she falters and stops.*]

MARK [*dead*]: All right. Let me give it to you in the face. How I actually killed her, your mother. How I actually finished her off. Short and physical.

LOIS: At least, he knows! He's the filthiest man I've met, but he knows something!

MARK: One night . . .

LOIS: He's not a phoney.

MARK: One night . . .

LOIS: He's garbage, but at least he's not a complete phoney.

MARK [*with sudden violence*]: Take your eyes off me! Get out of here! I can't speak!

[*He turns away.*]

LOIS [*now relentless*]: Do you know what a phoney is, Giddy? A person who says the family is obsolete, and all he really wishes is that David Askelon was his own son!

[GIDEON *turns to look at her.*]

Do you know what a phoney is? Someone who says Peace because there's no war in him. I don't mean he drove it out – I mean he never had it. It's easy to be chaste when you've got no cock, Giddy. It's easy to give up bloodshed, if you've got no blood to shed! Right? Dig that! I made an epigram! You see, I'm not so pompous as everyone says! . . . [*Icy.*] You know something? I don't believe your word on anything. Like when you say when you were young, you were attracted to boys and dogs and shit knows what? I tell you, I don't believe a fucking word. *I think you're exactly like me. You can't stand it!* You made that whole thing up just to teach a point. [*English accent.*] 'Sex Freedom is a jolly good thing!' But I'm willing to bet my ass you never did it at all. Everyone says how noble you were to give it up – just *imagine* what he went through to do it! . . . Well, yeah, I can imagine. It was like nothing! No wonder she left you, your wife. No wonder she just got out, poor stupid Enid. She found out what a phoney she was hitched to. What a phoney! Christ, at least he's alive up there! Not dead – as good as dead! – Dead thing! Dead old thing! Dead! Boring – dead! – ridiculous – Dead! phoney – Dead! – old – dead! dead! dead! DEAD!

[*Deliberately,* GIDEON *strikes her as she leans over him. She recoils. He rises. She retreats. He strikes her again more violently. She stares at him in horror.*
Pause.]

GIDEON: Are you satisfied? In your deep heart, are you satisfied?

[*She turns from him. Then he turns from her. They stand frozen.*
Pause.]

MARK [*flatly*]: One night. She lying upstairs; I below, turning over my book of love poems. I get up. I drive into town. I sit in the arcade. I see a girl. I signal. I drive her back to the villa. I go up with her, into your mother's room. She lying there, drinking coca-cola her favourite way, out of the bottle. Now barely able to speak, she turns to me with her usual smile for any new thing. The girl giggles. 'Don't be afraid,' I say. 'My wife enjoys this. It's for her we do it.' [*Pause.*] And so. Slowly. On the floor. At the foot of the bed from which she could not move. I saluted her with my ecstasies. [*Pause.*] During the whole time she held the bottle before her, as if she were offering me refreshment. It was next morning she groaned first thing on waking. Very exactly: once. As if she were clearing her throat. [*Pause.*] She didn't live three weeks after that. I remember she held the cola bottle night and day. Like a doll to a sick child.

> [*Silence. Then* DAVID *moves, quickly. His hands fly up, join violently above his head. For a long moment they stay up there, poised to smash his father down. Then he begins to tremble. Slowly his arms are lowered over his father's head. He pulls* MARK *to him, and kisses him on the face. They stay still.*
>
> *Below neither* LOIS *nor* GIDEON *moves.*]

LOIS [*low*]: Don't ever forgive me.

> [DAVID *releases* MARK. *He moves, and shuts the shrine on his mother's image.*]

Don't ever.

DAVID: Go down to him.

MARK: No.

DAVID: You *have* to.

MARK: You. You're his son where it matters.

DAVID: No. You are. [*Pause.*] Padre.

MARK: *Figlio.*

> [*They stare at each other.*]

DAVID: *Va.*

MARK: *Si.*

> [MARK *leaves the bedroom, and comes slowly downstairs.* DAVID *sits on the bed, exhausted.*]

LOIS [*quietly*]: That night we met in jail. I was reading John Stuart Mill. Where he asked himself that question: if all the wrongs in the world were put right, would you yourself be any happier? – and the answer came back No. You said, for you it would be Yes. [*Pause.*] I never heard anything better than that.

[*She turns and sees* MARK *watching them both. He moves towards them. She ignores him, and walks straight by him up the stairs.* GIDEON *does not move. The girl hesitates outside the bedroom door – looks in – sees* DAVID *– enters.* DAVID *does not look at her. Pause.*]

MARK [*seeing the bowl of soup*]: You haven't even eaten.

LOIS: Hey.

DAVID: Hay is for horses.

LOIS: Sure.

MARK: I warned you. I did. [*With fury.*] *You talk about life! –*

[LOIS *turns her face to the wall, but does not leave.*]

No. *We* talk about life – the knowers. And look at us. You are the only possible thing I've ever met. D'you wonder I hate you?

DAVID [*woodenly*]: Why, Lois?

MARK: D'you wonder I love you?

DAVID: Why?

LOIS [*as woodenly*]: I don't know.

DAVID: Did you enjoy it, at least?

LOIS [*quietly: with absolute frankness*]: I don't know what enjoy means.

MARK: I wish I was an animal, and could live without a dream. I wish I was a child, and could live in a Church. But I'm a man, and I've known you. Where else can I go?

LOIS: I don't know who I am, David.

[MARK *moves forward and thrusts his outstretched hand before the motionless* GIDEON.]

MARK: Here! This. This tool for making. A killer's hand. It's all you've got . . . Take it.

[GIDEON *ignores it, staring straight ahead.*]

What will it do without you? Squeeze some more napalm out of my cock? Drive some more Red tanks over dreaming heads? Wear the Pope's ring, and dip a gold pen in the sick of starving children it's helped create. Sign me Governor of Louisibama, and decree at parties for the blind, white guests must be separated from black by

charitable hands, since they can't see to do God's work for themselves. Don't leave me with this God's hand, Giddy.

LOIS [*quietly*]: I'm no place, David. No place at all.

DAVID: Shrivings is a place.

LOIS: No.

DAVID: It has to be.

LOIS: It's nowhere.

DAVID [*violently*]: It has to be! IT HAS TO BE!

[*The girl turns. He turns round to her. They stare at one another.*]

MARK: Have you no word for me? No word at all?

GIDEON: Dust.

[*Appalled,* MARK *sits down at the table. He takes up a spoon. He dips
it in the soup, and presents it to* GIDEON.]

MARK: Peace!

[GIDEON *sits rigid.*

Above, DAVID *suddenly stretches out his arm to* LOIS. *She looks at it
without expression: motionless.*

A long pause.

Then, very slowly, GIDEON *begins to lower his head to the spoon held
before him. He does not look at* MARK. *He opens his mouth, and
drinks.*

The light fades.]

CURTAIN

Equus

A NOTE ON THE TEXT

WHAT appears in this text is a description of the first production of *Equus* at the National Theatre in July 1973. In making this description, I am partly satisfying myself, but also partly bowing to demand.

When people buy the published text of a new play, they mostly want to recall the experience they received in the theatre. That experience is composed, of course, not merely of the words they heard, but the gestures they saw, and the lighting, and the look of the thing.

There are, however, evils attendant on this sort of description. It can imprison a play in one particular stylization. Just as seriously, it can do a real injustice to the original Director, by incorporating his ideas without truly acknowledging them. Worse, if the Director is as inventive as John Dexter, it can actually seem to minimize those ideas, just by flatly setting down on paper what was far from flat on the stage, and listing inexpressively details of his work which, in accumulation, became deeply expressive.

Dexter directs powerfully through suggestion. Into the theatrical, spaces he contrives, flows the communal imagination of an audience. He enables it to charge the action of a play with electric life. He is a master of gesture and of economy. Aesthetically, his founding fathers are Noh Drama and Berthold Brecht: the plain plank; the clear light; the great pleasure in a set-piece. I do not mean by this that he would ever direct a single minute of physical action which detracted from the meaning of a play, or in some grand visual sense subverted it – he sharply dislikes effect isolated from context – but he is naturally and rightly drawn to plays which demand elaborate physical actions to complete them.

The Royal Hunt of the Sun and *Black Comedy*, both of which he directed, are such pieces: and so is *Equus*. Their visual action is to me as much a part of the play as the dialogue. I suppose my head has always been full of images. The gold masks staring hopefully and then in gathering despair at the sky, at the end of *The Royal Hunt of the Sun*, had been part of my imagination ever since I first saw a Peruvian funeral mask with its elongated eyes and red-smeared cheeks. Brindsley Miller in the lit-up darkness of *Black Comedy*, slowly moving the spiky legs of a Regency chair one inch before the innocent face of his spinster neighbour, had tiptoed that very journey in my head as I sat at my desk. But such images, like the Field of Ha-ha in *Equus* with its mist and nettles, still have to be externalized. In John Dexter's courageous and precise staging, they acquire a vibrant and unforgettable life.

While I am confessing debts, let me mention John Napier who created the tough, bright masks of horsedom; Andy Phillips who lit them superbly; and above all, Claude Chagrin, who animated them. She created, with the help of six human actors, a stable of Superhorses to stalk through the mind.

Finally, out of a fine company I must set down the names of three actors who made the first performance of this play live with a very special intensity. Alec McCowen's Dysart touched audiences deeply with its dry agony. Peter Firth's Alan left them sighing with admiration. Nicholas Clay's horse Nugget was, quite simply, unforgettable.

Rehearsing a play is making the word flesh. Publishing a play is reversing the process. I can only hope this book is not too unjust to these brilliant people.

P.S.

A NOTE ON THE PLAY

ONE weekend over two years ago, I was driving with a friend through bleak countryside. We passed a stable. Suddenly he was reminded by it of an alarming crime which he had heard about recently at a dinner party in London. He knew only one horrible detail, and his complete mention of it could barely have lasted a minute – but it was enough to arouse in me an intense fascination.

The act had been committed several years before by a highly disturbed young man. It had deeply shocked a local bench of magistrates. It lacked, finally, any coherent explanation.

A few months later my friend died. I could not verify what he had said, or ask him to expand it. He had given me no name, no place, and no time. I don't think he knew them. All I possessed was his report of a dreadful event, and the feeling it engendered in me. I knew very strongly that I wanted to interpret it in some entirely personal way. I had to create a mental world in which the deed could be made comprehensible.

Every person and incident in *Equus* is of my own invention, save the crime itself; and even that I modified to accord with what I feel to be acceptable theatrical proportion. I am grateful now that I have never received confirmed details of the real story, since my concern has been more and more with a different kind of exploration.

I have been lucky, in doing final work on the play, to have enjoyed the advice and expert comment of a distinguished child psychiatrist. Through him I have tried to keep things real in a more naturalistic sense. I have also come to perceive that psychiatrists are an immensely varied breed, professing immensely varied methods and techniques. Martin Dysart is simply one doctor in one hospital. I must take responsibility for him, as I do for his patient.

P.S.

EQUUS

Characters:

MARTIN DYSART, *a psychiatrist*

ALAN STRANG

FRANK STRANG, *his father*

DORA STRANG, *his mother*

HESTHER SALOMON, *a magistrate*

JILL MASON

HARRY DALTON, *a stable owner*

A YOUNG HORSEMAN

A NURSE

SIX ACTORS – *including the Young Horseman, who also plays Nugget –
appear as Horses.*

Equus was first presented by The National Theatre at The Old Vic
Theatre on 26 July 1973, with the following cast:

MARTIN DYSART	Alec McCowen
NURSE	Louie Ramsay
HESTHER SALOMON	Gillian Barge
ALAN STRANG	Peter Firth
FRANK STRANG	Alan MacNaughtan
DORA STRANG	Jeanne Watts
HORSEMAN	Nicholas Clay
HARRY DALTON	David Healy
JILL MASON	Doran Godwin

and
Neil Cunningham, David Graham, David Kincaid, Maggie Riley,
Rosalind Shanks, Veronica Sowerby, Harry Waters

PRODUCTION	John Dexter
DESIGN	John Napier
MUSIC	Marc Wilkinson
LIGHTING	Andy Phillips
MOVEMENT	Claude Chagrin
ASSISTANT TO THE PRODUCER	Kenneth Mackintosh
STAGE MANAGER	Diana Boddington
DEPUTY STAGE MANAGERS	Phil Robins
	Tony Walters
ASSISTANT STAGE MANAGERS	Elizabeth Markham
	Terry Oliver

The main action of the play takes place in Rokeby Psychiatric Hospital in southern England. The time is the present.

The play is divided into numbered scenes, indicating a change of time or locale or mood. The action, however, is continuous.

THE SETTING

A SQUARE of wood set on a circle of wood.

The square resembles a railed boxing ring. The rail, also of wood, encloses three sides. It is perforated on each side by an opening. Under the rail are a few vertical slats, as if in a fence. On the downstage side there is no rail. The whole square is set on ball bearings, so that by slight pressure from actors standing round it on the circle, it can be made to turn round smoothly by hand.

On the square are set three little plain benches, also of wood. They are placed parallel with the rail, against the slats, but can be moved out by the actors to stand at right angles to them.

Set into the floor of the square, and flush with it, is a thin metal pole, about a yard high. This can be raised out of the floor, to stand upright. It acts as a support for the actor playing Nugget, when he is ridden.

In the area outside the circle stand benches. Two downstage left and right are curved to accord with the circle. The left one is used by Dysart as a listening and observing post when he is out of the square, and also by Alan as his hospital bed. The right one is used by Alan's parents, who sit side by side on it. (Viewpoint is from the main body of the audience.)

Further benches stand upstage, and accommodate the other actors. All the cast of *Equus* sits on stage the entire evening. They get up to perform their scenes, and return when they are done to their places around the set. They are witnesses, assistants – and especially a Chorus.

Upstage, forming a backdrop to the whole, are tiers of seats in the fashion of a dissecting theatre, formed into two railed-off blocks, pierced by a central tunnel. In these blocks sit members of the audience. During the play, Dysart addresses them directly from time to time, as he addresses the main body of the theatre. No other actor ever refers to them.

To left and right, downstage, stand two ladders on which are suspended horse masks.

The colour of all benches is olive green.

Above the stage hangs a battery of lights, set in a huge metal ring. Light cues, in this version, will be only of the most general description.

THE HORSES

THE actors wear track-suits of chestnut velvet. On their feet are light strutted hooves, about four inches high, set on metal horse-shoes. On their hands are gloves of the same colour. On their heads are tough masks made of alternating bands of silver wire and leather; their eyes are outlined by leather blinkers. The actors' own heads are seen beneath them: no attempt should be made to conceal them.

Any literalism which could suggest the cosy familiarity of a domestic animal – or worse, a pantomime horse – should be avoided. The actors should never crouch on all fours, or even bend forward. They must always – except on the one occasion where Nugget is ridden – stand upright, as if the body of the horse extended invisibly behind them. Animal effect must be created entirely mimetically, through the use of legs, knees, neck, face, and the turn of the head which can move the mask above it through all the gestures of equine wariness and pride. Great care must also be taken that the masks are put on before the audience with very precise timing – the actors watching each other, so that the masking has an exact and ceremonial effect.

THE CHORUS

REFERENCES are made in the text to the Equus Noise. I have in mind a choric effect, made by all the actors sitting round upstage, and composed of humming, thumping, and stamping – though never of neighing or whinnying. This Noise heralds or illustrates the presence of Equus the God.

ACT ONE

I

Darkness.
Silence.
Dim light up on the square. In a spotlight stands ALAN STRANG, *a lean boy of seventeen, in sweater and jeans. In front of him, the horse* NUGGET. ALAN's *pose represents a contour of great tenderness: his head is pressed against the shoulder of the horse, his hands stretching up to fondle its head. The horse in turn nuzzles his neck.*
The flame of a cigarette lighter jumps in the dark. Lights come up slowly on the circle. On the left bench, downstage, MARTIN DYSART, *smoking. A man in his mid-forties.*

DYSART: With one particular horse, called Nugget, he embraces. The animal digs its sweaty brow into his cheek, and they stand in the dark for an hour – like a necking couple. And of all nonsensical things – I keep thinking about the *horse*! Not the boy: the horse, and what it may be trying to do. I keep seeing that huge head kissing him with its chained mouth. Nudging through the metal some desire absolutely irrelevant to filling its belly or propagating its own kind. What desire could that be? Not to stay a horse any longer? Not to remain reined up for ever in those particular genetic strings? Is it possible, at certain moments we cannot imagine, a horse can add its sufferings together – the non-stop jerks and jabs that are its daily life – and turn them into grief? What use is grief to a horse?

[ALAN *leads* NUGGET *out of the square and they disappear together up the tunnel, the horse's hooves scraping delicately on the wood.*

DYSART *rises, and addresses both the large audience in the theatre and the smaller one on stage.*]

You see, I'm lost. What use, I should be asking, are questions like these to an overworked psychiatrist in a provincial hospital? They're worse than useless; they are, in fact, subversive.

[*He enters the square. The light grows brighter.*]

The thing is, I'm desperate. You see, I'm wearing that horse's head myself. That's the feeling. All reined up in old language and old assumptions, straining to jump clean-hoofed on to a whole new track of being I only suspect is there. I can't see it, because my educated, average head is being held at the wrong angle. I can't jump because the bit forbids it, and my own basic force – my horse-power, if you like – is too little. The only thing I know for sure is this: a horse's head is finally unknowable to me. Yet I handle children's heads – which I must presume to be more complicated, at least in the area of my chief concern . . . In a way, it has nothing to do with this boy. The doubts have been there for years, piling up steadily in this dreary place. It's only the extremity of this case that's made them active. I know that. The *extremity* is the point! All the same, whatever the reason, they are now, these doubts, not just vaguely worrying – but intolerable . . . I'm sorry. I'm not making much sense. Let me start properly; in order. It began one Monday last month, with Hesther's visit.

2

[*The light gets warmer.*
He sits. NURSE *enters the square.*]

NURSE: Mrs Salomon to see you, Doctor.

DYSART: Show her in, please.

[NURSE *leaves and crosses to where* HESTHER *sits.*]

Some days I blame Hesther. She brought him to me. But of course that's nonsense. What is he but a last straw? a last symbol? If it hadn't been him, it would have been the next patient, or the next. At least, I suppose so.

[HESTHER *enters the square: a woman in her mid-forties.*]

HESTHER: Hallo, Martin.

[DYSART *rises and kisses her on the cheek.*]

DYSART: Madam Chairman! Welcome to the torture chamber!

HESTHER: It's good of you to see me right away.

DYSART: You're a welcome relief. Take a couch.

HESTHER: It's been a day?

DYSART: No – just a fifteen-year-old schizophrenic, and a girl of eight thrashed into catatonia by her father. Normal, really ... You're in a state.

HESTHER: Martin, this is the most shocking case I ever tried.

DYSART: So you said on the phone.

HESTHER: I mean it. My bench wanted to send the boy to prison. For life, if they could manage it. It took me two hours solid arguing to get him sent to you instead.

DYSART: Me?

HESTHER: I mean, to hospital.

DYSART: Now look, Hesther. Before you say anything else, I can take no more patients at the moment. I can't even cope with the ones I have.

HESTHER: You must.

DYSART: Why?

HESTHER: Because most people are going to be disgusted by the whole thing. Including doctors.

DYSART: May I remind you I share this room with two highly competent psychiatrists?

HESTHER: Bennett and Thoroughgood. They'll be as shocked as the public.

DYSART: That's an absolutely unwarrantable statement.

HESTHER: Oh, they'll be cool and exact. And underneath they'll be revolted, and immovably English. Just like my bench.

DYSART: Well, what am I? Polynesian?

HESTHER: You know exactly what I mean! ... [*Pause.*] Please, Martin. It's vital. You're this boy's only chance.

DYSART: Why? What's he done? Dosed some little girl's Pepsi with Spanish Fly? What could possibly throw your bench into two-hour convulsions?

HESTHER: He blinded six horses with a metal spike.

[*A long pause.*]

DYSART: Blinded?

HESTHER: Yes.

DYSART: All at once, or over a period?

HESTHER: All on the same night.

DYSART: Where?

HESTHER: In a riding stable near Winchester. He worked there at week-ends.

DYSART: How old?

HESTHER: Seventeen.

DYSART: What did he say in Court?

HESTHER: Nothing. He just sang.

DYSART: Sang?

HESTHER: Any time anyone asked him anything.

[*Pause.*]

Please take him, Martin. It's the last favour I'll ever ask you.

DYSART: No, it's not.

HESTHER: No, it's not – and he's probably abominable. All I know is, he needs you badly. Because there really is nobody within a hundred miles of your desk who can handle him. And perhaps understand what this is about. Also ...

DYSART: What?

HESTHER: There's something very special about him.

DYSART: In what way?

HESTHER: Vibrations.

DYSART: You and your vibrations.

HESTHER: They're quite startling. You'll see.

DYSART: When does he get here?

HESTHER: Tomorrow morning. Luckily there was a bed in Neville

Ward. I know this is an awful imposition, Martin. Frankly I didn't
know what else to do.

[*Pause.*]

DYSART: Can you come in and see me on Friday?

HESTHER: Bless you!

DYSART: If you come after work I can give you a drink. Will six
thirty be all right?

HESTHER: You're a dear. You really are.

DYSART: Famous for it.

HESTHER: Goodbye.

DYSART: By the way, what's his name?

HESTHER: Alan Strang.

[*She leaves and returns to her seat.*]

DYSART [*to audience*]: What did I expect of him? Very little, I promise
you. One more dented little face. One more adolescent freak. The
usual unusual. One great thing about being in the adjustment
business: you're never short of customers.

[NURSE *comes down the tunnel, followed by* ALAN. *She enters the
square.*]

NURSE: Alan Strang, Doctor.

[*The boy comes in.*]

DYSART: Hallo. My name's Martin Dysart. I'm pleased to meet
you.

[*He puts out his hand. Alan does not respond in any way.*]

That'll be all, Nurse, thank you.

3

[NURSE *goes out and back to her place.*

DYSART *sits, opening a file.*]

So: did you have a good journey? I hope they gave you lunch at
least. Not that there's much to choose between a British Rail meal
and one here.

[ALAN *stands staring at him.*]

DYSART: Won't you sit down?

[*Pause. He does not.* DYSART *consults his file.*]

Is this your full name? Alan Strang?

[*Silence.*]

And you're seventeen. Is that right? Seventeen? . . . Well?

ALAN [*singing low*]: Double your pleasure,

Double your fun

With Doublemint, Doublemint

Doublemint gum.

DYSART [*unperturbed*]: Now, let's see. You work in an electrical shop
during the week. You live with your parents, and your father's a
printer. What sort of things does he print?

ALAN [*singing louder*]: Double your pleasure

Double your fun

With Doublemint, Doublemint

Doublemint gum.

DYSART: I mean does he do leaflets and calendars? Things like
that?

[*The boy approaches him, hostile.*]

ALAN [*singing*]: Try the taste of Martini

The most beautiful drink in the world.

It's the right one –

The bright one –

That's Martini!

DYSART: I wish you'd sit down, if you're going to sing. Don't you
think you'd be more comfortable?

[*Pause.*]

ALAN [*singing*]: There's only one 'T' in Typhoo!

In packets and in teabags too.

Any way you make it, you'll find it's true:

There's only one 'T' in Typhoo!

DYSART [*appreciatively*]: Now that's a good song. I like it better than
the other two. Can I hear that one again?

[ALAN *starts away from him, and sits on the upstage bench.*]

ALAN [*singing*]: Double your pleasure
Double your fun
With Doublemint, Doublemint
Doublemint gum.

DYSART [*smiling*]: You know I was wrong. I really do think that one's better. It's got such a catchy tune. Please do that one again.

[*Silence. The boy glares at him.*]

I'm going to put you in a private bedroom for a little while. There are one or two available, and they're rather more pleasant than being in a ward. Will you please come and see me tomorrow? . . . [*He rises.*] By the way, which parent is it who won't allow you to watch television? Mother or father? Or is it both? [*Calling out of the door.*] Nurse!

[ALAN *stares at him.* NURSE *comes in.*]

NURSE: Yes, Doctor?

DYSART: Take Strang here to Number Three, will you? He's moving in there for a while.

NURSE: Very good, Doctor.

DYSART [*to* ALAN]: You'll like that room. It's nice.

[*The boy sits staring at* DYSART.

DYSART *returns the stare.*]

NURSE: Come along, young man. This way . . . I said this way, please.

[*Reluctantly* ALAN *rises and goes to* NURSE, *passing dangerously close to* DYSART, *and out through the left door.* DYSART *looks after him, fascinated.*]

4

[NURSE *and patient move on to the circle, and walk downstage to the bench where the doctor first sat, which is to serve also as* ALAN's *bed.*]

NURSE: Well now; isn't this nice? You're lucky to be in here, you know, rather than the ward. That ward's a noisy old place.

ALAN [*singing*]: Let's go where you wanna go – Texaco!

NURSE [*contemplating him*]: I hope you're not going to make a nuisance of yourself. You'll have a much better time of it here, you know, if you behave yourself.

ALAN: Fuck off.

NURSE [*tight*]: That's the bell there. The lav's down the corridor.

[*She leaves him, and goes back to her place.*

ALAN lies down.]

5

[*DYSART stands in the middle of the square and addresses the audience. He is agitated.*]

DYSART: That night, I had this very explicit dream. In it I'm a chief priest in Homeric Greece. I'm wearing a wide gold mask, all noble and bearded, like the so-called Mask of Agamemnon found at Mycenae. I'm standing by a thick round stone and holding a sharp knife. In fact, I'm officiating at some immensely important ritual sacrifice, on which depends the fate of the crops or of a military expedition. The sacrifice is a herd of children: about 500 boys and girls. I can see them stretching away in a long queue, right across the plain of Argos. I know it's Argos because of the red soil. On either side of me stand two assistant priests, wearing masks as well: lumpy, pop-eyed masks, such as also were found at Mycenae. They are enormously strong, these other priests, and absolutely tireless. As each child steps forward, they grab it from behind and throw it over the stone. Then, with a surgical skill which amazes even me, I fit in the knife and slice elegantly down to the navel, just like a seamstress following a pattern. I part the flaps, sever the inner tubes, yank them out and throw them hot and steaming on to the floor. The other two then study the pattern they make, as if they were reading hieroglyphics. It's obvious to me that I'm tops as chief priest. It's this unique talent for carving that has got me where I am. The only thing is, unknown to them, I've started to feel distinctly nauseous. And with each victim, it's getting worse. My face is going green behind the mask. Of course, I redouble my efforts to look professional – cutting and snipping for all I'm worth: mainly because I know that if ever those two assistants so much as glimpse my distress – and the implied doubt that this repetitive and smelly work is doing any social good at all – I will be the next across the stone. And then, of course – the damn mask begins to slip. The priests both turn and look at it – it slips some more – they see the green sweat running down my face – their gold pop-eyes suddenly fill up with blood – they tear the knife out of my hand . . . and I wake up.

6

[HESTHER *enters the square. Light grows warmer.*]

HESTHER: That's the most indulgent thing I ever heard.

DYSART: You think?

HESTHER: Please don't be ridiculous. You've done the most superb work with children. You must know that.

DYSART: Yes, but do the children?

HESTHER: Really!

DYSART: I'm sorry.

HESTHER: So you should be.

DYSART: I don't know why you listen. It's just professional menopause. Everyone gets it sooner or later. Except you.

HESTHER: Oh, of course. I feel totally fit to be a magistrate all the time.

DYSART: No, you don't – but then that's you feeling unworthy to fill a job. I feel the job is unworthy to fill me.

HESTHER: Do you seriously?

DYSART: More and more. I'd like to spend the next ten years wandering very slowly around the *real* Greece . . . Anyway, all this dream nonsense is your fault.

HESTHER: Mine?

DYSART: It's that lad of yours who started it off. Do you know it's his face I saw on every victim across the stone?

HESTHER: Strang?

DYSART: He has the strangest stare I ever met.

HESTHER: Yes.

DYSART: It's exactly like being accused. Violently accused. But what of? . . . Treating him is going to be unsettling. Especially in my present state. His singing was direct enough. His speech is more so.

HESTHER [*surprised*]: He's talking to you, then?

DYSART: Oh yes. It took him two more days of commercials, and then he snapped. Just like that – I suspect it has something to do with his nightmares.

[NURSE *walks briskly round the circle, a blanket over her arm, a clipboard of notes in her hand.*]

HESTHER: He has nightmares?

DYSART: Bad ones.

NURSE: We had to give him a sedative or two, Doctor. Last night it was exactly the same.

DYSART [*to* NURSE]: What does he do? Call out?

NURSE [*to desk*]: A lot of screaming, Doctor.

DYSART [*to* NURSE]: Screaming?

NURSE: One word in particular.

DYSART [*to* NURSE]: You mean a special word?

NURSE: Over and over again. [*Consulting clipboard.*] It sounds like 'Ek'.

HESTHER: Ek?

NURSE: Yes, Doctor. Ek . . . 'Ek!' he goes. 'Ek!'

HESTHER: How weird.

NURSE: When I woke him up he clung to me like he was going to break my arm.

[*She stops at* ALAN's *bed. He is sitting up. She puts the blanket over him, and returns to her place.*]

DYSART: And then he bursts in – just like that – without knocking or anything. Fortunately, I didn't have a patient with me.

ALAN [*jumping up*]: *Dad!*

HESTHER: What?

DYSART: The answer to a question I'd asked him two days before. Spat out with the same anger as he sang the commercials.

HESTHER: Dad what?

ALAN: Who hates telly.

[*He lies downstage on the circle, as if watching television.*]

HESTHER: You mean his dad forbids him to watch?

DYSART: Yes.

ALAN: It's a dangerous drug.

HESTHER: Oh, really!

[FRANK *stands up and enters the scene downstage on the circle. A man in his fifties.*]

FRANK [*to* ALAN]: It may not look like that, but that's what it is. Absolutely fatal mentally, if you receive my meaning.

[DORA *follows him on. She is also middle aged.*]

DORA: That's a little extreme, dear, isn't it?

FRANK: You sit in front of that thing long enough, you'll become stupid for life – like most of the population. [*To* ALAN.] The thing is, it's a *swiz*. It seems to be offering you something, but actually it's taking something away. Your intelligence and your concentration, every minute you watch it. That's a true swiz, do you see?

[*Seated on the floor,* ALAN *shrugs.*]

I don't want to sound like a spoilsport, old chum – but there really is no substitute for reading. What's the matter; don't you like it?

ALAN: It's all right.

FRANK: I know you think it's none of my beeswax, but it really is you know ... Actually, it's a disgrace when you come to think of it. You the son of a printer, and never opening a book! If all the world was like you, I'd be out of a job, if you receive my meaning!

DORA: All the same, times change, Frank.

FRANK [*reasonably*]: They change if you let them change, Dora. Please return that set in the morning.

ALAN [*crying out*]: No!

DORA: Frank! No!

FRANK: I'm sorry, Dora, but I'm not having that thing in the house a moment longer. I told you I didn't want it to begin with.

DORA: But, dear, everyone watches television these days!

FRANK: Yes, and what do they watch? Mindless violence! Mindless jokes! Every five minutes some laughing idiot selling you something you don't want, just to bolster up the economic system. [To ALAN.] I'm sorry, old chum.

[He leaves the scene and sits again in his place.]

HESTHER: He's a Communist, then?

DYSART: Old-type Socialist, I'd say. Relentlessly self-improving.

HESTHER: They're *both* older than you'd expect.

DYSART: So I gather.

DORA [looking after FRANK]: Really, dear, you are very extreme!

[She leaves the scene too, and again sits beside her husband.]

HESTHER: She's an ex-school teacher, isn't she?

DYSART: Yes. The boy's proud of that. We got on to it this afternoon.

ALAN [belligerently, standing up]: She knows more than you.

[HESTHER crosses and sits by DYSART. During the following, the boy walks round the circle, speaking to DYSART but not looking at him. DYSART replies in the same manner.]

DYSART [to ALAN]: Does she?

ALAN: I bet I do too. I bet I know more history than you.

DYSART [to ALAN]: Well, I bet you don't.

ALAN: All right: who was the Hammer of the Scots?

DYSART [to ALAN]: I don't know: who?

ALAN: King Edward the First. Who never smiled again?

DYSART [to ALAN]: I don't know: who?

ALAN: You don't know anything, do you? It was Henry the First. I know all the Kings.

DYSART [to ALAN]: And who's your favourite?

ALAN: John.

DYSART [to ALAN]: Why?

ALAN: Because he put out the eyes of that smarty little –

[Pause.]

[*Sensing he has said something wrong.*] Well, he didn't really. He was prevented, because the gaoler was merciful!

HESTHER: Oh dear.

ALAN: *He was prevented!*

DYSART: Something odder was to follow.

ALAN: Who said 'Religion is the opium of the people'?

HESTHER: Good Lord!

[ALAN *giggles.*]

DYSART: The odd thing was, he said it with a sort of guilty snigger. The sentence is obviously associated with some kind of tension.

HESTHER: What did you say?

DYSART: I gave him the right answer. [*To* ALAN.] Karl Marx.

ALAN: No.

DYSART [*to* ALAN]: Then who?

ALAN: Mind your own beeswax.

DYSART: It's probably his dad. He may say it to provoke his wife.

HESTHER: And you mean she's religious?

DYSART: She could be. I tried to discover – none too successfully.

ALAN: Mind your own beeswax!

[ALAN *goes back to bed and lies down in the dark.*]

DYSART: However, I shall find out on Sunday.

HESTHER: What do you mean?

DYSART [*getting up*]: I want to have a look at his home, so I invited myself over.

HESTHER: Did you?

DYSART: If there's any tension over religion, it should be evident on a Sabbath evening! I'll let you know.

[*He kisses her cheek and they part, both leaving the square.* HESTHER *sits in her place again;* DYSART *walks round the circle, and greets* DORA *who stands waiting for him downstage.*]

DYSART [*shaking hands*]: Mrs Strang.

DORA: Mr Strang's still at the Press, I'm afraid. He should be home in a minute.

DYSART: He works Sundays as well?

DORA: Oh, yes. He doesn't set much store by Sundays.

DYSART: Perhaps you and I could have a little talk before he comes in.

DORA: Certainly. Won't you come into the living-room?

[*She leads the way into the square. She is very nervous.*]

Please . . .

[*She motions him to sit, then holds her hands tightly together.*]

DYSART: Mrs Strang, have you any idea how this thing could have occurred?

DORA: I can't imagine, Doctor. It's all so unbelievable! . . . Alan's always been such a gentle boy. He loves animals! Especially horses.

DYSART: Especially?

DORA: Yes. He even has a photograph of one up in his bedroom. A beautiful white one, looking over a gate. His father gave it to him a few years ago, off a calendar he'd printed – and he's never taken it down . . . And when he was seven or eight, I used to have to read him the same book over and over, all *about* a horse.

DYSART: Really?

DORA: Yes; it was called Prince, and no one could ride him.

[ALAN *calls from his bed, not looking at his mother.*]

ALAN [*excited, younger voice*]: Why not? . . . Why not? . . . Say it! In his voice!

DORA: He loved the idea of animals talking.

DYSART: Did he?

ALAN: *Say it! Say it! . . . Use his voice!*

DORA ['*proud*' *voice*]: 'Because I am faithful!'

[ALAN *giggles.*]

'My name is Prince, and I'm a Prince among horses! Only my young Master can ride me! Anyone else – I'll *throw off!*'

[ALAN *giggles louder.*]

And then I remember I used to tell him a funny thing about falling off horses. Did you know that when Christian cavalry first appeared in the New World, the pagans thought horse and rider was one person?

DYSART: Really?

ALAN [sitting up, amazed]: One person?

DORA: Actually, they thought it must be a god.

ALAN: *A god!*

DORA: It was only when one rider fell off, they realized the truth.

DYSART: That's fascinating. I never heard that before ... Can you remember anything else like that you may have told him about horses?

DORA: Well, not really. They're in the Bible, of course. 'He saith among the trumpets, Ha, ha.'

DYSART: Ha, ha?

DORA: The Book of Job. Such a noble passage. *You* know – [Quoting.] 'Hast thou given the horse strength?'

ALAN [responding]: 'Hast thou clothed his neck with thunder?'

DORA [to ALAN]: 'The glory of his nostrils is terrible!'

ALAN: 'He swallows the ground with fierceness and rage!'

DORA: 'He saith among the trumpets –'

ALAN [trumpeting]: 'Ha! Ha!'

DORA [to DYSART]: Isn't that splendid?

DYSART: It certainly is.

ALAN [trumpeting]: Ha! Ha!

DORA: And then, of course, we saw an awful lot of Westerns on the television. He couldn't have enough of those.

DYSART: But surely you don't have a set, do you? I understood Mr Strang doesn't approve.

DORA [conspiratorially]: He doesn't ... I used to let him slip off in the afternoons to a friend next door.

DYSART [smiling]: You mean without his father's knowledge?

DORA: What the eye does not see, the heart does not grieve over, does it? Anyway, Westerns are harmless enough, surely?

[FRANK *stands up and enters the square.*

ALAN *lies back under the blanket.*]

[*To* FRANK.] Oh, hallo dear. This is Dr Dysart.

FRANK [*shaking hands*]: How d'you do?

DYSART: How d'you do?

DORA: I was just telling the Doctor, Alan's always adored horses.

FRANK [*tight*]: We assumed he did.

DORA: You know he did, dear. Look how he liked that photograph you gave him.

FRANK [*startled*]: What about it?

DORA: Nothing dear. Just that he pestered you to have it as soon as he saw it. Do you remember? [*To* DYSART.] We've always been a horsey family. At least my side of it has. My grandfather used to ride every morning on the downs behind Brighton, all dressed up in bowler hat and jodhpurs! He used to look splendid. Indulging in equitation, he called it.

[FRANK *moves away from them and sits wearily.*]

ALAN [*trying the word*]: Equitation ...

DORA: I remember I told him how that came from *equus*, the Latin word for horse. Alan was fascinated by that word, I know. I suppose because he'd never come across one with two 'u's together before.

ALAN [*savouring it*]: *Equus!*

DORA: I always wanted the boy to ride himself. He'd have so enjoyed it.

DYSART: But surely he did?

DORA: No.

DYSART: Never?

DORA: He didn't care for it. He was most definite about not wanting to.

DYSART: But he must have had to at the stables? I mean, it would be part of the job.

DORA: You'd have thought so, but no. He absolutely wouldn't, would he, dear?

FRANK [*dryly*]: It seems he was perfectly happy raking out manure.

DYSART: Did he ever give a reason for this?

DORA: No. I must say we both thought it most peculiar, but he wouldn't discuss it. I mean, you'd have thought he'd be longing to get out in the air after being cooped up all week in that dreadful shop. Electrical and kitchenware! Isn't *that* an environment for a sensitive boy, Doctor? . . .

FRANK: Dear, have you offered the doctor a cup of tea?

DORA: Oh dear, no, I haven't! . . . And you must be dying for one.

DYSART: That would be nice.

DORA: Of course it would . . . Excuse me . . .

[*She goes out – but lingers on the circle, eavesdropping near the right door.* ALAN *stretches out under his blanket and sleeps.* FRANK *gets up.*]

FRANK: My wife has romantic ideas, if you receive my meaning.

DYSART: About her family?

FRANK: She thinks she married beneath her. I daresay she did. I don't understand these things myself.

DYSART: Mr Strang, I'm fascinated by the fact that Alan wouldn't ride.

FRANK: Yes, well that's him. He's always been a weird lad, I have to be honest. Can you imagine spending your week-ends like that – just cleaning out stalls – with all the things that he could have been doing in the way of Further Education?

DYSART: Except he's hardly a scholar.

FRANK: How do we know? He's never really tried. His mother indulged him. She doesn't care if he can hardly write his own name, and she a school teacher that was. Just as long as he's happy, she says . . .

[DORA *wrings her hands in anguish.*

FRANK *sits again.*]

DYSART: Would you say she was closer to him than you are?

FRANK: They've always been thick as thieves. I can't say I entirely approve – especially when I hear her whispering that Bible to him hour after hour, up there in his room.

DYSART: Your wife is religious?

FRANK: Some might say excessively so. Mind you, that's her business.

But when it comes to dosing it down the boy's throat – well, frankly, he's my son as well as hers. She doesn't see that. Of course, that's the funny thing about religious people. They always think their susceptibilities are more important than non-religious.

DYSART: And you're non-religious, I take it?

FRANK: I'm an atheist, and I don't mind admitting it. If you want my opinion, it's the Bible that's responsible for all this.

DYSART: Why?

FRANK: Well, look at it yourself. A boy spends night after night having this stuff read into him; an innocent man tortured to death – thorns driven into his head – nails into his hands – a spear jammed through his ribs. It can mark anyone for life, that kind of thing. I'm not joking. The boy was absolutely fascinated by all that. He was always mooning over religious pictures. I mean real kinky ones, if you receive my meaning. I had to put a stop to it once or twice! . . . [*Pause.*] Bloody religion – it's our only real problem in this house, but it's insuperable; I don't mind admitting it.

[*Unable to stand any more,* DORA *comes in again.*]

DORA [*pleasantly*]: You must excuse my husband, Doctor. This one subject is something of an obsession with him, isn't it, dear? You must admit.

FRANK: Call it what you like. All that stuff to me is just bad sex.

DORA: And what has that got to do with Alan?

FRANK: Everything! . . . [*Seriously.*] Everything, Dora!

DORA: I don't understand. What are you saying?

[*He turns away from her.*]

DYSART [*calmingly*]: Mr Strang, exactly how informed do you judge your son to *be* about sex?

FRANK [*tight*]: I don't know.

DYSART: You didn't actually instruct him yourself?

FRANK: Not in so many words, no.

DYSART: Did *you*, Mrs Strang?

DORA: Well, I spoke a little, yes. I had to. I've been a teacher, Doctor, and I know what happens if you don't. They find out through magazines and dirty books.

DYSART: What sort of thing did you tell him? I'm sorry if this is embarrassing.

DORA: I told him the biological facts. But I also told him what I believed. That sex is not *just* a biological matter, but spiritual as well. That if God willed, he would fall in love one day. That his task was to prepare himself for the most important happening of his life. And after that, if he was lucky, he might come to know a higher love still . . . I simply . . . don't understand . . . *Alan!* . . .

[*She breaks down in sobs.*

Her husband gets up and goes to her.]

FRANK [*embarrassed*]: There now. There now, Dora. Come on!

DORA [*with sudden desperation*]: All right – laugh! Laugh, as usual!

FRANK [*kindly*]: No one's laughing, Dora.

[*She glares at him. He puts his arms round her shoulders.*]

No one's laughing, are they Doctor?

[*Tenderly, he leads his wife out of the square, and they resume their places on the bench.*

Lights grow much dimmer.]

8

[*A strange noise begins.* ALAN *begins to murmur from his bed. He is having a bad nightmare, moving his hands and body as if frantically straining to tug something back.*

DYSART *leaves the square as the boy's cries increase.*]

ALAN: Ek! . . . Ek! . . . Ek! . . .

[*Cries of* Ek! *on tape fill the theatre, from all around.*

DYSART *reaches the foot of* ALAN's *bed as the boy gives a terrible cry –*

EK!

– and wakes up. The sounds snap off. ALAN *and the Doctor stare at each other. Then abruptly* DYSART *leaves the area and re-enters the square.*]

[*Lights grow brighter.*

DYSART sits on his bench, left, and opens his file. ALAN gets out of bed, leaves his blanket, and comes in. He looks truculent.]

DYSART: Hallo. How are you this morning?

[*ALAN stares at him.*]

Come on: sit down.

[*ALAN crosses the stage and sits on the bench, opposite.*]

Sorry if I gave you a start last night. I was collecting some papers from my office, and I thought I'd look in on you. Do you dream often?

ALAN: Do *you*?

DYSART: It's my job to ask the questions. Yours to answer them.

ALAN: Says who?

DYSART: Says me. Do you dream often?

ALAN: Do you?

DYSART: Look – Alan.

ALAN: I'll answer if you answer. In turns.

[*Pause.*]

DYSART: Very well. Only we have to speak the truth.

ALAN [*mocking*]: Very well.

DYSART: So. Do you dream often?

ALAN: Yes. Do you?

DYSART: Yes. Do you have a special dream?

ALAN: No. Do you?

DYSART: Yes. What was your dream about last night?

ALAN: Can't remember. What's yours about?

DYSART: I said the truth.

ALAN: That is the truth. What's yours about? The special one.

DYSART: Carving up children.

[*ALAN smiles.*]

My turn!

ALAN: What?

DYSART: What is your first memory of a horse?

ALAN: What d'you mean?

DYSART: The first time one entered your life, in any way.

ALAN: Can't remember.

DYSART: Are you sure?

ALAN: Yes.

DYSART: You have no recollection of the first time you noticed a horse?

ALAN: I told you. Now it's my turn. Are you married?

DYSART [controlling himself]: I am.

ALAN: Is she a doctor too?

DYSART: It's my turn.

ALAN: Yes, well what?

DYSART: What is Ek?

[Pause.]

You shouted it out last night in your sleep. I thought you might like to talk about it.

ALAN [singing]: Double Diamond works wonders,

Works wonders, works wonders!

DYSART: Come on, now. You can do better than that.

ALAN [singing louder]: Double Diamond works wonders,

Works wonders

For you!

DYSART: All right. Good morning.

ALAN: What d'you mean?

DYSART: We're finished for today.

ALAN: But I've only had ten minutes.

DYSART: Too bad.

[He picks up a file and studies it.

ALAN lingers.]

Didn't you hear me? I said, Good morning.

ALAN: That's not fair!

DYSART: No?

ALAN [savagely]: The Government pays you twenty quid an hour to see me. I know. I heard downstairs.

DYSART: Well, go back there and hear some more.

ALAN: *That's not fair!*

[*He springs up, clenching his fists in a sudden violent rage.*]

You're a – you're a – You're a swiz! . . . Bloody swiz! . . . Fucking swiz!

DYSART: Do I have to call Nurse?

ALAN: She puts a finger on me, I'll bash her!

DYSART: She'll bash you much harder, I can assure you. Now go away.

[*He reads his file.* ALAN *stays where he is, emptily clenching his hands. He turns away.*

A pause.

A faint hum starts from the CHORUS.]

ALAN [*sullenly*]: On a beach . . .

10

[*He steps out of the square, upstage, and begins to walk round the circle. Warm light glows on it.*]

DYSART: What?

ALAN: Where I saw a horse. Swizzy.

[*Lazily he kicks at the sand, and throws stones at the sea.*]

DYSART: How old were you?

ALAN: How should I know? . . . Six.

DYSART: Well, go on. What were you doing there?

ALAN: Digging.

[*He throws himself on the ground, downstage centre of the circle, and starts scuffing with his hands.*]

DYSART: A sandcastle?

ALAN: Well, what else?

DYSART [*warningly*]: And?

ALAN: Suddenly I heard this noise. Coming up behind me.

[*A young* HORSEMAN *issues in slow motion out of the tunnel. He*

*carries a riding crop with which he is urging on his invisible horse,
down the right side of the circle.*

The hum increases.]

DYSART: What noise?

ALAN: Hooves. Splashing.

DYSART: Splashing?

ALAN: The tide was out and he was galloping.

DYSART: Who was?

ALAN: This fellow. Like a college chap. He was on a big horse –
urging him on. I thought he hadn't seen me. I called out: Hey!

[*The* HORSEMAN *goes into* natural time, *charging fast round the
downstage corner of the square straight at* ALAN.]

and they just swerved in time!

HORSEMAN [*reining back*]: Whoa! ... Whoa there! *Whoa!* ...
Sorry! I didn't see you! ... Did I scare you?

ALAN: No!

HORSEMAN [*looking down on him*]: That's a terrific castle!

ALAN: What's his name?

HORSEMAN: Trojan. You can stroke him, if you like. He won't
mind.

[*Shyly* ALAN *stretches up on tip-toe, and pats an invisible shoulder.*]
[*Amused.*] You can hardly reach down there. Would you like to
come up?

[ALAN *nods, eyes wide.*]

All right. Come round this side. You always mount a horse from
the left. I'll give you a lift. O.K.?

[ALAN *goes round on the other side.*]

Here we go, now. Just do nothing. Upsadaisy!

[ALAN *sets his foot on the* HORSEMAN's *thigh, and is lifted by him up
on to his shoulders.*

The hum from the CHORUS *becomes exultant. Then stops.*]

All right?

[ALAN *nods.*]

Good. Now all you do is hold onto his mane.

[*He holds up the crop, and* ALAN *grips on to it.*]

Tight now. And grip with your knees. All right?
All set? . . . Come on, then, Trojan. Let's go!

[*The* HORSEMAN *walks slowly upstage round the circle, with* ALAN's *legs tight round his neck.*]

DYSART: How was it? Was it wonderful?

[ALAN *rides in silence.*]

Can't you remember?

HORSEMAN: Do you want to go faster?

ALAN: Yes!

HORSEMAN: O.K. All you have to do is say 'Come on, Trojan – bear me away!' . . . Say it, then!

ALAN: Bear me away!

[*The* HORSEMAN *starts to run with* ALAN *round the circle.*]

DYSART: You went fast?

ALAN: Yes!

DYSART: Weren't you frightened?

ALAN: No!

HORSEMAN: Come on now, Trojan! Bear us away! Hold on! Come on now! . . .

[*He runs faster.* ALAN *begins to laugh. Then suddenly, as they reach again the right downstage corner,* FRANK *and* DORA *stand up in alarm.*]

DORA: Alan!

FRANK: Alan!

DORA: Alan, stop!

[FRANK *runs round after them.* DORA *follows behind.*]

FRANK: Hey, you! You! . . .

HORSEMAN: Whoa, boy! . . . Whoa! . . .

[*He reins the horse round, and wheels to face the parents. This all goes fast.*]

FRANK: What do you imagine you are doing?

HORSEMAN [*ironic*]: 'Imagine?'

FRANK: What is my son doing up there?

HORSEMAN: Water-skiing!

[DORA *joins them, breathless.*]

DORA: Is he all right, Frank? . . . He's not hurt?

FRANK: Don't you think you should ask permission before doing a stupid thing like that?

HORSEMAN: What's stupid?

ALAN: It's lovely, dad!

DORA: Alan, come down here!

HORSEMAN: The boy's perfectly safe. Please don't be hysterical.

FRANK: Don't you be la-di-da with me, young man! Come down here, Alan. You heard what your mother said.

ALAN: No.

FRANK: Come down at once. Right this moment.

ALAN: No . . . NO!

FRANK [in a fury]: I said – this moment!

[He pulls ALAN from the horseman's shoulders. The boy shrieks, and falls to the ground.]

HORSEMAN: Watch it!

DORA: Frank!

[She runs to her son, and kneels. The HORSEMAN skitters.]

HORSEMAN: Are you mad? D'you want to terrify the horse?

DORA: He's grazed his knee. Frank – the boy's hurt!

ALAN: I'm not! I'm not!

FRANK: What's your name?

HORSEMAN: Jesse James.

DORA: Frank, he's bleeding!

FRANK: I intend to report you to the police for endangering the lives of children.

HORSEMAN: Go right ahead!

DORA: Can you stand, dear?

ALAN: Oh, stop it! . . .

FRANK: You're a public menace, d'you know that? How dare you pick up children and put them on dangerous animals.

HORSEMAN: Dangerous?

FRANK: Of course dangerous. Look at his eyes. They're rolling.

HORSEMAN: So are yours!

FRANK: In my opinion that is a dangerous animal. In my considered opinion you are both dangers to the safety of this beach.

HORSEMAN: And in my opinion, you're a stupid fart!

DORA: Frank, leave it!

FRANK: What did you say?

DORA: It's not important, Frank – really!

FRANK: *What did you say?*

HORSEMAN: Oh bugger off! Sorry, chum! Come on, Trojan!

[*He urges his horse straight at them, then wheels it and gallops off round the right side of the circle and away up the tunnel, out of sight. The parents cry out, as they are covered with sand and water.* FRANK *runs after him, and round the left side of the circle, with his wife following after.*]

ALAN: Splash, splash, splash! All three of us got covered with water! Dad got absolutely soaked!

FRANK [*shouting after the* HORSEMAN]: Hooligan! Filthy hooligan!

ALAN: I wanted to laugh!

FRANK: Upper-class riff-raff! That's all they are, people who go riding! That's what they *want* – trample on ordinary people!

DORA: Don't be absurd, Frank.

FRANK: It's why they do it. It's why they bloody do it!

DORA [*amused*]: Look at you. You're covered!

FRANK: Not as much as you. There's sand all over your hair!

[*She starts to laugh.*]

[*Shouting.*] Hooligan! Bloody hooligan!

[*She starts to laugh more. He tries to brush the sand out of her hair.*]

What are you laughing at? It's not funny. It's not funny at all, Dora!

[*She goes off, right, still laughing.* ALAN *edges into the square, still on the ground.*]

It's just not funny! . . .

[FRANK *returns to his place on the beach, sulky. Abrupt silence.*]

ALAN: And that's all I remember.

DYSART: And a lot, too. Thank you . . . You know, I've never been on a horse in my life.

ALAN [*not looking at him*]: Nor me.

DYSART: You mean, after that?

ALAN: Yes.

DYSART: But you must have done at the stables?

ALAN: No.

DYSART: Never?

ALAN: No.

DYSART: How come?

ALAN: I didn't care to.

DYSART: Did it have anything to do with falling off like that, all those years ago?

ALAN [*tight*]: I just didn't care to, that's all.

DYSART: Do you think of that scene often?

ALAN: I suppose.

DYSART: Why, do you think?

ALAN: 'Cos it's funny.

DYSART: Is that all?

ALAN: What else? My turn . . . I told you a secret; now you tell me one.

DYSART: All right. I have patients who've got things to tell me, only they're ashamed to say them to my face. What do you think I do about that?

ALAN: What?

DYSART: I give them this little tape recorder.

[*He takes a small tape recorder and microphone from his pocket.*]

They go off to another room, and send me the tape through Nurse. They don't have to listen to it with me.

ALAN: That's stupid.

DYSART: All you do is press this button, and speak into this. It's very simple. Anyway, your time's up for today. I'll see you tomorrow.

ALAN [*getting up*]: Maybe.

DYSART: Maybe?

ALAN: If I feel like it.

[*He is about to go out. Then suddenly he returns to* DYSART *and takes the machine from him.*]

It's stupid.

[*He leaves the square and goes back to his bed.*]

II

DORA [*calling out*]: Doctor!

[*DORA re-enters and comes straight on to the square from the right. She wears an overcoat, and is nervously carrying a shopping bag.*]

DYSART: That same evening, his mother appeared.

DORA: Hallo, Doctor.

DYSART: Mrs Strang!

DORA: I've been shopping in the neighbourhood. I thought I might just look in.

DYSART: Did you want to see Alan?

DORA [*uncomfortably*]: No, no . . . Not just at the moment. Actually, it's more you I wanted to see.

DYSART: Yes?

DORA: You see, there's something Mr Strang and I thought you ought to know. We discussed it, and it might just be important.

DYSART: Well, come and sit down.

DORA: I can't stay more than a moment. I'm late as it is. Mr Strang will be wanting his dinner.

DYSART: Ah. [*Encouragingly.*] So, what was it you wanted to tell me?

[*She sits on the upstage bench.*]

DORA: Well, do you remember that photograph I mentioned to you. The one Mr Strang gave Alan to decorate his bedroom a few years ago?

DYSART: Yes. A horse looking over a gate, wasn't it?

DORA: That's right. Well, actually, it took the place of another kind of picture altogether.

DYSART: What kind?

DORA: It was a reproduction of Our Lord on his way to Calvary. Alan found it in Reeds Art Shop, and fell absolutely in love with it. He insisted on buying it with his pocket money, and hanging it at the foot of his bed where he could see it last thing at night. My husband was very displeased.

DYSART: Because it was religious?

DORA: In all fairness I must admit it was a little extreme. The Christ was loaded down with chains, and the centurions were really laying on the stripes. It certainly would not have been my choice, but I don't believe in interfering too much with children, so I said nothing.

DYSART: But Mr Strang did?

DORA: He stood it for a while, but one day we had one of our tiffs about religion, and he went upstairs, tore it off the boy's wall and threw it in the dustbin. Alan went quite hysterical. He cried for days without stopping – and he was not a crier, you know.

DYSART: But he recovered when he was given the photograph of the horse in its place?

DORA: He certainly seemed to. At least, he hung it in exactly the same position, and we had no more of that awful weeping.

DYSART: Thank you, Mrs Strang. That *is* interesting ... Exactly how long ago was that? Can you remember?

DORA: It must be five years ago, Doctor. Alan would have been about twelve. How is he, by the way?

DYSART: Bearing up.

[*She rises.*]

DORA: Please give him my love.

DYSART: You can see him any time you want, you know.

DORA: Perhaps if I could come one afternoon without Mr Strang. He and Alan don't exactly get on at the moment, as you can imagine.

DYSART. Whatever you decide, Mrs Strang ... Oh, one thing.

DORA: Yes?

DYSART: Could you describe that photograph of the horse in a little more detail for me? I presume it's still in his bedroom?

DORA: Oh, yes. It's a most remarkable picture, really. You very rarely see a horse taken from that angle – absolutely head on. That's what makes it so interesting.

DYSART: Why? What does it look like?

DORA: Well, it's most extraordinary. It comes out all eyes.

DYSART: Staring straight at you?

DORA: Yes, that's right . . .

[*An uncomfortable pause.*]

I'll come and see him one day very soon, Doctor. Goodbye.

[*She leaves, and resumes her place by her husband.*]

DYSART [*to audience*]: It was then – that moment – I felt real alarm. What was it? The shadow of a giant head across my desk? . . . At any rate, the feeling got worse with the stable-owner's visit.

12

[DALTON *comes in to the square: heavy-set, mid-fifties.*]

DALTON: Dr Dysart?

DYSART: Mr Dalton. It's very good of you to come.

DALTON: It is, actually. In my opinion the boy should be in prison. Not in a hospital at the tax-payers' expense.

DYSART: Please sit down.

[DALTON *sits.*]

This must have been a terrible experience for you.

DALTON: Terrible? I don't think I'll ever get over it. Jill's had a nervous breakdown.

DYSART: Jill?

DALTON: The girl who worked for me. Of course, she feels responsible in a way. Being the one who introduced him in the first place.

DYSART: He was introduced to the stable by a girl?

DALTON: Jill Mason. He met her somewhere, and asked for a job. She told him to come and see me. I wish to Christ she never had.

DYSART: But when he first appeared he didn't seem in any way peculiar?

DALTON: No, he was bloody good. He'd spend hours with the horses cleaning and grooming them, way over the call of duty. I thought he was a real find.

DYSART: Apparently, during the whole time he worked for you, he never actually rode.

DALTON: That's true.

DYSART: Wasn't that peculiar?

DALTON: Very . . . *If* he didn't.

DYSART: What do you mean?

[DALTON *rises.*]

DALTON: Because on and off, that whole year, I had the feeling the horses were being taken out at night.

DYSART: At night?

DALTON: There were just odd things I noticed. I mean too often one or other of them would be sweaty first thing in the morning, when it wasn't sick. Very sweaty, too. And its stall wouldn't be near as mucky as it should be if it had been in all night. I never paid it much mind at the time. It was only when I realized I'd been hiring a loony, I came to wonder if he hadn't been riding all the time, behind our backs.

DYSART: But wouldn't you have noticed if things had been disturbed?

DALTON: Nothing ever was. Still, he's a neat worker. That wouldn't prove anything.

DYSART: Aren't the stables locked at night?

DALTON: Yes.

DYSART: And someone sleeps on the premises?

DALTON: Me and my son.

DYSART: Two people?

DALTON: I'm sorry, Doctor. It's obviously just my fancy. I tell you, this thing has shaken me so bad, I'm liable to believe anything. If there's nothing else, I'll be going.

DYSART: Look: even if you were right, why should anyone do that? Why would any boy prefer to ride by himself at night, when he could go off with others during the day?

DALTON: Are you asking me? He's a loony, isn't he?

[DALTON *leaves the square and sits again in his place.* DYSART *watches him go.*]

ALAN: It was *sexy*.

DYSART: His tape arrived that evening.

[ALAN *is sitting on his bed holding the tape recorder.* NURSE *approaches briskly, takes the machine from him – gives it to* DYSART *in the square – and leaves again, resuming her seat.* DYSART *switches on the tape.*]

ALAN: That's what you want to know, isn't it? All right: it was. I'm talking about the beach. That time when I was a kid. What I told you about . . .

[*Pause. He is in great emotional difficulty.*

DYSART *sits on the left bench listening, file in hand.* ALAN *rises and stands directly behind him, but on the circle, as if recording the ensuing speech. He never, of course, looks directly at the Doctor.*]

I was pushed forward on the horse. There was sweat on my legs from his neck. The fellow held me tight, and let me turn the horse which way I wanted. All that power going any way you wanted . . . His sides were all warm, and the smell . . . Then suddenly I was on the ground, where Dad pulled me. I could have bashed him . . .

[*Pause.*]

Something else. When the horse first appeared, I looked up into his mouth. It was huge. There was this chain in it. The fellow pulled it, and cream dripped out. I said 'Does it hurt?' And he said – the horse said – said –

[*He stops, in anguish.* DYSART *makes a note in his file.*]

[*Desperately.*] It was always the same, after that. Every time I heard one clop by, I had to run and see. Up a country lane or anywhere. They sort of pulled me. I couldn't take my eyes off them. Just to watch their skins. The way their necks twist, and sweat shines in the folds . . . [*Pause.*] I can't remember when it started. Mum reading to me about Prince who no one could ride, except one boy. Or the white horse in Revelations. 'He that sat upon him was called Faithful and True. His eyes were as flames of fire, and he had a name written that no man knew but himself' . . . Words like reins Stirrup. Flanks . . . 'Dashing his spurs against his charger's flanks!'

... Even the words made me feel – Years, I never told anyone. Mum wouldn't understand. She likes 'Equitation'. Bowler hats and jodhpurs! 'My grandfather dressed for the horse,' she says. What does that mean? The horse isn't dressed. It's the most naked thing you ever saw! More than a dog or a cat or anything. Even the most broken down old nag has got its *life*! To put a bowler on it is *filthy*! ... Putting them through their paces! Bloody gymkhanas! ... No one understands! ... Except cowboys. They do. I wish I was a cowboy. They're free. They just swing up and then it's miles of grass ... I bet all cowboys are *orphans*! ... I bet they are!

NURSE: Mr Strang to see you, Doctor.

DYSART [*in surprise*]: Mr Strang? Show him up, please.

ALAN: No one ever says to cowboys 'Receive my meaning'! They wouldn't dare. Or 'God' all the time. [*Mimicking his mother.*] 'God sees you, Alan. God's got eyes everywhere –'

[*He stops abruptly.*]

I'm not doing any more! ... I hate this! ... You can whistle for any more. I've had it!

[*He returns angrily to his bed, throwing the blanket over him.*

DYSART *switches off the tape.*]

14

[FRANK STRANG *comes into the square, his hat in his hand. He is nervous and embarrassed.*]

DYSART [*welcoming*]: Hallo, Mr Strang.

FRANK: I was just passing. I hope it's not too late.

DYSART: Of course not. I'm delighted to see you.

FRANK: My wife doesn't know I'm here. I'd be grateful to you if you didn't enlighten her, if you receive my meaning.

DYSART: Everything that happens in this room is confidential, Mr Strang.

FRANK: I hope so ... I hope so ...

DYSART [*gently*]: Do you have something to tell me?

FRANK: As a matter of fact I have. Yes.

DYSART: Your wife told me about the photograph.

FRANK: I know, it's not that! It's *about* that, but it's – worse ... I wanted to tell you the other night, but I couldn't in front of Dora. Maybe I should have. It might show her where all that stuff leads to, she drills into the boy behind my back.

DYSART: What kind of thing is it?

FRANK: Something I witnessed.

DYSART: Where?

FRANK: At home. About eighteen months ago.

DYSART: Go on.

FRANK: It was late. I'd gone upstairs to fetch something. The boy had been in bed hours, or so I thought.

DYSART: Go on.

FRANK: As I came along the passage I saw the door of his bedroom was ajar. I'm sure he didn't know it was. From inside I heard the sound of this chanting.

DYSART: Chanting?

FRANK: Like the Bible. One of those lists his mother's always reading to him.

DYSART: What kind of list?

FRANK: Those Begats. So-and-so begat, you know. Genealogy.

DYSART: Can you remember what Alan's list sounded like?

FRANK: Well, the *sort* of thing. I stood there absolutely astonished. The first word I heard was ...

ALAN [*rising and chanting*]: Prince!

DYSART: Prince?

FRANK: Prince begat Prince. That sort of nonsense.

[ALAN *moves slowly to the centre of the circle, downstage.*]

ALAN: And Prance begat Prankus! And Prankus begat Flankus!

FRANK: I looked through the door, and he was standing in the moon-light in his pyjamas, right in front of that big photograph.

DYSART: The horse with the huge eyes?

FRANK: Right.

ALAN: Flankus begat Spankus. And Spankus begat Spunkus the Great, who lived three score years!

FRANK: It was all like that. I can't remember the exact names, of course. Then suddenly he knelt down.

DYSART: In front of the photograph?

FRANK: Yes. Right there at the foot of his bed.

ALAN [*kneeling*]: And Legwus begat Neckwus. And Neckwus begat Fleckwus, the King of Spit. And Fleckwus spoke out of his chinkle-chankle!

[*He bows himself to the ground.*]

DYSART: What?

FRANK: I'm sure that was the word. I've never forgotten it. Chinkle-chankle.

[ALAN *raises his head and extends his hands up in glory.*]

ALAN: And he said 'Behold – I give you Equus, my only begotten son!'

DYSART: Equus?

FRANK: Yes. No doubt of that. He repeated that word several times. 'Equus my only begotten son.'

ALAN [*reverently*]: Ek . . . wus!

DYSART [*suddenly understanding: almost 'aside'*]: Ek . . . Ek . . .

FRANK [*embarrassed*]: And then . . .

DYSART: Yes: what?

FRANK: He took a piece of string out of his pocket. Made up into a noose. And put it in his mouth.

[ALAN *bridles himself with invisible string, and pulls it back.*]
And then with his other hand he picked up a coat hanger. A wooden coat hanger, and – and –

DYSART: Began to beat himself?

[ALAN, *in mime, begins to thrash himself, increasing the strokes in speed and viciousness.*
Pause.]

FRANK: You see why I couldn't tell his mother . . . Religion. Religion's at the bottom of all this!

DYSART: What did you do?

243

FRANK: Nothing. I coughed – and went back downstairs.
  [*The boy starts guiltily – tears the string from his mouth – and scrambles back to bed.*]
DYSART: Did you ever speak to him about it later? Even obliquely?
FRANK [*unhappily*]: I can't speak of things like that, Doctor. It's not in my nature.
DYSART [*kindly*]: No. I see that.
FRANK: But I thought you ought to know. So I came.
DYSART [*warmly*]: Yes. I'm very grateful to you. Thank you.
  [*Pause.*]
FRANK: Well, that's it . . .
DYSART: Is there anything else?
FRANK [*even more embarrassed*]: There is actually. One thing.
DYSART: What's that?
FRANK: On the night that he did it – that awful thing in the stable –
DYSART: Yes?
FRANK: That very night, he was out with a girl.
DYSART: How d'you know that?
FRANK: I just know.
DYSART [*puzzled*]: Did he tell you?
FRANK: I can't say any more.
DYSART: I don't quite understand.
FRANK: Everything said in here is confidential, you said.
DYSART: Absolutely.
FRANK: Then ask him. Ask him about taking a girl out, that very night he did it . . . [*Abruptly.*] Goodbye, Doctor.
  [*He goes.* DYSART *looks after him.*
  FRANK *resumes his seat.*]

15

[ALAN *gets up and enters the square.*]
DYSART: Alan! Come in. Sit down. [*Pleasantly.*] What did you do last night?

ALAN: Watched telly.

DYSART: Any good?

ALAN: All right.

DYSART: Thanks for the tape. It was excellent.

ALAN: I'm not making any more.

DYSART: One thing I didn't quite understand. You began to say something about the horse on the beach talking to you.

ALAN: That's stupid. Horses don't talk.

DYSART: So I believe.

ALAN: I don't know what you mean.

DYSART: Never mind. Tell me something else. Who introduced you to the stable to begin with?

[*Pause.*]

ALAN: Someone I met.

DYSART: Where?

ALAN: Bryson's.

DYSART: The shop where you worked?

ALAN: Yes.

DYSART: That's a funny place for you to be. Whose idea was that?

ALAN: Dad.

DYSART: I'd have thought he'd have wanted you to work with him.

ALAN: I haven't the aptitude. And printing's a failing trade. If you receive my meaning.

DYSART [*amused*]: I see . . . What did your mother think?

ALAN: Shops are common.

DYSART: And you?

ALAN: I loved it.

DYSART: Really?

ALAN [*sarcastic*]: Why not? You get to spend every minute with electrical things. It's fun.

[NURSE, DALTON *and the actors playing horses call out to him as* CUSTOMERS, *seated where they are. Their voices are aggressive and demanding. There is a constant background mumbling, made up of trade names, out of which can clearly be distinguished the italicized words, which are shouted out.*]

CUSTOMER: *Philco!*

ALAN [*to* DYSART]: Of course it might just drive you off your chump.

CUSTOMER: I want to buy a hot-plate. I'm told the *Philco* is a good make!

ALAN: I think it is, madam.

CUSTOMER: *Remington* ladies' shavers?

ALAN: I'm not sure, madam.

CUSTOMER: *Robex* tableware?

CUSTOMER: *Croydex?*

CUSTOMER: *Volex?*

CUSTOMER: *Pifco* automatic toothbrushes?

ALAN: I'll find out, sir.

CUSTOMER: Beautiflor!

CUSTOMER: Windowlene!

CUSTOMER: I want a *Philco* transistor radio!

CUSTOMER: This isn't a *Remington!* I wanted a *Remington!*

ALAN: Sorry.

CUSTOMER: Are you a dealer for *Hoover?*

ALAN: Sorry.

CUSTOMER: I wanted the heat-retaining *Pifco!*

ALAN: *Sorry!*

[JILL *comes into the square; a girl in her early twenties, pretty and middle class. She wears a sweater and jeans. The mumbling stops.*]

JILL: Hallo.

ALAN: Hallo.

JILL: Have you any blades for a clipping machine?

ALAN: Clipping?

JILL: To clip horses.

[*Pause. He stares at her, open-mouthed.*]
What's the matter?

ALAN: You work at Dalton's stables. I've seen you.

[*During the following, he mimes putting away a pile of boxes on a shelf in the shop.*]

JILL: I've seen you too, haven't I? You're the boy who's always staring into the yard around lunch-time.

LAN: Me?

JILL: You're there most days.

ALAN: Not me.

JILL [*amused*]: Of course it's you. Mr Dalton was only saying the other day: 'Who's that boy keeps staring in at the door?' Are you looking for a job or something?

ALAN [*eagerly*]: Is there one?

JILL: I don't know.

ALAN: I can only do week-ends.

JILL: That's when most people ride. We can always use extra hands. It'd mainly be mucking out.

ALAN: I don't mind.

JILL: Can you ride?

ALAN: No . . . No . . . I don't want to.

[*She looks at him curiously.*]

Please.

JILL: Come up on Saturday. I'll introduce you to Mr Dalton.

[*She leaves the square.*]

DYSART: When was this? About a year ago?

ALAN: I suppose.

DYSART: And she did?

ALAN: Yes.

[*Briskly he moves the three benches to form three stalls in the stable.*]

16

[*Rich light falls on the square.
An exultant humming from the* CHORUS.
*Tramping is heard. Three actors playing horses rise from their places.
Together they unhook three horse masks from the ladders to left and
right, put them on with rigid timing, and walk with swaying horse-
motion into the square. Their metal hooves stamp on the wood. Their
masks turn and toss high above their heads – as they will do sporadically
throughout all horse scenes – making the steel gleam in the light.*

For a moment they seem to converge on the boy as he stands in the middle of the stable, but then they swiftly turn and take up positions as if tethered by the head, with their invisible rumps towards him, one by each bench.

ALAN *is sunk in this glowing world of horses. Lost in wonder, he starts almost involuntarily to kneel on the floor in reverence – but is sharply interrupted by the cheery voice of* DALTON, *coming into the stable, followed by* JILL. *The boy straightens up guiltily.*]

DALTON: First thing to learn is drill. Learn it and keep to it. I want this place neat, dry and clean at all times. After you've mucked out, Jill will show you some grooming. What we call strapping a horse.

JILL: I think Trooper's got a stone.

DALTON: Yes? Let's see.

[*He crosses to the horse by the left bench, who is balancing one hoof on its tip. He picks up the hoof.*]

You're right. [*To* ALAN.] See this? This V here. It's what's called a frog. Sort of shock-absorber. Once you pierce that, it takes ages to heal – so you want to watch for it. You clean it out with this. What we call a hoof-pick.

[*He takes from his pocket an invisible pick.*]

Mind how you go with it. It's very sharp. Use it like this.

[*He quickly takes the stone out.*]

See?

[ALAN *nods, fascinated.*]

You'll soon get the hang of it. Jill will look after you. What she doesn't know about stables, isn't worth knowing.

JILL [*pleased*]: Oh yes, I'm sure!

DALTON [*handing* ALAN *the pick*]: Careful how you go with that. The main rule is, anything you don't know: ask. Never pretend you know something when you don't. [*Smiling.*] Actually, the main rule is: enjoy yourself. All right?

ALAN: Yes, sir.

DALTON: Good lad. See you later.

[*He nods to them cheerfully, and leaves the square.* ALAN *clearly puts the invisible hoof-pick on the rail, downstage left.*]

JILL: All right, let's start on some grooming. Why don't we begin with him? He looks as if he needs it.

[*They approach* NUGGET, *who is standing to the right. She pats him.* ALAN *sits and watches her.*]

This is Nugget. He's my favourite. He's as gentle as a baby, aren't you? But terribly fast if you want him to be.

[*During the following, she mimes both the actions and the objects, which she picks up from the right bench.*]

Now this is the dandy, and we start with that. Then you move on to the body brush. This is the most important, and you use it with this curry-comb. Now you always groom the same way: from the ears downward. Don't be afraid to do it hard. The harder you do it, the more the horse loves it. Push it right through the coat: like this.

[*The boy watches in fascination as she brushes the invisible body of* NUGGET, *scraping the dirt and hair off on to the invisible curry-comb. Now and then the horse mask moves very slightly in pleasure.*]

Down towards the tail and right through the coat. See how he loves it? I'm giving you a lovely massage, boy, aren't I? . . . You try.

[*She hands him the brush. Gingerly he rises and approaches* NUGGET. *Embarrassed and excited, he copies her movements, inexpertly.*]

Keep it nice and easy. Never rush. Down towards the tail and right through the coat. That's it. Again. Down towards the tail and right through the coat . . . Very good. Now you keep that up for fifteen minutes and then do old Trooper. Will you?

[ALAN *nods.*]

You've got a feel for it. I can tell. It's going to be nice teaching you. See you later.

[*She leaves the square and resumes her place.*

ALAN *is left alone with the horses.*

They all stamp. He approaches NUGGET *again, and touches the horse's shoulder. The mask turns sharply in his direction. The boy pauses, then moves his hand gently over the outline of the neck and back. The mask is reassured. It stares ahead unmoving. Then* ALAN *lifts his palm to his face and smells it deeply, closing his eyes.*

DYSART *rises from his bench, and begins to walk slowly upstage round the circle.*]

DYSART: Was that good? Touching them.

[ALAN *gives a faint groan.*]

ALAN: Mmm.

DYSART: It must have been marvellous, being near them at last . . . Stroking them . . . Making them fresh and glossy . . . Tell me . . .

[*Silence.* ALAN *begins to brush* NUGGET]

How about the girl? Did you like her?

ALAN [*tight*]: All right.

DYSART: Just all right?

[ALAN *changes his position, moving round* NUGGET's *rump so that his back is to the audience. He brushes harder.* DYSART *comes downstage around the circle, and finally back to his bench.*]

Was she friendly?

ALAN: Yes.

DYSART: Or stand-offish?

ALAN: Yes.

DYSART: Well which?

ALAN: What?

DYSART: Which was she?

[ALAN *brushes harder.*]

Did you take her out? Come on now: tell me. Did you have a date with her?

ALAN: What?

DYSART [*sitting*]: Tell me if you did.

[*The boy suddenly explodes in one of his rages.*]

ALAN [*yelling*]: TELL ME!

[*All the masks toss at the noise.*]

DYSART: What?

ALAN: *Tell me, tell me, tell me, tell me!*

[ALAN *storms out of the square, and downstage to where* DYSART *sits. He is raging. During the ensuing, the horses leave by all three openings.*]

On and on, sitting there! Nosey Parker! That's all you are! Bloody
Nosey Parker! Just like Dad. On and on and bloody on! Tell me,
tell me, tell me! . . . Answer this. Answer that. Never stop! –
[*He marches round the circle and back into the square.* DYSART *rises
and enters it from the other side.*]

17

[*Lights brighten.*]
DYSART: I'm sorry.
[ALAN *slams about what is now the office again, replacing the benches
to their usual position.*]
ALAN: All right, it's my turn now. You tell me! Answer me!
DYSART: We're not playing that game now.
ALAN: We're playing what I say.
DYSART: All right. What do you want to know?
[*He sits.*]
ALAN: Do *you* have dates?
DYSART: I told you. I'm married.
[ALAN *approaches him, very hostile.*]
ALAN: I know. Her name's Margaret. She's a dentist! You see, I
found out! What made you go with her? Did you use to bite her
hands when she did you in the chair?
[*The boy sits next to him, close.*]
DYSART: That's not very funny.
ALAN: Do you have girls behind her back?
DYSART: No.
ALAN: Then what? Do you fuck her?
DYSART: That's enough now.
[*He rises and moves away.*]
ALAN: Come on, tell me! Tell me, tell me!
DYSART: I said that's enough now.
[ALAN *rises too and walks around him.*]

I bet you don't. I bet you never touch her. Come on, tell me.
You've got no kids, have you? Is that because you don't fuck?

DYSART [*sharp*]: Go to your room. Go on: quick march.

[*Pause.* ALAN *moves away from him, insolently takes up a packet of*
DYSART's *cigarettes from the bench, and extracts one.*]

Give me those cigarettes.

[*The boy puts one in his mouth.*]

[*Exploding.*] Alan, *give them to me*!

[*Reluctantly* ALAN *shoves the cigarette back in the packet, turns and
hands it to him.*]

Now go!

[ALAN *bolts out of the square, and back to his bed.* DYSART, *unnerved,
addresses the audience.*]

Brilliant! Absolutely brilliant! The boy's on the run, so he gets
defensive. What am *I*, then? ... Wicked little bastard – he knew
exactly what questions to try. He'd actually marched himself
round the hospital, making inquiries about my wife. Wicked and –
of course, perceptive. Ever since I made that crack about carving up
children, he's been aware of me in an absolutely specific way. Of
course, there's nothing novel in that. Advanced neurotics can be
dazzling at that game. They aim unswervingly at your area of
maximum vulnerability ... Which I suppose is as good a way as
any of describing Margaret.

[*He sits.* HESTHER *enters the square.*
Light grows warmer.]

18

HESTHER: Now stop it.

DYSART: Do I embarrass you?

HESTHER: I suspect you're about to.

[*Pause.*]

DYSART: My wife doesn't understand me, Your Honour.

HESTHER: Do you understand her?

DYSART: No. Obviously I never did.

HESTHER: I'm sorry. I've never liked to ask but I've always imagined you weren't exactly compatible.

[*She moves to sit opposite.*]

DYSART: We were. It actually worked for a bit. I mean for both of us. We worked for each other. She actually for me through a kind of briskness. A clear, red-headed, inaccessible briskness which kept me keyed up for months. Mind you, if you're kinky for Northern Hygienic, as I am, you can't find anything much more compelling than a Scottish Lady Dentist.

HESTHER: It's *you* who are wicked, you know!

DYSART: Not at all. She got exactly the same from me. Antiseptic proficiency. I was like that in those days. We suited each other admirably. I see us in our wedding photo: Doctor and Doctor Mac Brisk. We were brisk in our wooing, brisk in our wedding, brisk in our disappointment. We turned from each other briskly into our separate surgeries; and now there's damn all.

HESTHER: You have no children, have you?

DYSART: No, we didn't go in for them. Instead, she sits beside our salmon-pink, glazed brick fireplace, and knits things for orphans in a home she helps with. And I sit opposite, turning the pages of art books on Ancient Greece. Occasionally, I still trail a faint scent of my enthusiasm across her path. I pass her a picture of the sacred acrobats of Crete leaping through the horns of running bulls – and she'll say: 'Och, Martin, what an *absurred* thing to be doing! The Highland Games, now there's *norrmal* sport!' Or she'll observe, just after I've told her a story from the Iliad: 'You know, when you come to think of it, Agamemnon and that lot were nothing but a bunch of ruffians from the Gorbals, only with fancy names!' [*He rises.*] You get the picture. She's turned into a Shrink. The familiar domestic monster. Margaret Dysart: the Shrink's Shrink.

HESTHER: That's cruel, Martin.

DYSART: Yes. Do you know what it's like for two people to live in the same house as if they were in different parts of the world? Mentally, she's always in some drizzly kirk of her own inheriting:

and I'm in some Doric temple – clouds tearing through pillars – eagles bearing prophecies out of the sky. She finds all that repulsive. All my wife has ever taken from the Mediterranean – from that whole vast intuitive culture – are four bottles of Chianti to make into lamps, and two china condiment donkeys labelled Sally and Peppy.

[*Pause.*]

[*More intimately.*] I wish there was one person in my life I could show. One instinctive, absolutely unbrisk person I could take to Greece, and stand in front of certain shrines and sacred streams and say 'Look! Life is only comprehensible through a thousand local Gods. And not just the old dead ones with names like Zeus – no, but living Geniuses of Place and Person! And not just Greece but modern England! Spirits of certain trees, certain curves of brick wall, certain chip shops, if you like, and slate roofs – just as of certain frowns in people and slouches' . . . I'd say to them – 'Worship as many as you can see – and more will appear!' . . . If I had a son, I bet you he'd come out exactly like his mother. Utterly worshipless. Would you like a drink?

HESTHER: No, thanks. Actually, I've got to be going. As usual . . .

DYSART: Really?

HESTHER: Really. I've got an Everest of papers to get through before bed.

DYSART: You never stop, do you?

HESTHER: Do you?

DYSART: This boy, with his stare. He's trying to save himself through me.

HESTHER: I'd say so.

DYSART: What am I trying to do to him?

HESTHER: Restore him, surely?

DYSART: To what?

HESTHER: A normal life.

DYSART: Normal?

HESTHER: It still means something.

DYSART: Does it?

HESTHER: Of course.

DYSART: You mean a normal boy has one head: a normal head has two ears?

HESTHER: You know I don't.

DYSART: Then what else?

HESTHER [*lightly*]: Oh, stop it.

DYSART: No, what? You tell me.

HESTHER [*rising: smiling*]: I won't be put on the stand like this, Martin. You're really disgraceful! . . . [*Pause.*] You know what I mean by a normal smile in a child's eyes, and one that isn't – even if I can't exactly define it. Don't you?

DYSART: Yes.

HESTHER: Then we have a duty to that, surely? Both of us.

DYSART: *Touché* . . . I'll talk to you.

HESTHER: Dismissed?

DYSART: You said you had to go.

HESTHER: I do . . . [*She kisses his cheek.*] Thank you for what you're doing . . . You're going through a rotten patch at the moment. I'm sorry . . . I suppose one of the few things one can do is simply hold on to priorities.

DYSART: Like what?

HESTHER: Oh – children before grown-ups. Things like that.

[*He contemplates her.*]

DYSART: You're really quite splendid.

HESTHER: Famous for it. Good night.

[*She leaves him.*]

DYSART [*to himself – or to the audience*]: Normal! . . . Normal!

19

[ALAN *rises and enters the square. He is subdued.*]

DYSART: Good afternoon.

ALAN: Afternoon.

DYSART: I'm sorry about our row yesterday.

ALAN: It was stupid.

DYSART: It was.

ALAN: What I said, I mean.

DYSART: How are you sleeping?

[ALAN *shrugs.*]

You're not feeling well, are you?

ALAN: All right.

DYSART: Would you like to play a game? It could make you feel better.

ALAN: What kind?

DYSART: It's called *Blink.* You have to fix your eyes on something: say, that little stain over there on the wall – and I tap this pen on the desk. The first time I tap it, you close your eyes. The next time you open them. And so on. Close, open, close, open, till I say stop.

ALAN: How can that make you feel better?

DYSART: It relaxes you. You'll feel as though you're talking to me in your sleep.

ALAN: It's stupid.

DYSART: You don't have to do it, if you don't want to.

ALAN: I didn't say I didn't want to.

DYSART: Well?

ALAN: I don't mind.

DYSART: Good. Sit down and start watching that stain. Put your hands by your sides, and open the fingers wide.

[*He opens the left bench and* ALAN *sits on the end of it.*]

The thing is to feel comfortable, and relax absolutely . . . Are you looking at the stain?

ALAN: Yes.

DYSART: Right. Now try and keep your mind as blank as possible.

ALAN: That's not difficult.

DYSART: Ssh. Stop talking . . . On the first tap, close. On the second, open. Are you ready?

[ALAN *nods.* DYSART *taps his pen on the wooden rail.* ALAN *shuts his eyes.* DYSART *taps again.* ALAN *opens them. The taps are evenly spaced. After four of them the sound cuts out, and is replaced by a louder, metallic sound, on tape.* DYSART *talks through this, to the audience – the light changes to cold – while the boy sits in front of him, staring at the wall, opening and shutting his eyes.*]

The Normal is the good smile in a child's eyes – all right. It is also the dead stare in a million adults. It both sustains and kills – like a God. It is the Ordinary made beautiful; it is also the Average made lethal. The Normal is the indispensable, murderous God of Health, and I am his Priest. My tools are very delicate. My compassion is honest. I have honestly assisted children in this room. I have talked away terrors and relieved many agonies. But also – beyond question – I have cut from them parts of individuality repugnant to this God, in both his aspects. Parts sacred to rarer and more wonderful Gods. And at what length ... Sacrifices to Zeus took at the most, surely, sixty seconds each. Sacrifices to the Normal can take as long as sixty months.

[*The natural sound of the pencil resumes.*

Light changes back.]

[*To* ALAN.] Now your eyes are feeling heavy. You want to sleep, don't you? You want a long, deep sleep. Have it. Your head is heavy. Very heavy. Your shoulders are heavy. Sleep.

[*The pencil stops.* ALAN's *eyes remain shut and his head has sunk on his chest.*]

Can you hear me?

ALAN: Mmm.

DYSART: You can speak normally. Say Yes, if you can.

ALAN: Yes.

DYSART: Good boy. Now raise your head, and open your eyes.

[*He does so.*]

Now, Alan, you're going to answer questions I'm going to ask you. Do you understand?

ALAN: Yes.

DYSART: And when you wake up, you are going to remember everything you tell me. All right?

ALAN: Yes.

DYSART: Good. Now I want you to think back in time. You are on that beach you told me about. The tide has gone out, and you're making sandcastles. Above you, staring down at you, is that great horse's head, and the cream dropping from it. Can you see that?

ALAN: Yes.

DYSART: You ask him a question. 'Does the chain hurt?'

ALAN: Yes.

DYSART: Do you ask him aloud?

ALAN: No.

DYSART: And what does the horse say back?

ALAN: 'Yes.'

DYSART: Then what do you say?

ALAN: 'I'll take it out for you.'

DYSART: And he says?

ALAN: 'It never comes out. They have me in chains.

DYSART: Like Jesus?

ALAN: Yes!

DYSART: Only his name isn't Jesus, is it?

ALAN: No.

DYSART: What is it?

ALAN: No one knows but him and me.

DYSART: You can tell me, Alan. Name him.

ALAN: Equus.

DYSART: Thank you. Does he live in all horses or just some?

ALAN: All.

DYSART: Good boy. Now: you leave the beach. You're in your bedroom at home. You're twelve years old. You're in front of the picture. You're looking at Equus from the foot of your bed. Would you like to kneel down?

ALAN: Yes.

DYSART [*encouragingly*]: Go on, then.

[ALAN *kneels.*]

Now tell me. Why is Equus in chains?

ALAN: For the sins of the world.

DYSART: What does he say to you?

ALAN: 'I see you.' 'I will save you.'

DYSART: How?

ALAN: 'Bear you away. Two shall be one.'

DYSART: Horse and rider shall be one beast?

ALAN: One person!

DYSART: Go on.

ALAN: 'And my chinkle-chankle shall be in thy hand.'

DYSART: Chinkle-chankle? That's his mouth chain?

ALAN: Yes.

DYSART: Good. You can get up ... Come on.

   [ALAN *rises*.]

  Now: think of the stable. What is the stable? His Temple? His
  Holy of Holies?

ALAN: Yes.

DYSART: Where you wash him? Where you tend him, and brush
  him with many brushes?

ALAN: Yes.

DYSART: And there he spoke to you, didn't he? He looked at you
  with his gentle eyes, and spake unto you?

ALAN: Yes.

DYSART: What did he say? 'Ride me?' 'Mount me, and ride me
  forth at night?'

ALAN: Yes.

DYSART: And you obeyed?

ALAN: Yes.

DYSART: How did you learn? By watching others?

ALAN: Yes.

DYSART: It must have been difficult. You bounced about?

ALAN: Yes.

DYSART: But he showed you, didn't he? Equus showed you the way.

ALAN: No!

DYSART: He didn't?

ALAN: He showed me nothing! He's a mean bugger! Ride – or fall!
  That's Straw Law.

DYSART: Straw Law?

ALAN: He was born in the straw, and this is his law.

DYSART: But you managed? You mastered him?

ALAN: Had to!

DYSART: And then you rode in secret?

ALAN: Yes.

DYSART: How often?

ALAN: Every three weeks. More, people would notice.

DYSART: On a particular horse?

ALAN: No.

DYSART: How did you get into the stable?

ALAN: Stole a key. Had it copied at Bryson's.

DYSART: Clever boy.

[ALAN *smiles.*]

Then you'd slip out of the house?

ALAN: Midnight! On the stroke!

DYSART: How far's the stable?

ALAN: Two miles.

[*Pause.*]

DYSART: Let's do it! Let's go riding! ... Now!

[*He stands up, and pushes in his bench.*]

You are there now, in front of the stable door.

[ALAN *turns upstage.*]

That key's in your hand. Go and open it.

20

[ALAN *moves upstage, and mimes opening the door.*
Soft light on the circle.
Humming from the CHORUS: *the Equus noise.*
*The horse actors enter, raise high their masks, and put them on all
together. They stand around the circle –* NUGGET *in the mouth of the
tunnel.*]

DYSART: Quietly as possible. Dalton may still be awake. Sssh ...
Quietly ... Good. Now go in.

[ALAN *steps secretly out of the square through the central opening on to the circle, now glowing with a warm light. He looks about him. The horses stamp uneasily; their masks turn towards him.]*

You are on the inside now. All the horses are staring at you. Can you see them?

ALAN [*excited*]: Yes!

DYSART: Which one are you going to take?

ALAN: Nugget.

[ALAN *reaches up and mimes leading* NUGGET *carefully round the circle downstage with a rope, past all the horses on the right.]*

DYSART: What colour is Nugget?

ALAN: Chestnut.

[*The horse picks his way with care.* ALAN *halts him at the corner of the square.]*

DYSART: What do you do, first thing?

ALAN: Put on his sandals.

DYSART: Sandals?

[*He kneels, downstage centre.]*

ALAN: Sandals of majesty! . . . Made of sack.

[*He picks up the invisible sandals, and kisses them devoutly.]*

Tie them round his hooves.

[*He taps* NUGGET's *right leg; the horse raises it and the boy mimes tying the sack round it.]*

DYSART: All four hooves?

ALAN: Yes.

DYSART: Then?

ALAN: Chinkle-chankle.

[*He mimes picking up the bridle and bit.]*

He doesn't like it so late, but he takes it for my sake. He bends for me. He stretches forth his neck to it.

[NUGGET *bends his head down.* ALAN *first ritually puts the bit into his own mouth, then crosses, and transfers it into* NUGGET's. *He reaches up and buckles on the bridle. Then he leads him by the invisible reins, across the front of the stage and up round the left side of the circle.* NUGGET *follows obediently.]*

ALAN: Buckle and lead out.

DYSART: No saddle?

ALAN: Never.

DYSART: Go on.

ALAN: Walk down the path behind. He's quiet. Always is, this bit. Meek and mild legs. At least till the field. Then there's trouble.

[*The horse jerks back. The mask tosses.*]

DYSART: What kind?

ALAN: Won't go in.

DYSART: Why not?

ALAN: It's his place of Ha Ha.

DYSART: What?

ALAN: Ha Ha.

DYSART: Make him go into it.

ALAN [*whispering fiercely*]: Come on! . . . Come on! . . .

[*He drags the horse into the square as DYSART steps out of it.*]

21

[NUGGET *comes to a halt staring diagonally down what is now the field. The Equus noise dies away. The boy looks about him.*]

DYSART [*from the circle*]: Is it a big field?

ALAN: Huge!

DYSART: What's it like?

ALAN: Full of mist. Nettles on your feet.

[*He mimes taking off his shoes – and the sting.*]

Ah!

DYSART [*going back to his bench*]: You take your shoes off?

ALAN: Everything.

DYSART: All your clothes?

ALAN: Yes.

[*He mimes undressing completely in front of the horse. When he is finished, and obviously quite naked, he throws out his arms and shows himself fully to his God, bowing his head before NUGGET.*]

DYSART: Where do you leave them?

ALAN: Tree hole near the gate. No one could find them.

[*He walks upstage and crouches by the bench, stuffing the invisible clothes beneath it.* DYSART *sits again on the left bench, downstage beyond the circle.*]

DYSART: How does it feel now?

ALAN [*holds himself*]: Burns.

DYSART: Burns?

ALAN: The mist!

DYSART: Go on. Now what?

ALAN: The Manbit.

[*He reaches again under the bench and draws out an invisible stick.*]

DYSART: Manbit?

ALAN: The stick for my mouth.

DYSART: Your mouth?

ALAN: To bite on.

DYSART: Why? What for?

ALAN: So's it won't happen too quick.

DYSART: Is it always the same stick?

ALAN: Course. Sacred stick. Keep it in the hole. The Ark of the Manbit.

DYSART: And now what? . . . What do you do now?

[*Pause. He rises and approaches* NUGGET.]

ALAN: Touch him!

DYSART: Where?

ALAN [*in wonder*]: All over. Everywhere. Belly. Ribs. His ribs are of ivory. Of great value! . . . His flank is cool. His nostrils open for me. His eyes shine. They can see in the dark . . . *Eyes!* –

[*Suddenly he dashes in distress to the farthest corner of the square.*]

DYSART: Go on! . . . Then?

[*Pause.*]

ALAN: Give sugar.

DYSART: A lump of sugar?

[ALAN *returns to* NUGGET.]

ALAN: His Last Supper.

DYSART: Last before what?

ALAN: Ha Ha.

[*He kneels before the horse, palms upward and joined together.*]

DYSART: Do you say anything when you give it to him?

ALAN [*offering it*]: Take my sins. Eat them for my sake . . . He always does.

[NUGGET *bows the mask into* ALAN's *palm, then takes a step back to eat.*]

And then he's ready.

DYSART: You can get up on him now?

ALAN: Yes!

DYSART: Do it, then. Mount him.

[ALAN, *lying before* NUGGET, *stretches out on the square. He grasps the top of the thin metal pole embedded in the wood. He whispers his God's name ceremonially.*]

ALAN: Equus! . . . Equus! . . . Equus!

[*He pulls the pole upright. The actor playing* NUGGET *leans forward and grabs it. At the same instant all the other horses lean forward around the circle, each placing a gloved hand on the rail.* ALAN *rises and walks right back to the upstage corner, left.*]

Take me!

[*He runs and jumps high on to* NUGGET's *back.*]

[*Crying out.*] Ah!

DYSART: What is it?

ALAN: Hurts!

DYSART: Hurts?

ALAN: Knives in his skin! Little knives – all inside my legs.

[NUGGET *mimes restiveness.*]

ALAN: Stay, Equus. No one said Go! . . . That's it. He's good. Equus the Godslave, Faithful and True. Into my hands he commends himself – naked in his chinkle-chankle. [*He punches* NUGGET.] Stop it! . . . He wants to go so badly.

DYSART: Go, then. Leave me behind. Ride away now, Alan. Now! . . . Now you are alone with Equus.

[ALAN *stiffens his body.*]

ALAN [*ritually*]: Equus – son of Fleckwus – son of Neckwus –¬ *Walk.*
[*A hum from the* CHORUS.
*Very slowly the horses standing on the circle begin to turn the square
by gently pushing the wooden rail.* ALAN *and his mount start to
revolve. The effect, immediately, is of a statue being slowly turned
round on a plinth. During the ride however the speed increases, and the
light decreases until it is only a fierce spotlight on horse and rider, with
the overspill glinting on the other masks leaning in towards them.*]
Here we go. The King rides out on Equus, mightiest of horses.
Only I can ride him. He lets me turn him this way and that. His
neck comes out of my body. It lifts in the dark. Equus, my Godslave! . . . Now the King commands you. Tonight, we ride against
them all.

DYSART: Who's all?

ALAN: My foes and His.

DYSART: Who are your foes?

ALAN: The Hosts of Hoover. The Hosts of Philco. The Hosts of
Pifco. The House of Remington and all its tribe!

DYSART: Who are His foes?

ALAN: The Hosts of Jodhpur. The Hosts of Bowler and Gymkhana.
All those who show him off for their vanity. Tie rosettes on his
head for their vanity! Come on, Equus. Let's get them! . . . *Trot!*
[*The speed of the turning square increases.*]
Stead-y! Stead-y! Stead-y! Stead-y! Cowboys are watching! Take
off their stetsons. They know who we are. They're admiring us!
Bowing low unto us! Come on now – show them! *Canter!* . . .
CANTER!
[*He whips* NUGGET.]
And Equus the Mighty rose against All!
His enemies scatter, his enemies fall!
TURN!
Trample them, trample them,
Trample them, trample them,
TURN!

TURN!!
TURN!!!

[*The Equus noise increases in volume.*]

[*Shouting.*] WEE!... WAA!... WONDERFUL!...

I'm stiff! Stiff in the wind!

My mane, stiff in the wind!

My flanks! *My* hooves!

Mane on my legs, on my flanks, like whips!

Raw!

Raw!

I'm raw! Raw!

Feel me on you! *On* you! *On* you! *On* you!

I want to be *in* you!

I want to BE you forever and ever! –

Equus, I love you!

Now! –

Bear me away!

Make us One Person!

[*He rides* EQUUS *frantically.*]

One Person! One Person! One Person! One Person!

[*He rises up on the horse's back, and calls like a trumpet.*]

Ha-HA!... Ha-HA!... Ha-HA!

[*The trumpet turns to great cries.*]

HA-HA! HA-HA! HA-HA! HA-HA! HA!... HA!...
HAAAAA!

[*He twists like a flame.*

Silence.

The turning square comes to a stop in the same position it occupied at the opening of the Act.

Slowly the boy drops off the horse's back on to the ground.

He lowers his head and kisses NUGGET's *hoof.*

Finally he flings back his head and cries up to him.]

AMEN!

[NUGGET *snorts, once.*]

BLACKOUT

ACT TWO

Darkness.
Lights come slowly up on ALAN *kneeling in the night at the hooves of*
NUGGET. *Slowly he gets up, climbing lovingly up the body of the horse*
until he can stand and kiss it.
DYSART *sits on the downstage bench where he began Act One.*

DYSART: With one particular horse, called Nugget, he embraces. He
showed me how he stands with it afterwards in the night, one hand
on its chest, one on its neck, like a frozen tango dancer, inhaling its
cold sweet breath. 'Have you noticed', he said, 'about horses: how
they'll stand one hoof on its end, like those girls in the ballet?'
  [ALAN *leads* NUGGET *out of the square.* DYSART *rises. The horse*
  walks away up the tunnel and disappears. The boy comes downstage
  and sits on the bench DYSART *has vacated.* DYSART *crosses down-*
  stage and moves slowly up round the circle, until he reaches the central
  entrance to the square.]
Now he's gone off to rest, leaving me alone with Equus. I can hear
the creature's voice. It's calling me out of the black cave of the
Psyche. I shove in my dim little torch, and there he stands – waiting
for me. He raises his matted head. He opens his great square teeth,
and says – [*Mocking.*] ' *Why?* . . . Why Me? . . . Why – ultimately –
Me? . . . Do you really imagine you can account for Me? Totally,
infallibly, inevitably account for Me? . . . Poor Doctor Dysart!'
  [*He enters the square.*]
Of course I've stared at such images before. Or been stared at by
them, whichever way you look at it. And weirdly often now with
me the feeling is that *they* are staring at *us* – that in some quite

palpable way they precede us. Meaningless, but unsettling . . . In either case, this one is the most alarming yet. It asks questions I've avoided all my professional life. [*Pause.*] A child is born into a world of phenomena all equal in their power to enslave. It sniffs – it sucks – it strokes its eyes over the whole uncomfortable range. Suddenly one strikes. Why? Moments snap together like magnets, forging a chain of shackles. Why? I can trace them. I can even, with time, pull them apart again. But why at the start they were ever magnetized at all – just those particular moments of experience and no others – I don't know. *And nor does anyone else.* Yet *if* I don't know – if I can never know that – then what am I doing here? I don't mean clinically doing or socially doing – I mean *fundamentally*! These questions, these Whys, are fundamental – yet they have no place in a consulting room. So then, do I? . . . This is the feeling more and more with me – No Place. Displacement . . . 'Account for me,' says staring Equus. 'First account for Me! . . .' I fancy this is more than menopause.

[NURSE *rushes in.*]

NURSE: Doctor! . . . Doctor! There's a terrible scene with the Strang boy. His mother came to visit him, and I gave her the tray to take in. He threw it at her. She's saying the most dreadful things.

[ALAN *springs up, down left.* DORA *springs up, down right. They face each other across the bottom end of the stage. It is observable that at the start of this Act* FRANK *is not sitting beside his wife on their bench. It is hopefully not observable that he is placed among the audience upstage, in the gloom, by the central tunnel.*]

DORA: Don't you dare! *Don't you dare!*

DYSART: Is she still there?

NURSE: Yes!

[*He quickly leaves the square, followed by the* NURSE. DORA *moves towards her son.*]

DORA: Don't you look at me like that! I'm not a doctor, you know, who'll take anything. Don't you dare give me that stare, young man!

[*She slaps his face.* DYSART *joins them.*]

DYSART: Mrs Strang!

DORA: I know your stares. They don't work on me!

DYSART [to her]: Leave this room.

DORA: What did you say?

DYSART: I tell you to leave here at once.

[DORA hesitates. Then:]

DORA: Good-bye, Alan.

[She walks past her son, and round into the square. DYSART follows her. Both are very upset. ALAN returns to his bench and NURSE to her place.]

23

[Lights up on the square.]

DYSART: I must ask you never to come here again.

DORA: Do you think I want to? Do you think I want to?

DYSART: Mrs Strang, what on earth has got into you? Can't you see the boy is highly distressed?

DORA [ironic]: Really?

DYSART: Of course! He's at a most delicate stage of treatment. He's totally exposed. Ashamed. Everything you can imagine!

DORA [exploding]: And me? What about me? ... What do you think I am? ... I'm a parent, of course – so it doesn't count. That's a dirty word in here, isn't it, 'parent'?

DYSART: You know that's not true.

DORA: Oh, I know. I know, all right! I've heard it all my life. It's our fault. Whatever happens, we did it. Alan's just a little victim. He's really done nothing at all! [Savagely.] What do you have to do in this world to get any sympathy – blind animals?

DYSART: Sit down, Mrs Strang.

DORA [ignoring him: more and more urgently]: Look, Doctor: you don't have to live with this. Alan is one patient to you: one out of many. He's my son. I lie awake every night thinking about it. Frank lies there beside me. I can hear him. Neither of us sleeps all night. You come to us and say, who forbids television? who does what behind whose back? – as if we're criminals. Let me tell you something. We're not criminals. We've done nothing wrong. We loved Alan. We gave him the best love we could. All right, we quarrel sometimes – all parents quarrel – we always make it up. My husband is a good man. He's an upright man, religion or no religion. He cares for his home, for the world, and for his boy. Alan had love and care and treats, and as much fun as any boy in the world. I know about loveless homes: I was a teacher. Our home wasn't loveless. I know about privacy too – not invading a child's privacy. All right, Frank may be at fault there – he digs into him too much – but nothing in excess. He's not a bully . . . [*Gravely.*] No, doctor. Whatever's happened has happened *because of Alan.* Alan is himself. Every soul is itself. If you added up everything we ever did to him, from his first day on earth to this, you wouldn't find why he did this terrible thing – because that's *him*; not just all of our things added up. Do you understand what I'm saying? I want you to understand, because I lie awake and awake thinking it out, and I want you to know that I deny it absolutely what he's doing now, staring at me, attacking me for what *he's* done, for what *he* is! [*Pause: calmer.*] You've got your words, and I've got mine. You call it a complex, I suppose. But if you knew God, Doctor, you would know about the Devil. You'd know the Devil isn't made by what mummy says and daddy says. The Devil's *there.* It's an old-fashioned word, but a true thing . . . I'll go. What I did in there was inexcusable. I only know he was my little Alan, and then the Devil came.

[*She leaves the square, and resumes her place.* DYSART *watches her go, then leaves himself by the opposite entrance, and approaches* ALAN.]

[*Seated on his bench, the boy glares at him.*]

DYSART: I thought you liked your mother.

[*Silence.*]

She doesn't know anything, you know. I haven't told her what you told me. You do know that, don't you?

ALAN: It was lies anyway.

DYSART: What?

ALAN: You and your pencil. Just a con trick, that's all.

DYSART: What do you mean?

ALAN: Made me say a lot of lies.

DYSART: Did it? . . . Like what?

ALAN: All of it. Everything I said. Lot of lies.

[*Pause.*]

DYSART: I see.

ALAN: You ought to be locked up. Your bloody tricks.

DYSART: I thought you liked tricks.

ALAN: It'll be the drug next. I know.

[DYSART *turns, sharply.*]

DYSART: What drug?

ALAN: I've heard. I'm not ignorant. I know what you get up to in here. Shove needles in people, pump them full of truth drug, so they can't help saying things. That's next, isn't it?

[*Pause.*]

DYSART: Alan, do you know why you're here?

ALAN: So you can give me truth drugs.

[*He glares at him.*

DYSART *leaves abruptly, and returns to the square.*]

[HESTHER *comes in simultaneously from the other side.*]

DYSART [*agitated*]: He actually thinks they exist! And of course he wants one.

HESTHER: It doesn't sound like that to me.

DYSART: Of course he does. Why mention them otherwise? He wants a way to speak. To finally tell me what happened in that stable. Tape's too isolated, and hypnosis is a trick. At least that's the pretence.

HESTHER: Does he still say that today?

DYSART: I haven't seen him. I cancelled his appointment this morning, and let him stew in his own anxiety. Now I am almost tempted to play a real trick on him.

HESTHER [*sitting*]: Like what?

DYSART: The old placebo.

HESTHER: You mean a harmless pill?

DYSART: Full of *alleged* Truth Drug. Probably an aspirin.

HESTHER: But he'd deny it afterwards. Same thing all over.

DYSART: No. Because he's ready to abreact.

HESTHER: Abreact?

DYSART: Live it all again. He won't be able to deny it after that, because he'll have shown me. Not just told me – but acted it out in front of me.

HESTHER: Can you get him to do that?

DYSART: I think so. He's nearly done it already. Under all that glowering, he trusts me. Do you realize that?

HESTHER [*warmly*]: I'm sure he does.

DYSART: Poor bloody fool.

HESTHER: Don't start that again.

    [*Pause.*]

DYSART [*quietly*]: Can you think of anything worse one can do to anybody than take away their worship?

HESTHER: Worship?

DYSART: Yes, that word again!

HESTHER: Aren't you being a little extreme?

DYSART: Extremity's the point.

HESTHER: Worship isn't destructive, Martin. I know that.

DYSART: I don't. I only know it's the core of his life. What else has he got? Think about him. He can hardly read. He knows no physics or engineering to make the world real for him. No paintings to show him how others have enjoyed it. No music except television jingles. No history except tales from a desperate mother. No friends. Not one kid to give him a joke, or make him know himself more moderately. He's a modern citizen for whom society doesn't exist. He lives *one hour* every three weeks – howling in a mist. And after the service kneels to a slave who stands over him obviously and unthrowably his master. With my body I thee worship! . . . Many men have less vital with their wives.

[*Pause.*]

HESTHER: All the same, they don't usually blind their wives, do they?

DYSART: Oh, come on!

HESTHER: Well, do they?

DYSART [*sarcastically*]: You mean he's dangerous? A violent, dangerous madman who's going to run round the country doing it again and again?

HESTHER: I mean he's in pain, Martin. He's been in pain for most of his life. That much, at least, you *know*.

DYSART: Possibly.

HEATHER: *Possibly?!* . . . That cut-off little figure you just described must have been in pain for years.

DYSART [*doggedly*]: Possibly.

HESTHER: And you can take it away.

DYSART: Still – possibly.

HESTHER: Then that's enough. That simply has to be enough for you, surely?

DYSART: No!

HESTHER: Why not?

DYSART: Because it's his.

HESTHER: I don't understand.

DYSART: His pain. His own. He made it.

[*Pause.*]

[*Earnestly.*] Look ... to go through life and call it yours – *your life* – you first have to get your own pain. Pain that's unique to you. You can't just dip into the common bin and say 'That's enough!' ... He's done that. All right, he's sick. He's full of misery and fear. He was dangerous, and could be again, though I doubt it. But that boy has known a passion more ferocious than I have felt in any second of my life. And let me tell you something: I envy it.

HESTHER: You can't.

DYSART [*vehemently*]: Don't you see? That's the Accusation! That's what his stare has been saying to me all this time. '*At least I galloped! When did you?*' ... [*Simply.*] I'm jealous, Hesther. Jealous of Alan Strang.

HESTHER: That's absurd.

DYSART: Is it? ... I go on about my wife. That smug woman by the fire. Have you thought of the fellow on the other side of it? The finicky, critical husband looking through his art books on mythical Greece. What worship has *he* ever known? Real worship! Without worship you shrink, it's as brutal as that ... I shrank my *own* life. No one can do it for you. I settled for being pallid and provincial, out of my own eternal timidity. The old story of bluster, and do bugger-all ... I imply that we can't have children; but actually, it's only me. I had myself tested behind her back. The lowest sperm count you could find. And I never told her. That's all I need – her sympathy mixed with resentment ... I tell everyone Margaret's the puritan, I'm the pagan. Some pagan! Such wild returns I make to the womb of civilization. Three weeks a year in the Peleponnese, every bed booked in advance, every meal paid for by vouchers, cautious jaunts in hired Fiats, suitcase crammed with Kao-Pectate! Such a fantastic surrender to the primitive. And I use that word endlessly: 'primitive'. 'Oh, the primitive world,' I say. 'What instinctual truths were lost with it!' And while I sit there, baiting a poor unimaginative woman with the word, that freaky boy tries to conjure the reality! I sit looking at pages of centaurs trampling the soil of Argos – and outside my window he is trying to *become one*, in a Hampshire field! . . . I watch that woman knitting, night after night – a woman I haven't *kissed* in six years – and he stands in the dark for an hour, sucking the sweat off his God's hairy cheek! [*Pause.*] Then in the morning, I put away my books on the cultural shelf, close up the kodachrome snaps of Mount Olympus, touch my reproduction statue of Dionysus for luck – and go off to hospital to treat him for insanity. Do you see?

HESTHER: The boy's in pain, Martin. That's all I see. In the end . . . I'm sorry.

> [*He looks at her.* ALAN *gets up from his bench and stealthily places an envelope in the left-hand entrance of the square, then goes back and sits with his back to the audience, as if watching television.*
>
> HESTHER *rises.*]

HESTHER: That stare of his. Have you thought it might not be accusing you at all?

DYSART: What then?

HESTHER: Claiming you.

DYSART: For what?

HESTHER [*mischievously*]: A new God.

> [*Pause.*]

DYSART: Too conventional, for him. Finding a religion in Psychiatry is really for very ordinary patients.

> [*She laughs.*]

HESTHER: Maybe he just wants a new Dad. Or is that too conventional too? . . . Since you're questioning your profession anyway, perhaps you ought to try it and see.

DYSART [*amused*]: I'll talk to you.

HESTHER: Goodbye.

> [*She smiles, and leaves him.*]

[DYSART *becomes aware of the letter lying on the floor. He picks it up, opens and reads it.*]

ALAN [*speaking stiffly, as* DYSART *reads*]: 'It is all true, what I said after you tapped the pencil. I'm sorry if I said different. Post Scriptum: I know why I'm in here.'

[*Pause.*]

DYSART [*calling, joyfully*]: Nurse!

[NURSE *comes in.*]

NURSE: Yes, Doctor?

DYSART [*trying to conceal his pleasure*]: Good evening!

NURSE: You're in late tonight.

DYSART: Yes! . . . Tell me, is the Strang boy in bed yet?

NURSE: Oh, no, Doctor. He's bound to be upstairs looking at television. He always watches to the last possible moment. He doesn't like going to his room at all.

DYSART: You mean he's still having nightmares?

NURSE: He had a bad one last night.

DYSART: Would you ask him to come down here, please?

NURSE [*faint surprise*]: Now?

DYSART: I'd like a word with him.

NURSE [*puzzled*]: Very good, Doctor.

DYSART: If he's not back in his room by lights out, tell Night Nurse not to worry. I'll see he gets back to bed all right. And would you phone my home and tell my wife I may be in late?

NURSE: Yes, Doctor.

DYSART: Ask him to come straight away, please.

[NURSE *goes to the bench, taps* ALAN *on the shoulder, whispers her message in his ear, and returns to her place.* ALAN *stands up and pauses for a second – then steps into the square.*]

[*He stands in the doorway, depressed.*]

DYSART: Hallo.

ALAN: Hallo.

DYSART: I got your letter. Thank you. [*Pause.*] Also the Post Scriptum.

ALAN [*defensively*]: That's the right word. My mum told me. It's Latin for 'After-writing'.

DYSART: How are you feeling?

ALAN: All right.

DYSART: I'm sorry I didn't see you today.

ALAN: You were fed up with me.

DYSART: Yes. [*Pause.*] Can I make it up to you now?

ALAN: What d'you mean?

DYSART: I thought we'd have a session.

ALAN [*startled*]: Now?

DYSART: Yes! At dead of night! . . . Better than going to sleep, isn't it?

[*The boy flinches.*]

Alan – look. Everything I say has a trick or a catch. Everything I do is a trick or a catch. That's all I know to do. But they work – and you know that. Trust me.

[*Pause.*]

ALAN: You got another trick, then?

DYSART: Yes.

ALAN: A truth drug?

DYSART: If you like.

ALAN: What's it do?

DYSART: Make it easier for you to talk.

ALAN: Like you can't help yourself?

DYSART: That's right. Like you have to speak the truth at all costs. And all of it.

[*Pause.*]

ALAN [*slyly*]: Comes in a needle, doesn't it?

DYSART: No.

ALAN: Where is it?

DYSART [*indicating his pocket*]: In here.

ALAN: Let's see.

[DYSART *solemnly takes a bottle of pills out of his pocket.*]

DYSART: There.

ALAN [*suspicious*]: That really it?

DYSART: It is . . . Do you want to try it?

ALAN: No.

DYSART: I think you do.

ALAN: I don't. Not at all.

DYSART: Afterwards you'd sleep. You'd have no bad dreams all night. Probably many nights, from then on . . .

[*Pause.*]

ALAN: How long's it take to work?

DYSART: It's instant. Like coffee.

ALAN [*half believing*]: It isn't!

DYSART: I promise you . . . Well?

ALAN: Can I have a fag?

DYSART: Pill first. Do you want some water?

ALAN: No.

[DYSART *shakes one out on to his palm.* ALAN *hesitates for a second – then takes it and swallows it.*]

DYSART: Then you can chase it down with this. Sit down.

[*He offers him a cigarette, and lights it for him.*]

ALAN [*nervous*]: What happens now?

DYSART: We wait for it to work.

ALAN: What'll I feel first?

DYSART: Nothing much. After a minute, about a hundred green snakes should come out of that cupboard singing the Hallelujah Chorus.

ALAN [*annoyed*]: *I'm serious!*

DYSART [*earnestly*]: You'll feel nothing. Nothing's going to happen now but what you want to happen. You're not going to say anything to me but what you want to say. Just relax. Lie back and finish your fag.

[ALAN *stares at him. Then accepts the situation, and lies back.*]

DYSART: Good boy.

ALAN: I bet this room's heard some funny things.

DYSART: It certainly has.

ALAN: I like it.

DYSART: This room?

ALAN: Don't you?

DYSART: Well, there's not much to like, is there?

ALAN: How long am I going to be in here?

DYSART: It's hard to say. I quite see you want to leave.

ALAN: No.

DYSART: You don't?

ALAN: Where would I go?

DYSART: Home ...

[*The boy looks at him.* DYSART *crosses and sits on the rail upstage, his feet on the bench. A pause.*]

Actually, I'd like to leave this room and never see it again in my life.

ALAN [*surprise*]: Why?

DYSART: I've been in it too long.

ALAN: Where would you go?

DYSART: Somewhere.

ALAN: Secret?

DYSART: Yes. There's a sea – a great sea – I love ... It's where the Gods used to go to bathe.

ALAN: What Gods?

DYSART: The old ones. Before they died.

ALAN: Gods don't die.

DYSART: Yes, they do.

[*Pause.*]

There's a village I spent one night in, where I'd like to live. It's all white.

ALAN: How would you Nosey Parker, though? You wouldn't have a room for it any more.

DYSART: I wouldn't mind. I don't actually enjoy being a Nosey Parker, you know.

ALAN: Then why do it?

DYSART: Because you're unhappy.

ALAN: So are you.

[DYSART *looks at him sharply.* ALAN *sits up in alarm.*]

Oooh, I didn't mean that!

DYSART: Didn't you?

ALAN: Here – is that how it works? Things just slip out, not feeling anything?

DYSART: That's right.

ALAN: But it's so quick!

DYSART: I told you; it's instant.

ALAN [*delighted*]: It's wicked, isn't it? I mean, you can say anything under it.

DYSART: Yes.

ALAN: Ask me a question.

DYSART: Tell me about Jill.

[*Pause. The boy turns away.*]

ALAN: There's nothing to tell.

DYSART: Nothing?

ALAN: No.

DYSART: Well, for example – is she pretty? You've never described her.

ALAN: She's all right.

DYSART: What colour hair?

ALAN: Dunno.

DYSART: Is it long or short?

ALAN: Dunno.

DYSART [*lightly*]: You must know that.

ALAN: I don't remember. *I don't!*

[DYSART *rises and comes down to him. He takes the cigarette out of his hand.*]

DYSART [*firmly*]: Lie back . . . Now listen. You have to do this. And now. You are going to tell me everything that happened with this girl. And not just *tell* me – *show* me. Act it out, if you like – even more than you did when I tapped the pencil. I want you to feel free to do absolutely anything in this room. The pill will help you. I will help you . . . Now, where does she live?

[*A long pause.*]

ALAN [*tight*]: Near the stables. About a mile.

[DYSART *steps down out of the square as* JILL *enters it. He sits again on the downstage bench.*]

28

[*The light grows warmer.*]

JILL: It's called The China Pantry.

[*She comes down and sits casually on the rail. Her manner is open and lightly provocative. During these scenes* ALAN *acts directly with her, and never looks over at* DYSART *when he replies to him.*]

When Daddy disappeared, she was left without a bean. She had to earn her own living. I must say she did jolly well, considering she was never trained in business.

DYSART: What do you mean, 'disappeared'?

ALAN [*to* DYSART]: He ran off. No one ever saw him again.

JILL: Just left a note on her dressing table saying 'Sorry. I've had it.' Just like that. She never got over it. It turned her right off men. All my dates have to be sort of secret. I mean, she knows about them, but I can't ever bring anyone back home. She's so rude to them.

ALAN [*to* DYSART]: She was always looking.

DYSART: At you?

ALAN [*to* DYSART]: Saying stupid things.

[*She jumps off the bench.*]

JILL: You've got super eyes.

ALAN [*to* DYSART]: Anyway, *she* was the one who had them.

[*She sits next to him. Embarrassed, the boy tries to move away as far as he can.*]

JILL: There was an article in the paper last week saying what points about boys fascinate girls. They said Number One is bottoms. I think it's eyes every time ... They fascinate you too, don't they?

ALAN: Me?

JILL [sly]: Or is it only horses' eyes?

ALAN [startled]: What d'you mean?

JILL: I saw you staring into Nugget's eyes yesterday for ages. I spied on you through the door!

ALAN [hotly]: There must have been something in it!

JILL: You're a real Man of Mystery, aren't you?

ALAN [to DYSART]: Sometimes, it was like she knew.

DYSART: Did you ever hint?

ALAN [to DYSART]: Course not!

JILL: I love horses' eyes. The way you can see yourself in them. D'you find them sexy?

ALAN [outraged]: What?!

JILL: Horses.

ALAN: Don't be daft!
  [He springs up, and away from her.]

JILL: Girls do. I mean, they go through a period when they pat them and kiss them a lot. I know I did. I suppose it's just a substitute, really.

ALAN [to DYSART]: That kind of thing, all the time. Until one night ...

DYSART: Yes? What?

ALAN [to DYSART: defensively]: She did it! Not me. It was her idea, the whole thing! ... She got me into it!

DYSART: What are you saying? 'One night': go on from there.
  [A pause.]

ALAN [to DYSART]: Saturday night. We were just closing up.

JILL: How would you like to take me out?

ALAN: What?

JILL [coolly]: How would you like to take me out tonight?

ALAN: I've got to go home.

JILL: What for?

[*He tries to escape upstage.*]

ALAN: They expect me.

JILL: Ring up and say you're going out.

ALAN: I can't.

JILL: Why?

ALAN: They expect me.

JILL: Look. Either we go out together and have some fun, or you go back to your boring home, *as usual*, and I go back to mine. That's the situation, isn't it?

ALAN: Well ... where would we go?

JILL: The pictures! There's a skinflick over in Winchester! I've never seen one, have you?

ALAN: No.

JILL: Wouldn't you like to? *I* would. All those heavy Swedes, panting at each other! ... What d'you say?

ALAN [*grinning*]: Yeh! ...

JILL: Good! ...

[*He turns away.*]

DYSART: Go on, please.

[*He steps off the square.*]

ALAN [*to* DYSART]: I'm tired now!

DYSART: Come on now. You can't stop there.

[*He storms round the circle to* DYSART, *and faces him directly.*]

ALAN: I'm *tired*! I want to go to bed!

DYSART [*sharply*]: Well, you can't. I want to hear about the film.

ALAN [*hostile*]: Hear what? ... *What*? ... It was bloody awful!

[*The actors playing horses come swiftly on to the square, dressed in sports coats or raincoats. They move the benches to be parallel with the audience, and sit on them – staring out front.*]

DYSART: Why?

ALAN: Nosey Parker!

DYSART: *Why*?

ALAN: *Because*! ... Well – we went into the Cinema!

[*A burst of Rock music, instantly fading down. Lights darken.*
ALAN *re-enters the square.* JILL *rises and together they grope their way to the downstage bench, as if in a dark auditorium.*]

ALAN [*to* DYSART]: The whole place was full of men. Jill was the only girl.

[*They push by a patron seated at the end, and sit side by side, staring up at the invisible screen, located above the heads of the main audience. A spotlight hits the boy's face.*]

We sat down and the film came on. It was daft. Nothing happened for ages. There was this girl Brita, who was sixteen. She went to stay in this house, where there was an older boy. He kept giving her looks, but she ignored him completely. In the end she took a shower. She went into the bathroom and took off all her clothes. The lot. Very slowly ... What she didn't know was the boy was looking through the door all the time ... [*He starts to become excited.*] It was fantastic! The water fell on her breasts, bouncing down her ...

[FRANK *steps into the square furtively from the back, hat in hand, and stands looking about for a place.*]

DYSART: Was that the first time you'd seen a girl naked?

ALAN [*to* DYSART]: Yes! You couldn't see everything, though ...
[*Looking about him.*] All round me they were all looking. All the men – staring up like they were in church. Like they were a sort of congregation. And then – [*He sees his father.*] *Ah!*

[*At the same instant* FRANK *sees him.*]

FRANK: Alan!

ALAN: God!

JILL: What is it?

ALAN: *Dad!*

JILL: *Where?*

ALAN: At the back! *He saw me!*

JILL: You sure?

ALAN: Yes!

FRANK [*calling*]: Alan!

ALAN: Oh God!

[*He tries to hide his face in the girl's shoulder. His father comes down the aisle towards him.*]

FRANK: Alan! You can hear me! Don't pretend!

PATRONS: *Ssssh!*

FRANK [*approaching the row of seats*]: Do I have to come and fetch you out? ... Do I? ...

[*Cries of 'Sssh!' and 'Shut up!'*]

Do I, Alan?

ALAN [*through gritted teeth*]: Oh fuck!

[*He gets up as the noise increases.* JILL *gets up too and follows him.*]

DYSART: You went?

ALAN [*to* DYSART]: What else could I do? He kept shouting. Everyone was saying Shut up!

[*They go out, right, through the group of* PATRONS – *who rise protesting as they pass, quickly replace the benches and leave the square.* DYSART *enters it.*]

30

[*Light brightens from the cinema, but remains cold: streets at night. The three walk round the circle downstage in a line:* FRANK *leading, wearing his hat. He halts in the middle of the left rail, and stands staring straight ahead of him, rigid with embarrassment.*

ALAN *is very agitated.*]

ALAN [*to* DYSART]: We went into the street, all three of us. It was weird. We just stood there by the bus stop – like we were three people in a queue, and we didn't know each other. Dad was all white and sweaty. He didn't look at us at all. It must have gone on for about five minutes. I tried to speak. I said – [*To his father.*] I – I – I've never been there before. Honest ... Never ... [*To* DYSART.] He didn't seem to hear. Jill tried.

JILL: It's true, Mr Strang. It wasn't Alan's idea to go there. It was mine.

ALAN [*to* DYSART]: He just went on staring, straight ahead. It was awful.

JILL: I'm not shocked by films like that. I think they're just silly.

ALAN [*to* DYSART]: The bus wouldn't come. We just stood and stood . . . Then suddenly he spoke.

[FRANK *takes off his hat.*]

FRANK [*stiffly*]: I'd like you to know something. Both of you. I came here tonight to see the Manager. He asked me to call on him for business purposes. I happen to be a printer, Miss. A picture house needs posters. That's entirely why I'm here. To discuss posters. While I was waiting I happened to glance in, that's all. I can only say I'm going to complain to the council. I had no idea they showed films like this. I'm certainly going to refuse my services.

JILL [*kindly*]: Yes, of course.

FRANK: So long as that's understood.

ALAN [*to* DYSART]: Then the bus came along.

FRANK: Come along now, Alan.

[*He moves away downstage.*]

ALAN: No.

FRANK [*turning*]: No fuss, please. Say good night to the young lady.

ALAN [*timid but firm*]: No. I'm stopping here . . . I've got to see her home . . . It's proper.

[*Pause.*]

FRANK [*as dignified as possible*]: Very well. I'll see you when you choose to return. Very well then . . . Yes . . .

[*He walks back to his original seat, next to his wife. He stares across the square at his son – who stares back at him. Then, slowly, he sits.*]

ALAN [*to* DYSART]: And he got in, and we didn't. He sat down and looked at me through the glass. And I saw . . .

DYSART [*soft*]: What?

ALAN [*to* DYSART]: His face. It was scared.

DYSART: Of you?

ALAN [*to* DYSART]: It was terrible. We had to walk home. Four miles. I got the shakes.

DYSART: You were scared too?

ALAN [*to* DYSART]: It was like a hole had been drilled in my tummy. A hole – right here. And the air was getting in!

[*He starts to walk upstage, round the circle.*]

31

[*The girl stays still.*]

JILL [*aware of other people looking*]: Alan . . .

ALAN [*to* DYSART]: People kept turning round in the street to look.

JILL: Alan!

ALAN [*to* DYSART]: I kept seeing him, just as he drove off. Scared of me . . . And me scared of *him* . . . I kept thinking – all those airs he put on! . . . 'Receive my meaning. Improve your mind!' . . . All those nights he said he'd be in late. 'Keep my supper hot, Dora!' 'Your poor father: he works so hard!' . . . Bugger! Old bugger! . . . Filthy old bugger!

[*He stops, clenching his fists.*]

JILL: Hey! Wait for me!

[*She runs after him. He waits.*]

What are you thinking about?

ALAN: Nothing.

JILL: Mind my own beeswax?

[*She laughs.*]

ALAN [*to* DYSART] And suddenly she began to laugh.

JILL: I'm sorry. But it's pretty funny, when you think of it.

ALAN [*bewildered*]: What?

JILL: Catching him like that! I mean, it's terrible – but it's very funny.

ALAN: Yeh!

[*He turns from her.*]

JILL: No, wait! . . . I'm sorry. I know you're upset. But it's not the end of the world, is it? I mean, what was he doing? Only what we were. Watching a silly film. It's a case of like father like son, I'd say! . . . I mean, when that girl was taking a shower, you were pretty interested, weren't you?

[*He turns round and looks at her.*]

We keep saying old people are square. Then when they suddenly aren't – we don't like it!

DYSART: What did you think about that?

ALAN [*to* DYSART]: I don't know. I kept looking at all the people in the street. They were mostly men coming out of pubs. I suddenly thought – *they all do it! All of them!* . . . They're not just Dads – they're people with pricks! . . . And Dad – he's not just Dad either. He's a man with a prick too. You know, I'd never thought about it.

[*Pause.*]

We went into the country.

[*He walks again.* JILL *follows. They turn the corner and come down-stage, right.*]

We kept walking. I just thought about Dad, and how he was nothing special – just a poor old sod on his own.

[*He stops.*]

[*To* JILL: *realizing it.*] Poor old sod!

JILL: That's right!

ALAN [*grappling with it*]: I mean, what else has he got? . . . He's got mum, of course, but well – she – she – she –

JILL: She doesn't give him anything?

ALAN: That's right. I bet you . . . She doesn't give him anything. That's right . . . That's really right! . . . She likes Ladies and Gentlemen. Do you understand what I mean?

JILL [*mischievously*]: Ladies and gentlemen aren't naked?

ALAN: That's right! Never! . . . *Never!* That would be disgusting! She'd have to put bowler hats on them! . . . Jodhpurs!

[*She laughs.*]

DYSART: Was that the first time you ever thought anything like that about your mother? . . . I mean, that she was unfair to your dad?

ALAN [*to* DYSART]: Absolutely!

DYSART: How did you feel?

ALAN [*to* DYSART]: Sorry. I mean for him. Poor old sod, that's what I felt – he's just like me! He hates ladies and gents just like me! Posh things – and la-di-da. He goes off by himself at night, and does his own secret thing which no one'll know about, just like me! There's no difference – he's just the same as me – just the same! –
[*He stops in distress, then bolts back a little upstage.*]
Christ!

DYSART [*sternly*]: Go on.

ALAN [*to* DYSART]: I can't.

DYSART: Of course you can. You're doing wonderfully.

ALAN [*to* DYSART]: No, please. *Don't make me!*

DYSART [*firm*]: Don't think: just answer. You were happy at that second, weren't you? When you realized about your dad. How lots of people have secrets, not just you?

ALAN [*to* DYSART]: Yes.

DYSART: You felt sort of free, didn't you? I mean, free to do anything?

ALAN [*to* DYSART, *looking at* JILL]: Yes!

DYSART: What was she doing?

ALAN [*to* DYSART]: Holding my hand.

DYSART: And that was good?

ALAN [*to* DYSART]: Oh, yes!

DYSART: Remember what you thought. *As if it's happening to you now. This very moment* . . . What's in your head?

ALAN [*to* DYSART]: Her eyes. *She's* the one with eyes! . . . I keep looking at them, because I really want –

DYSART: To look at her breasts?

ALAN [*to* DYSART]: Yes.

DYSART: Like in the film.

ALAN [*to* DYSART]: Yes . . . Then she starts to scratch my hand.

JILL: You're really very nice, you know that?

ALAN [*to* DYSART]: Moving her nails on the back. Her face so warm. Her eyes.

DYSART: You want her very much?

ALAN [*to* DYSART]: Yes . . .

JILL: I love your eyes.

　　[*She kisses him.*]

　　[*Whispering.*] Let's go!

ALAN: Where?

JILL: I know a place. It's right near here.

ALAN: Where?

JILL: Surprise! ... Come on!

　　[*She darts away round the circle, across the stage and up the left side.*]
Come *on*!

ALAN [*to* DYSART]: She runs ahead. I follow. And then – and then –!
　　[*He halts.*]

DYSART: What?

ALAN [*to* DYSART]: I see what she means.

DYSART: What? ... Where are you? ... Where has she taken
　　you?

ALAN [*to* JILL]: *The Stables?*

JILL: Of course!

32

　　[CHORUS *makes a warning hum.*
　　The horses actors enter, and ceremonially put on their masks – first
　　raising them high above their heads. NUGGET *stands in the central*
　　tunnel.]

ALAN [*recoiling*]: No!

JILL: Where else? They're perfect!

ALAN: No!

　　[*He turns his head from her.*]

JILL: Or do you want to go home now and face your dad?

ALAN: No!

JILL: Then come on!

　　[*He edges nervously past the horse standing at the left, which turns its*
　　neck and even moves a challenging step after him.]

ALAN: Why not your place?

JILL: I can't. Mother doesn't like me bringing back boys. I told you
... Anyway, the Barn's better.

ALAN: No!

JILL: All that straw. It's cosy.

ALAN: No.

JILL: *Why not?*

ALAN: Them!

JILL: Dalton will be in bed ... What's the matter? ... Don't you
want to?

ALAN [*aching to*]: Yes!

JILL: So?

ALAN [*desperate*]: Them! ... Them! ...

JILL: *Who?*

ALAN [*low*]: Horses.

JILL: *Horses?* ... You're really dotty, aren't you? ... What do you
mean?

  [*He starts shaking.*]

Oh, you're freezing ... Let's get under the straw. You'll be warm
there.

ALAN [*pulling away*]: No!

JILL: What on earth's the matter with you? ...

  [*Silence. He won't look at her.*]

Look, if the sight of horses offends you, my lord, we can just shut
the door. You won't have to see them. All right?

DYSART: What door is that? In the barn?

ALAN [*to* DYSART]: Yes.

DYSART: So what do you do? You go in?

ALAN [*to* DYSART]: Yes.

33

[*A rich light falls.*
Furtively ALAN *enters the square from the top end, and* JILL *follows.*
The horses on the circle retire out of sight on either side. NUGGET

retreats up the tunnel and stands where he can just be glimpsed in the dimness.]

DYSART: Into the Temple? The Holy of Holies?

ALAN [*to* DYSART: *desperate*]: What else can I do? . . . I can't say! I can't tell her . . . [*To* JILL.] Shut it tight.

JILL: All right . . . You're crazy.

ALAN: Lock it.

JILL: Lock?

ALAN: Yes.

JILL: It's just an old door. What's the matter with you? They're in their boxes. They can't get out . . . Are you all right?

ALAN: Why?

JILL: You look weird.

ALAN: *Lock it!*

JILL: Ssssh! D'you want to wake up Dalton? . . . Stay there, idiot.
   [*She mimes locking a heavy door, upstage.*]

DYSART: Describe the barn, please.

ALAN [*walking round it: to* DYSART]: Large room. Straw everywhere. Some tools . . . [*As if picking it up off the rail where he left it in Act One.*] A hoof pick! . . .
   [*He 'drops' it hastily, and dashes away from the spot.*]

DYSART: *Go on.*

ALAN [*to* DYSART]: At the end this big door. Behind it –

DYSART: Horses.

ALAN [*to* DYSART]: Yes.

DYSART: How many?

ALAN [*to* DYSART]: Six.

DYSART: Jill closes the door so you can't see them?

ALAN [*to* DYSART]: Yes.

DYSART: And then? . . . What happens now? . . . Come on, Alan. Show me.

JILL: See, it's all shut. There's just us . . . Let's sit down. Come on.
   [*They sit together on the same bench, left.*]
   Hallo.

ALAN [*quickly*]: Hallo.

[*She kisses him lightly. He responds. Suddenly a faint trampling of hooves, off-stage, makes him jump up.*]

JILL: What is it?

[*He turns his head upstage, listening.*]

Relax. There's no one there. Come here.

[*She touches his hand. He turns to her again.*]

You're very gentle. I love that . . .

ALAN: So are you . . . I mean . . .

[*He kisses her spontaneously. The hooves trample again, harder. He breaks away from her abruptly towards the upstage corner.*]

JILL [*rising*]: What is it?

ALAN: Nothing!

[*She moves towards him. He turns and moves past her. He is clearly distressed. She contemplates him for a moment.*]

JILL [*gently*]: Take your sweater off.

ALAN: What?

JILL: I will, if you will.

[*He stares at her. A pause.*

She lifts her sweater over her head; he watches – then unzips his. They each remove their shoes, their socks, and their jeans. Then they look at each other diagonally across the square, in which the light is gently increasing.]

ALAN: You're . . . You're very . . .

JILL: So are you . . . [*Pause.*] Come here.

[*He goes to her. She comes to him. They meet in the middle, and hold each other, and embrace.*]

ALAN [*to* DYSART]: She put her mouth in mine. It was lovely! *Oh, it was lovely!*

[*They burst into giggles. He lays her gently on the floor in the centre of the square, and bends over her eagerly.*

Suddenly the noise of EQUUS *fills the place. Hooves smash on wood.* ALAN *straightens up, rigid. He stares straight ahead of him over the prone body of the girl.*]

DYSART: Yes, what happened then, Alan?

ALAN [*to* DYSART: *brutally*]: I put it in her!

DYSART: Yes?

ALAN [*to* DYSART]: I put it in her.

DYSART: You did?

ALAN [*to* DYSART]: Yes!

DYSART: Was it easy?

ALAN [*to* DYSART]: Yes.

DYSART: Describe it.

ALAN [*to* DYSART]: I told you.

DYSART: More exactly.

ALAN [*to* DYSART]: I put it in her!

DYSART: Did you?

ALAN [*to* DYSART]: All the way!

DYSART: Did you, Alan?

ALAN [*to* DYSART]: All the way. I shoved it. I put it in her all the way.

DYSART: Did you?

ALAN [*to* DYSART]: Yes!

DYSART: Did you?

ALAN [*to* DYSART]: Yes! . . . Yes!

DYSART: Give me the TRUTH! . . . Did you? . . . *Honestly?*

ALAN [*to* DYSART]: Fuck off!

[*He collapses, lying upstage on his face.* JILL *lies on her back motionless, her head downstage, her arms extended behind her. A pause.*]

DYSART [*gently*]: What was it? You couldn't? Though you wanted to very much?

ALAN [*to* DYSART]: I couldn't . . . see her.

DYSART: What do you mean?

ALAN [*to* DYSART]: Only Him. Every time I kissed her – *He* was in the way.

DYSART: Who?

[ALAN *turns on his back.*]

ALAN [*to* DYSART]: You *know* who! . . . When I touched her, I felt *Him.* Under me . . . His side, waiting for my hand . . . His flanks . . . I refused him. I looked. I looked right at her. . . . and I couldn't do it. When I shut my eyes, I saw Him at once. The streaks on his belly . . . [*With more desperation.*] I couldn't feel *her* flesh at all! I wanted the foam off his neck. His sweaty hide. Not flesh. *Hide! Horse-hide!* . . . Then I couldn't even kiss her.

[JILL *sits up.*]

JILL: What is it?

ALAN [*dodging her hand*]: No!

[*He scrambles up and crouches in the corner against the rails, like a little beast in a cage.*]

JILL: Alan!

ALAN: Stop it!

[JILL *gets up.*]

JILL: It's all right . . . It's all right . . . Don't worry about it. It often happens – honest . . . There's nothing wrong. I don't mind, you know . . . I don't at all.

[*He dashes past her downstage.*]

Alan, look at me . . . Alan? . . . Alan!

[*He collapses again by the rail.*]

ALAN: Get out! . . .

JILL: What?

ALAN [*soft*]: Out!

JILL: There's nothing wrong; believe me! It's very common.

ALAN: *Get out!*

[*He snatches up the invisible pick.*]

GET OUT!

JILL: Put that down!

ALAN: Leave me alone!

JILL: Put that down, Alan. It's very dangerous. Go on, please – drop it.

[*He 'drops' it, and turns from her.*]

ALAN: You ever tell anyone. Just you tell . . .

JILL: Who do you think I am? . . . I'm your friend – Alan . . .

[*She goes towards him.*]

Listen: you don't have to do anything. Try to realize that. Nothing at all. Why don't we just lie here together in the straw. And talk.

ALAN [*low*]: Please . . .

JILL: Just talk.

ALAN: *Please!*

JILL: All right, I'm going . . . Let me put my clothes on first.

[*She dresses, hastily.*]

ALAN: You tell anyone! . . . Just tell and see . . .

JILL: Oh, *stop it!* . . . I wish you could believe me. It's not in the least important.

[*Pause.*]

Anyway, I won't say anything. You know that. You know won't . . .

[*Pause. He stands with his back to her.*]

Good night, then, Alan . . . I wish – I really wish –

[*He turns on her, hissing. His face is distorted – possessed. In horrified alarm she turns – fumbles the door open – leaves the barn – shuts the door hard behind her, and dashes up the tunnel out of sight, past the barely visible figure of* NUGGET.]

34

[ALAN *stands alone, and naked.*

A faint humming and drumming. The boy looks about him in growing terror.]

DYSART: What?

ALAN [*to* DYSART]: He was there. Through the door. The door was shut, but he was there! . . . He'd seen everything. I could hear him. He was laughing.

DYSART: Laughing?

ALAN [*to* DYSART]: Mocking! . . . *Mocking!* . . .

[*Standing downstage he stares up towards the tunnel. A great silence weighs on the square.*]

[*To the silence: terrified.*] Friend . . . Equus the Kind . . . The Merciful! . . . *Forgive me!* . . .

[*Silence.*]

It wasn't me. Not really me. *Me!* . . . Forgive me! . . . Take me
back again! Please! . . . PLEASE!

[*He kneels on the downstage lip of the square, still facing the door,
huddling in fear.*]

I'll never do it again. I swear . . . I swear! . . .

[*Silence.*]

[*In a moan.*] *Please!!!* . . .

DYSART: And He? What does He say?

ALAN [*to* DYSART: *whispering*]: 'Mine! . . . You're mine! . . . I am
yours and you are mine!' . . . Then I see his eyes. They are rolling!

[NUGGET *begins to advance slowly, with relentless hooves, down the
central tunnel.*]

'I see you. I see you. Always! Everywhere! Forever!'

DYSART: Kiss anyone and I will see?

ALAN [*to* DYSART]: Yes!

DYSART: Lie with anyone and I will see?

ALAN [*to* DYSART]: Yes!

DYSART: And you will fail! Forever and ever you will *fail!* You will
see ME – and you will FAIL!

[*The boy turns round, hugging himself in pain. From the sides two
more horses converge with* NUGGET *on the rails.*

Their hooves stamp angrily. The EQUUS *noise is heard more terribly.*]

The Lord thy God is a Jealous God. He sees you. He sees you forever and ever, Alan. He sees you! . . . *He sees you!*

ALAN [*in terror*]: Eyes! . . . White eyes – never closed! Eyes like flames
– coming – coming! . . . God seest! God seest! . . . NO! . . .

[*Pause. He steadies himself. The stage begins to blacken.*]

[*Quieter.*] No more. No more, Equus.

[*He gets up. He goes to the bench. He takes up the invisible pick. He
moves slowly upstage towards* NUGGET, *concealing the weapon behind
his naked back, in the growing darkness. He stretches out his hand and
fondles* NUGGET's *mask.*]

[*Gently.*] Equus . . . Noble Equus . . . Faithful and True . . . Godslave . . . Thou – God – Seest – NOTHING!

[*He stabs out* NUGGET's *eyes. The horse stamps in agony. A great screaming begins to fill the theatre, growing ever louder.* ALAN *dashes at the other two horses and blinds them too, stabbing over the rails. Their metal hooves join in the stamping.*

Relentlessly, as this happens, three more horses appear in cones of light: not naturalistic animals like the first three, but dreadful creatures out of nightmare. Their eyes flare – their nostrils flare – their mouths flare. They are archetypal images – judging, punishing, pitiless. They do not halt at the rail, but invade the square. As they trample at him, the boy leaps desperately at them, jumping high and naked in the dark, slashing at their heads with arms upraised.

The screams increase. The other horses follow into the square. The whole place is filled with cannoning, blinded horses – and the boy dodging among them, avoiding their slashing hooves as best he can. Finally they plunge off into darkness and away out of sight. The noise dies abruptly, and all we hear is ALAN *yelling in hysteria as he collapses on the ground – stabbing at his own eyes with the invisible pick.*]

ALAN: Find me! ... Find me! ... Find me! ...

KILL ME! ... KILL ME! ...

35

[*The light changes quickly back to brightness.*

DYSART *enters swiftly, hurls a blanket on the left bench, and rushes over to* ALAN. *The boy is having convulsions on the floor.* DYSART *grabs his hands, forces them from his eyes, scoops him up in his arms and carries him over to the bench.* ALAN *hurls his arms round* DYSART *and clings to him, gasping and kicking his legs in a dreadful frenzy.*

DYSART *lays him down and presses his head back on the bench. He keeps talking – urgently talking – soothing the agony as he can.*]

DYSART: Here ... Here ... Ssssh ... Ssssh ... Calm now ... Lie back. *Just lie back!* Now breathe in deep. Very deep. In ... Out ... In ... Out ... That's it ... In. Out ... In ... Out ...

[*The boy's breath is drawn into his body with a harsh rasping sound, which slowly grows less.* DYSART *puts the blanket over him.*]

Keep it going . . . That's a good boy . . . Very good boy . . . It's all over now, Alan. It's all over. He'll go away now. You'll never see him again, I promise. You'll have no more bad dreams. No more awful nights. Think of that! . . . You are going to be well. I'm going to make you well, I promise you . . . You'll be here for a while, but I'll be here too, so it won't be so bad. Just trust me . . .

[*He stands upright. The boy lies still.*]

Sleep now. Have a good long sleep. You've earned it . . . Sleep. Just sleep . . . I'm going to make you well.

[*He steps backwards into the centre of the square. The light brightens some more.*

A pause.]

DYSART: I'm lying to you, Alan. He won't really go that easily. Just clop away from you like a nice old nag. Oh, no! When Equus leaves – if he leaves at all – it will be with your intestines in his teeth. And I don't stock replacements . . . If you knew anything, you'd get up this minute and run from me fast as you could.

[HESTHER *speaks from her place.*]

HESTHER: The boy's in pain, Martin.

DYSART: Yes.

HESTHER: And you can take it away.

DYSART: Yes.

HESTHER: Then that has to be enough for you, surely? . . . In the end!

DYSART [*crying out*]: *All right! I'll take it away!* He'll be delivered from madness. *What then?* He'll feel himself acceptable! *What then?* Do you think feelings like his can be simply re-attached, like plasters? Stuck on to other objects we select? *Look at him!* . . . My desire might be to make this boy an ardent husband – a caring citizen – a worshipper of abstract and unifying God. My achievement, however, is more likely to make a ghost! . . . Let me tell you exactly what I'm going to do to him!

[*He steps out of the square and walks round the upstage end of it, storming at the audience.*]

I'll heal the rash on his body. I'll erase the welts cut into his mind by flying manes. When that's done, I'll set him on a nice mini-scooter and send him puttering off into the Normal world where animals are treated *properly*: made extinct, or put into servitude, or tethered all their lives in dim light, just to feed it! I'll give him the good Normal world where we're tethered beside them – blinking our nights away in a non-stop drench of cathode-ray over our shrivelling heads! I'll take away his Field of Ha Ha, and give him Normal places for his ecstasy – multi-lane highways driven through the guts of cities, extinguishing Place altogether, *even the idea of Place!* He'll trot on his metal pony tamely through the concrete evening – and one thing I promise you: he will never touch hide again! With any luck his private parts will come to feel as plastic to him as the products of the factory to which he will almost certainly be sent. Who knows? He may even come to find sex funny. Smirky funny. Bit of grunt funny. Trampled and furtive and entirely in control. Hopefully, he'll feel nothing at his fork but Approved Flesh. *I doubt, however, with much passion! . . .* Passion, you see, can be destroyed by a doctor. It cannot be created.

[*He addresses* ALAN *directly, in farewell.*]

You won't gallop any more, Alan. Horses will be quite safe. You'll save your pennies every week, till you can change that scooter in for a car, and put the odd 50p on the gee-gees, quite forgetting that they were ever anything more to you than bearers of little profits and little losses. You will, however, be without pain. More or less completely without pain.

[*Pause.*

He speaks directly to the theatre, standing by the motionless body of ALAN STRANG, *under the blanket.*]

And now for me it never stops: that voice of Equus out of the cave – 'Why Me? . . . Why Me? . . . Account for Me!' . . . All right – I surrender! I say it! . . . In an ultimate sense I cannot know what I do in this place – yet I do ultimate things. Essentially I cannot know what I do – yet I do essential things. Irreversible, terminal things. I stand in the dark with a pick in my hand, striking at heads!

[*He moves away from* ALAN, *back to the downstage bench, and finally sits.*]

I need – more desperately than my children need me – a way of seeing in the dark. What way is this? . . . *What dark is this?* . . . I cannot call it ordained of God: I can't get that far. I will however pay it so much homage. There is now, in my mouth, this sharp chain. And it never comes out.

[*A long pause.*

DYSART *sits staring.*]

BLACKOUT

READ MORE IN PENGUIN

In every corner of the world, on every subject under the sun, Penguin represents quality and variety – the very best in publishing today.

For complete information about books available from Penguin – including Puffins, Penguin Classics and Arkana – and how to order them, write to us at the appropriate address below. Please note that for copyright reasons the selection of books varies from country to country.

In the United Kingdom: Please write to *Dept. JC, Penguin Books Ltd, FREEPOST, West Drayton, Middlesex UB7 OBR.*

If you have any difficulty in obtaining a title, please send your order with the correct money, plus ten per cent for postage and packaging, to *PO Box No. 11, West Drayton, Middlesex UB7 OBR*

In the United States: Please write to *Consumer Sales, Penguin USA, P.O. Box 999, Dept. 17109, Bergenfield, New Jersey 07621-0120.* VISA and MasterCard holders call 1-800-253-6476 to order all Penguin titles

In Canada: Please write to *Penguin Books Canada Ltd, 10 Alcorn Avenue, Suite 300, Toronto, Ontario M4V 3B2*

In Australia: Please write to *Penguin Books Australia Ltd, P.O. Box 257, Ringwood, Victoria 3134*

In New Zealand: Please write to *Penguin Books (NZ) Ltd, Private Bag 102902, North Shore Mail Centre, Auckland 10*

In India: Please write to *Penguin Books India Pvt Ltd, 706 Eros Apartments, 56 Nehru Place, New Delhi 110 019*

In the Netherlands: Please write to *Penguin Books Netherlands bv, Postbus 3507, NL-1001 AH Amsterdam*

In Germany: Please write to *Penguin Books Deutschland GmbH, Metzlerstrasse 26, 60594 Frankfurt am Main*

In Spain: Please write to *Penguin Books S. A., Bravo Murillo 19, 1° B, 28015 Madrid*

In Italy: Please write to *Penguin Italia s.r.l., Via Felice Casati 20, I–20124 Milano*

In France: Please write to *Penguin France S. A., 17 rue Lejeune, F–31000 Toulouse*

In Japan: Please write to *Penguin Books Japan, Ishikiribashi Building, 2–5–4, Suido, Bunkyo-ku, Tokyo 112*

In Greece: Please write to *Penguin Hellas Ltd, Dimocritou 3, GR–106 71 Athens*

In South Africa: Please write to *Longman Penguin Southern Africa (Pty) Ltd, Private Bag X08, Bertsham 2013*

BY THE SAME AUTHOR

Amadeus

Winner of the *Evening Standard* Drama Award as best play of 1979, and of the *Plays and Players'* London Theatre Critics Award.

'Shaffer works out his tremendous, his colossal, theme in language of great strength . . . those who go to it prepared to understand what it is about will have an experience that far transcends even its considerable value as drama' – *Bernard Levin*

Lettice and Lovage *and* **Yonadab**

Lettice and Lovage

Winner of the 1988 *Evening Standard* Drama Award for Best Comedy

'An original and often hilarious treatment of an important and theatrically neglected subject; combining uproarious farce with savage indignation' – Irving Wardle in *The Times*

Yonadab with a revised text

'*Yonadab*, Peter Shaffer's controversial play . . . once again the author of *Amadeus* explores the battle between the mundane and the transcendent . . . This is Shaffer's most daring, most personal, most honest play' – *Newsweek*

and

The Royal Hunt of the Sun
Four Plays
The Private Ear / The Public Eye;
White Liars; *Black Comedy*